Look who it is!

Look who it is!
ALAN CARR
My Story

HarperCollins*Publishers*

HarperCollins*Publishers*
77–85 Fulham Palace Road,
Hammersmith, London W6 8JB

www.harpercollins.co.uk

First published by HarperCollins*Publishers* 2008

3

A catalogue record of this book
is available from the British Library

HB ISBN-13 978-0-00-727822-0
HB ISBN-10 0-00-727822-5
PB ISBN-13 978-0-00-728116-9
PB ISBN-10 0-00-728116-1

Printed and bound in Great Britain by
Clays Ltd, St Ives plc

Mixed Sources
Product group from well-managed
forests and other controlled sources
www.fsc.org Cert no. SW-COC-1806
© 1996 Forest Stewardship Council

FSC is a non-profit international organisation established to promote the
responsible management of the world's forests. Products carrying the FSC
label are independently certified to assure consumers that they come
from forests that are managed to meet the social, economic and
ecological needs of present and future generations.

Find out more about HarperCollins and the environment at
www.harpercollins.co.uk/green

Contents

To Christine and Graham,
my wonderful parents

Preface

Even though he was wearing sunglasses, you could see Kanye West was staring at us thinking 'What the hell?' The camp one was wearing a gold lamé tracksuit, and the beardy one was wearing MC Hammer pantaloons made of tin foil. We looked like two oven-cooked turkeys that had just run a marathon. I think he thought we were simple.

It was whilst standing there in *The Friday Night Project* studio, explaining to Kanye West what 'dogging' was, that I had a flashback to when my life wasn't so surreal, wasn't so out there, wasn't so wig-based. Look at me now, for Christ's sake, standing in front of a mirror, my eyes following the line of my stockings up from my black stilettos to the silver-sequinned négligé. It's not a dream because I can actually hear myself saying '… but would Tina Turner wear this?' How did this happen? My life was becoming about as real as the plastic tits that had been rammed down the front of my top.

No one told me it would be like this – not that I'm complaining, I just didn't even know what 'it' was. I knew it would be a lot of smiling, waving, good press, bad press, people gossiping about me, but I didn't realise it would happen at this pace. My life had been pelting along at break-neck speed and, like the costume changes on *The Friday Night*

Project, sequins, feather boas and leather had been whizzing before my eyes, and I hadn't had time to absorb it.

It was only when the show finished and I sat in my dressing room and had made time for gentle reflection that I realised I'd been in front of millions of viewers dressed as a gimp. It's telling when you can recognise your outfits from other television programmes. There's something tragic sitting there of an evening watching *Heartbeat* and then suddenly blurting out, 'Hold on, I wore that wig when I was Rula Lenska!' *The Friday Night Project* has been a wonderful experience for me, albeit a wonderful experience with a learning curve reminiscent of a cliff face.

I walked into the studio on that cold January Thursday morning, not taking it particularly seriously. It was only when I saw the huge eight-foot portrait of my face next to Justin's, staring back at me, that it finally dawned on me what I had let myself in for. This was serious. It was like a punch in the stomach. I felt sick. The studio we were filming in didn't help, either. It was huge and imposing and bathed in harsh lighting. Looking out at row after row of empty seats, which in eight hours' time would be filled with excited and expectant faces, made the agony even worse. I'd only ever appeared in makeshift studios at the back of production offices, performing in shows that were destined for obscure satellite channels, where often the people in the studio would outnumber the viewing figures two to one. This vast space was all worryingly new to me. Even the rehearsals for *The Friday Night Project* were done in a room above a shopping centre in West London.

Preface

Admittedly, my acting didn't do the rehearsals justice. A lot of the time the rehearsals would consist of me stumbling over the words on the autocue wearing an ill-fitting wig – mind you, it hasn't done Brucie's career any harm, I suppose. The sketches are done one after the other, which is no hardship. But when you're whipping off clothes at a moment's notice, donning wigs, and having your breasts adjusted by a saveloy-fingered costumier, on a hot day, you could fool your body into thinking it's going through the change. If you have someone fabulous at presenting like the lovely Davina or Cilla, the rehearsal can fly by. But if we are saddled with, shall we say, some of our less literate showbiz friends, the show will be begging to be put out of its misery.

Thankfully, those shows are few and far between. But there I go again with my mocking, totally forgetting my first appearance on the first show of the first series at the beginning of January 2006. I wasn't so hot myself. As you can imagine, the nerves had gone full throttle, not helped by the three energy drinks I'd downed in quick succession in a vain attempt to salvage some vim from some part of my body which wasn't quivering with fear. The amount of energy drinks I consume before I go onto the studio floor is a bit of a joke with *The Friday Night Project* team. I love the buzz I get, plus it gives me the added bonus of coming up just as my 'Topical Barometer' does. Perfect timing.

So 7.15 p.m. finally came, which could only mean one thing: showtime. People forget how Justin and I and Princess, the production company that created *The Friday Night Project*, had to build things up after the previous series. We had been left with a vacuum. A familiar brand, but nothing to back it up, an empty shell that needed to be filled not only with 'stuff' but 'entertaining stuff'. After the last series Channel 4 had had a complete clear-out of the main hosts, and Justin and my good self had been chosen as the replacements.

Obviously, being relatively new faces, we were a gamble. Viewers would have to take a chance on us. We weren't as established as Jimmy Carr and, as we found out to our displeasure, on that first show we couldn't fill the seats in the studio – we had to cover up the empty places with a discreet black cover. Employing adept camera-work, the director managed to make the studio look full to the brim and fooled our lovely viewers at home that Thursday night at *The Friday Night Project* was party night. If you believed what you saw on the screen, we were the hottest ticket in town. Justin and I were obviously connecting with someone, though, because after a few shows we were filling all the seats. Not only that, they were turning people away at the door.

I have never watched *The Friday Night Project*, or any other programme I've been on, for that matter. I can't stand watching myself, I find it uncomfortable, I start begrudging my campness. The critics had slated the programme – it's a Friday late-night entertainment show, of course they're going to hate it! What were they expecting? *World in Action*? Even so, I could tell the show was going down well because, say what you want about the Great British Public, they're not backward in coming forward. If they like you, they will tell you they like you.

Shopping, eating, catching a show, attending a funeral, 'ALAN, WE LOVE YOU!' will come out of nowhere and pierce the atmosphere like a pin. You will look up and, more often than not, there will be a gaggle of girls wolf-whistling and waving, poking their heads out the back of a Cortina window – a bit like dogs do when they need some air.

We were starting to get audiences who were real fans. The first few shows had been uninspiring audience-wise, plus we had noticed that a handful of the seats in the studio were suspiciously vacant once the 'Coat of Cash' had happened. For those of you who don't know it, the 'Coat of Cash' is very simple. A 'celebrity', a term used loosely, runs into the audience with a coat covered in fivers and tenners, and the audience has to rip the money off. The audience go wild at this point, and it is pure chaos as people try to get their money's worth off the poor coat-wearer.

However, when it was over, the penny finally dropped: some cheeky bastards in the audience had grabbed the money off the coat, had got their bags and decided to go home. It seems some of the audience were using us as an ATM, handing out free money to people who didn't give two hoots about the show. Tight bastards. Thankfully, as the show's success grew, so did the enthusiasm of the audience, and we got people there who enjoyed the show whether they had grabbed a handful of fivers or not.

Over time the undesirables were ruthlessly rooted out. With this new burst of love from the audience, our confidence grew and so did the studio. We went up to the biggest one at London Studios. We were on hallowed ground. This was where Ant and Dec filmed their *Saturday Night Takeaway*, this was the pat on the back we needed.

Justin and I were both thrilled. I felt I had finally shaken off the demons that said I wasn't good enough. I had been so worried at the beginning of the run that I couldn't do it. Justin was naturally upbeat, enthusiastic and a born conversationalist. He made it look so easy, thriving in what is essentially the pretty stark surroundings of a studio. I doubted whether I could keep up with him, let alone possibly say anything that would make the final cut. Justin can literally talk about anything, plus, amazingly, sound like he gives a shit, which is a fantastic skill to have when you're faced with a dreary A-Lister intent on plugging their CD, perfume, clothing range, film. Delete where applicable. Whereas Justin can throw himself wholeheartedly into the conversation and chug it along with his cheeky chat and upbeat nature, I tend to switch off and look completely bored shitless which, I admit, isn't ideal. I bet you can't wait for the 'Alan Carr Chat Show', can you?

But I made a concerted effort to talk more, engage myself with the guest and earn my place upon the sofa. Believe it or not, towards the end of that first run I started to enjoy myself. I actually looked forward to the recording and, as it happens, I wasn't making a tit of myself. In fact, Justin and I were making quite a good partnership in this thing they call 'presenting'. We were doing just fine together, we were becoming a right old double act, and my fears that I was the new Syd Little had been unfounded.

Whether it's performing 'Doctor Who on Ice' with Billie Piper, or rapping on a mock R'n'B video with Mariah Carey, or singing a duet with Mel C at an EastEnders pub in Magaluf, it is only when it stops that you can finally take in the bizarreness of what I used to call my life. If I actually took it in whilst I was in the middle of these more surreal moments, I think my head would explode. Maybe after all it's a good thing that I let myself get swept away by it all. Maybe I'm afraid that if I pinched myself it would bring me round from this dream-like state, and I would wake up and find myself back packing shampoo in Northampton. Even after all I've been through, I still worry that it will end tomorrow and I'll get banished to some industrial estate in the middle of nowhere for having too much fun. So I do what I do best – I pop on my costume and carry on regardless.

So I'm back in the studio, and for the eighth time that day I change into my outfit. Staring at the monstrosity that looks back at me in the mirror, it's hard to comprehend firstly that the shy little boy from Northampton has come so far, and secondly that I would make such an ugly woman. Not disheartened, I slip on the négligé with no complaints, pop on the black stilettos, let Sue the make-up lady smear my lips with cherry-red lipstick, and I am ready.

With a quick glance in the mirror to see that Justine has pinned the shaggy brown wig to my head, I make my way to the back of the stage reciting the lyrics of 'Simply the Best' over and over again. As I pass through the backcloth to the wings, one of the stagehands mutters sarcastically, 'Look who it is!'

'Yes,' I say. 'It's Tina!'

Chapter One

KICK-OFF!

wish you were here ...

SEA SIDE TOWN

I remember running and touching a tree, any tree, and then running back to my father and then running to a tree that was a little bit further away and then back to my father and so on. I seemed to have spent my whole childhood breathless, touching trees. If there weren't trees available, Dad would bring bollards. There would be no escape from the tree touching.

Whilst I was running I would see all the other kids in the park having a kick-around, taking it in turns to be in goal, playing keepy-uppy, their playful laughter and squeals of joy slowly being drowned out by Dad's 'One, two, three, four! Quicker! You fat fairy!' from the other side of the park. He would shout using the same booming voice with just a hint of Geordie that he used every Saturday on the touchline to his own players. I would see them try to shout back, only to be blasted again with that voice, the fools. It would be like arguing with a hand-dryer.

I first started running to try and dislodge some of the puppy fat. It would be just a leisurely run around the fields, nothing too strenuous. Strangely, although I hated sports, I did enjoy running; bounding along the country lanes seemed to clear my head and sharpen my mind. I remember running after school around a field at the back of my house, and as I approached the winning line, which was in fact an old tree with a dangly branch, who did I spot emerging from behind a bush? Yes, my father, with a stopwatch.

'That's 29 minutes, 38 seconds. If you'd pushed yourself a bit harder on that hill, you would have made 28 minutes easy.'

Not only had he been spying on me running, I later found out he had tried to enrol me in the local boys' running team, the Overstone Phoenixes, without me knowing.

'What's the point of running if you're not up against someone?' he would say. 'There's no point, Alan, if there's no challenge!'

I was a twelve-year-old spectacle wearer with a weight problem. The only challenge I had was finding sports shorts with an elasticated waist. As my father would tell me, football wasn't about scoring goals, it was about discipline and fitness.

'Alan, see those kids over there?'

'What, the ones laughing and having fun?'

'They'll never be any good because they're just kicking the ball about. We're getting your thighs built up, so they will protect your knees and you won't get arthritis in later life.'

Dad sure knew how to inject a bit of fun into the proceedings. Arthritis prevention, anyone? Apparently, if I followed Dad's exercise routine and did the relevant amount of sit-ups every day, not only would I become a top professional footballer, I would be an athlete, an Adonis, from the top of my waxed Mohican down to the gold studs on the soles of my (limited edition) Adidas football boots. Well, that was the plan anyway.

I know what you're thinking: 'If you were forced to do so much exercise, how come you're so fat?' Well, for a start it's my glands and, to be frank, Dad put me off playing football. Obviously, I realise you have to do the groundwork, and put the effort in to succeed at your chosen field, but what he didn't understand was that a child has to be tempted into it in the first place. It is the exhilaration of scoring a goal that enchants a seven year old, an exhilaration that would then hopefully blossom into a career. No one becomes a pilot because they'd enjoyed an in-flight meal; no, they want to fly the bloody thing. My father had inadvertently managed to extract all the fun out of the game for me; on that playing field it was all work, work, work with him.

* * *

It's been stated in every interview I've ever done that my father was a football manager. They write about it as if it's a punch-line to a gag, but it's true, he has been involved in football all his life and in some respects it is his life, but what people don't realise is how deep football runs in our family. Almost everyone (well, everyone with a penis) has been a professional footballer at one time or another. Granddad Wilf played for Newcastle United and West Bromwich Albion (if you don't believe me, his photo is up on the wall as you enter the Hawthorns ground), an uncle played for PSV Eindhoven, cousins and nephews had tryouts at various football clubs up and down the country and of course there was my father, Graham Carr.

If you mention the words 'Graham Carr' to a Northamptonian of a certain age, their eyes mist up and a lump appears in their throat – Dad is a local hero. After taking Northampton Town, affectionately nicknamed the Cobblers, from the bottom of the Fourth Division up to the top of the Third Division in the late Eighties (with 103 goals and 99 points in their promotion season, no less), he became literally the talk of the town – just think Alex Ferguson, but on a budget.

Football chants honouring him would echo around the County Ground (Northampton Town Football Club's home): 'He's fat, he's round, his feet don't touch the ground, Graham Carr, Graham Carr!' or my personal favourite, 'He's got no hair, but we don't care, Graham, Graham, Carr, ooh ah!' I'm sad to say these chants were an apt description of my father. He *was* fat and round, well, maybe round's going a bit too far, but he definitely has a bit of a pot belly. He definitely has got no hair. He went bald in his early twenties, something that I am beginning to experience myself. I feel it is only a matter of time before I look in the mirror and see my father looking back.

I don't care, as long as he's not shouting out 'Touch the tree – Fatty!'

Those football chants came from a good place; the fans had a genuine affection for Dad. He had actually played for the Cobblers in the Sixties, their heyday, when they went all the way up from the Fourth Division to the First – and then back down again. He had been popular back then, too. His return as manager was the return of the prodigal son. Complete strangers would approach us as we sauntered around the town centre and take an interest in our lives.

Kick-off!

At first the novelty of having people come up to us and say positive things about the Cobblers was nice, but then inevitably they would turn their line of questioning to me.

'Does he play, Graham?' they would ask with a nod in my direction or, worse, ruffle my hair and say, 'What position do you want to play?'

I'd just smile sweetly and watch their face fall when my camp voice trilled, 'I'm not really into football,' then carry on listening to the Supremes on my Walkman.

To be honest, I don't think I've got the edge to be a footballer. When I look through Dad's scrapbooks at some of the newspaper clippings, I see a rock-hard defender – in the thick of the action, fearlessly performing sliding tackles and diving feet first onto some poor opponent's legs. In fact, old Cobblers fans talk of him in hushed tones, looking over their shoulders cautiously as if he might suddenly burst from the undergrowth and tackle them.

'He was terrifying alright', 'You'd know if your dad had tackled you', 'He could take a man down with ease' – please don't make your own jokes up. I suppose what I'm calling competitiveness, he'd probably call passion. In terms of sports, he doesn't understand why anyone would want to do something for fun.

Of course I'd love to be earning £75,000 a week, working two days a week and then spending the rest showing OK! magazine my beautiful mock-Tudor mansion. But you've got to remember that when I grew up in the Eighties, football was grim, men in cloth caps with no teeth shouting on terraces and throwing bananas at the black players. It wasn't the ghetto-fabulous existence that we all know and love today, with the fast cars and Louis Vuitton hand luggage. If I'd known I could have lived that kind of lifestyle, I would have endured my father's stomach crunches and star jumps. I'd have even touched a few more trees.

One thing that I have been pleased to see, though, is that when it's cold the Premiership players now wear gloves and leggings. This to me is a personal victory, as I'd proposed these changes at the age of twelve. But did Dad take these pioneering thoughts on board? No, he just said, 'Only poofs wear leggings.'

To be fair, though, if that competitiveness is the worst aspect of my father, then I've been very lucky indeed. I know Dad would get frustrated at my lack of sporting ability, but then again I was shit! Even the kindliest PE teacher would break out in an attack of Tourette's and start shouting profanities at me. I've had a PE teacher snap a hockey stick in frustration at one of my pitiful lobs.

You have to remember, I was the only boy at my Upper School to score an own goal at basketball – look, I got disorientated, and once you've seen one basket you've seen them all. But at times, I'll admit, I didn't really help myself. I remember shouting out at a Northampton Town Football match, 'He's behind you!' instead of 'Man on!' It wasn't deliberate, it's just that I got carried away. I guess you could say I was being passionate – like my father.

Having a dad in the footballing trade is a bit like having a parent in the army or in the circus: you have to go where the work is. So if there are any children of sergeant majors or bearded ladies reading this, then you'll know what I mean. I was actually born in Weymouth, Dorset, where Dad had made the leap from player to manager of Weymouth Football Club. To be exact I was born at the Portland Hospital on 14 June 1976. Six pounds ten. I was 'a beautiful baby boy'. These are my words. I don't know if anyone called me a beautiful baby boy, but I must have been beautiful at one stage, surely. I didn't have my glasses or teeth back then, so the odds must be quite good.

I wonder if, as I lay there kicking my little legs in the air in my cot, Dad was imagining little football boots at the end of them and that my little wrinkled hands would be ideal for throw-ins. Mum once told me of when she was heavily pregnant with me and in bed with Dad one night I gave an almighty kick from inside the womb, so hard in Dad's back that he woke up. It seems I had cruelly raised Dad's hopes, and I wasn't even born.

I've never been one of those people with a really great memory, and for someone as self-obsessed as me it's a shame. All those wonderful times when I was the centre of attention gone forever – it's enough to bring you to tears. In fact, I only have one memory of my first five years, and even that's a bit shaky because I have been known to absorb stuff off the telly and pass it off as my own life. I remember telling Mum about the time I stopped a woman from having a diamond-encrusted necklace stolen and she said, 'No, Alan, that was Poirot.' Then there's another time when I was with Dad at the seaside in Clacton, sitting on his lap as we slid down a helter-skelter. I remember the sky was blue and cloudless and the squawk of the seagulls made me jump and I cried. Even now I'm not sure whether we were down the tip on a sunny day or watching an episode of *Holiday*.

My early memories are all seaside-centric. When I try to recollect some of those days, I get little flashbulbs of a Punch and Judy show or the curve of a brightly coloured wind-breaker or of myself sitting on the beach sipping a bottle of tea, which apparently was my favourite drink as a toddler.

What I do know is my favourite donkey on Weymouth beach was Pepper and my parents would have to take a detour around the amusements because I would run off into the arcade and lose them among the noise and crowds. They would find me each time in the same motor car clutching the steering wheel.

It can be lovely to hear relations talking about your early years, the sentimentalism tugging on your heart strings, just the act of remembering warming you up.

'What do you remember about my childhood, Nan?' I asked recently, all dewy-eyed and expectant.

'You always jumped in shit!' she cackled.

Dogshit, donkey shit – any kind of shit, I would just love to step in it. There was one time when my parents had just bought me some brand new shoes from Clark's. I came out of the shop all excited. Then I spotted some dogshit and without any hesitation jumped in, both feet first. The shoes were so caked they had to be thrown in the bin, which still makes me feel guilty because I realise now how skint my parents were at the time and how they struggled to make ends meet. But why couldn't Nan talk about my first word or the first time I walked – away from a piece of dogshit?

Kick-off!

Other memories bustle for attention. Every morning when I was little, I would stand and look out of the window that overlooked Weymouth beach to watch my father go to work and wave at him as he got into his green Mazda. Sometimes, Dad would say that I would become distracted by the beach, and he would drive round again and again to try to get my attention. My eyes would finally leave what was happening on the beach and reconnect to my father in his car and I would carry on with my waving and he would drive off to work.

For someone who swore that they could never do Dad's job, our lives have eerily mirrored each other's. The ridiculous amount of travelling we both do is testament to that. I find it strangely comforting to know that if I'm in some weird village hall performing on the other side of the Pennines, he'll be somewhere twice as obscure up a mountain watching a football team in the Dordogne.

Funnily enough it was this incessant travel that bonded us: sitting around the dining table we would often discuss in great detail the benefits of the M40 or ask, 'Have you been on that new flyover yet?' while Mum's eyes would slowly glaze over and she'd try to stick her head in the oven. It also took me a while to recognise back then that the moodiness and sharp exchanges we'd get every Friday night weren't Dad being grumpy, but merely his anxiety about the game the next day. This is pretty similar to me now as anyone who's had the misfortune to approach me before I go on stage can testify, receiving a glare or a curt 'leave me alone' for their troubles.

* * *

Dad was away quite a bit when I was a kid, but that did mean I could spend a lot of time with my mother. Before my brother Gary was born it was often just us two in the house and the bond that usually connects mother and son became that little bit stronger. People say I look more like my mother than my father. Stop! Get that image of Olive from *On the Buses* out of your head – my mother is an attractive woman, I'll have you know. One thing that we share is our sense of humour, and growing up I remember the house just being full of laughter. My mother is very much like me when telling a story; she will get to her feet and start mimicking the person, taking on the different characters and voices.

I remember when my father was away at a match, asking my mother how she met him. She says she was sitting in the stands at Dartford Football Club watching a match where Dad was playing. When Dad scored a goal, he ran over to the stand and pulled a moonie at the supporters.

'What did you think about that?' I asked her.

'I thought, "What an idiot!"'

Well, I guess that's an icebreaker in anyone's book. Most romances start with a furtive glance across a crowded room, not by exposing yourself to your loved one. Anyway, my mother not only fell in love with that idiot, she married him.

Dad must have been doing something right at Weymouth, because he was asked to become manager of Dartford, so not for the last time in our lives we were on the move. Now when you're poor, having a beach on your doorstep and bright, delicious sunshine for what felt like 24 hours a day can take the edge off having empty pockets.

Dartford sadly didn't have any of these things going for it; the tunnel is a wonderful man-made phenomenon, admittedly, and the Thames can be a majestic thing up by the Houses of Parliament, but down near Dartford it looked as grey and weary as the people.

As it happens, we weren't there for long because Dad became manager of Nuneaton Town Football Club, so yet again we were on the move. Dad, Mum and I journeyed up the M1 in the Mazda. We stayed in Northampton instead of Nuneaton due to the fact Dad had played there in the Sixties and thought it would be a nice place to live.

He was right, it was nice, just nice. Not a little bit naughty, just nice. We moved onto the Moulton Leys estate and lived in a house in a cul-de-sac that overlooked a cornfield. The cul-de-sac was a perfect example of suburbia: young families, pets, people washing their cars every Sunday. We even had our own peeping Tom. He would walk his dog at night and throw a ball up the drives, go to get it and then try to catch a glimpse of a woman through the parted curtains. We knew this because we saw him most nights.

In fact, Mum and the woman across the road, Sue, tried to catch him out one night. Sue left her curtains open and her lights on to lure the pervert while Mum kept our house in darkness and looked out of the window to catch him red-eyed. After a few seductive curtain twitches from Sue had proved fruitless, Mum peered out a bit more closely, but it was only when she looked down that she realised he was actually peeping through her own window. She screamed and he ran off, which left us terrified but strangely excited. Mum quickly rang up Sue and they laughed about it together nervously, feeling triumphant and yet a little bit dirty.

Those were some of the things that Mum and I would get up to whilst Dad was away – stupid, silly things that would make us laugh. They say the devil makes work for idle hands, but he also dabbles in finding work for skint hands. If we'd been able to afford to go to the cinema, we wouldn't have had to amuse ourselves by capturing local sex pests like some kind of Hetty Wainthropp. The following Christmas, I got an Atari and that kept Mum and me busy till all hours playing PacMan, Space Invaders and Wizard of War.

I used to support Nuneaton Town Football Club and, believe it or not, I used to look forward to the matches, even though they were an unfashionable non-League side. I even used to go to the training nights, where I would have the whole football ground to myself and sit in whatever seat I wanted. I would even climb up the goal nets and splash about in the huge players' baths. I could do anything I wanted because Dad was the boss. I would obviously knacker myself out on those nights because I remember lying on the back seat of Dad's car with his sheepskin over me, driving back to Northampton and feeling very safe drifting off along those country lanes.

Mohammed Ali once came to Nuneaton Town Football Club when I was little. It's true, it's true – I've got photos and everything. The chairman, by some amazing wheeler dealing, got the boxing legend to officiate the ground. I didn't know who he was back then. I knew he was a boxer, but his fame had sort of passed me by. What I do remember is that he was upbeat, said hello to everyone and took the piss out of Dad's baldness, with Dad laughing along jovially. I remember him shaking slightly, which of course we now know was the beginning of Parkinson's. I just wish that at the time I'd understood the importance of meeting such an icon. I wonder if he feels the same about me now that I'm on the telly. I guess I'll never know.

We were getting quite a name for ourselves in our little cul-de-sac, mainly because we had brought a cat with us from Dartford, Big Puss. We were never inventive with names in our house, and if we're honest, cats don't do anything anyway, so Big Puss was quite an apt name. He was a big puss, just a big fat puss. And vicious. Ever since he'd moved to Northampton he'd been terrorising people and cats the length and breadth of the estate.

It was a miracle that he was even with us then. By the time we had arrived at Northampton and we were trying to find our house, he had eaten through the cardboard box that had been meant to hold him in and he wasn't happy. Mad with rage in fact, he pounced claws first onto Mum's face and in a moment of panic she threw him out of the car window.

I was distraught. Can you imagine first seeing your mum savaged by your own pet cat and then seeing it thrown out of a window? I was only five and could have been traumatised for life. I thought the last I would ever see of Big Puss would be his tail whizzing past the wing mirror, but then guess who stalks, six days later, around the side of the house? Big Puss! Via some amazing tracking system that cats seem to have in their head, he had traced us to our new home. What a clever cat! I shouted joyously, 'Big Puss! You're alive!' and ran over to cuddle him, and he bit me. That was Big Puss for you – hard as nails.

Big Puss would terrify the other cats in the neighbourhood, but that was too easy for him – it was the humans he loved to hurt. You would see him in the alley opposite, sprawled out against the wall, his fluffy ginger stomach just waiting to be stroked. A little girl or boy on a scooter would come over and touch that fluffy stomach and then he would pounce and a scream would ring out. Five minutes later the parent would be knocking on our door.

'D'you know what your cat's done? Look at that bite mark! And that's after I've mopped up the blood. That animal's a menace. What are you going to do about it?'

Mum's answer would always be: 'Well, you shouldn't have touched it.'

To be fair, she had a point.

Before long the Carrs' cat was enemy number one. We caught our next-door neighbour hitting him with a broom after he had attacked her Persian, and later he was even shot in the head with an airgun. Needless to say, he survived. If anything, the shooting just made him a bit more mental. It was only a speeding car in our village ten years later that finally killed him off. Big Puss was a nasty piece of work, but I still miss him.

Eventually the time came when I had to go to school. My first school was Booth Lower and it was on top of what then felt like a massive hill. It isn't a massive hill at all and now I always laugh at how short it is, but walking up it at the age of five it felt like Kilimanjaro.

I wasn't really ready to go to school. With Dad always being away training or playing the away games, I had bonded too closely with my mother and would start crying hysterically every time she dropped me off. It wasn't the actual dropping off that did it – it was seeing her pass by the window afterwards on her way back home. It was like watching her in slow motion, and once she'd crossed the window I would just bawl my heart out.

The teacher was quite sympathetic at first, but that soon changed when my tidal wave of tears flooded into the following week. 'Alan Carr, pull yourself together!' Mrs Bellinge roared at me – which made me cry even more. It got so bad that the teacher had to have words with my mother, but after a while, when I realised that my mother would actually be coming back to collect me, I stopped crying.

After that, though, I really got into this school lark. Every day seemed to be sunny and we would dress up and play games in the 'wild area', which felt like a jungle then but was actually a piece of land that the caretaker couldn't be bothered to look after.

I had started making friends, lots of friends. Tellingly, they were all girls. I had no interest in mixing or playing with the boys. I can't remember it being a conscious decision; like now, I just feel comfortable in female company. Sometimes the group of girls would grow and grow, and from afar it must have looked like a proper harem. It must have been alarming for my parents to see this seemingly endless conveyor belt of girls I would invite for tea.

'Can Sarah come for tea?'

'Can Kelly come to tea?'
'Can Justine come to tea?'
'Is Sarah your girlfriend?' Mum would ask.
'No.'
'Kelly?'
'No.'
'Justine?'
'No. Just friends.'
One of my best friends was Jenny, an intelligent boyish girl, who was teacher's pet. It was not long before she started coming to tea, like so many girls had. We had the same sense of humour and really got on. Little did I know, we had more in common than I thought. We lost touch when she went to Northampton School for Girls. I did see Jenny again, but it was in very strange circumstances. Unknown to me, she had had a sex change and became a homosexual called Daniel. Obviously, I never heard about that on Friends Reunited, so you can imagine my shock when I spotted her, sorry him, sitting on the Tube opposite me with a beard. I must have shocked the other commuters when I started jumping and pointing excitedly, shouting, 'Jenny! Jenny! It's you, isn't it, Jenny?' Anyway, that's what the future held, but back then we were just two innocent seven-year-old misfits enjoying each other's company in the playground.

Straight after the football season ended, we'd always go on holiday – to shiver on the Norfolk coast, sheltering from the wind and rain on a caravan park in Great Yarmouth. Great Yarmouth was grey, windswept and grim. I lost track of how many Frisbees I lost one 'summer'. Dad would buy one from the park shop and pass it to me, I would get ready, all excited, to pass it back to him, and as soon as it left my fingers the gale force wind would whisk it off to Calais.

I will never forget my first night in Great Yarmouth. It's hard enough to sleep in those bunk beds, especially with the nylon sheets and rough blankets that smell of corned beef. Ugh! I'll never forget the texture of those scratchy blankets up against my skin – it was like having sex with a leper. (Not that I knew about that then.) And then I was rudely awakened by the caravan rocking.

My indignation was soon replaced by fear, and with my runaway imagination I just knew it was a gang of thugs trying to tip us over into the sea.

I called out to Mum: 'Someone's rocking the caravan. Help!'

'Just go to sleep,' she said.

'No, no, it's rocking even more. Help me! Please, someone!'

'It's the wind. Go back to sleep!' shouted Dad, oblivious to the gang of ne'er-do-wells intent on killing us.

I realised that my parents, normally so vigilant about strange noises and goings-on, really didn't care. All I could hear from their room was giggling and muffled laughter, as the caravan rocked even more.

I don't know what finished first, the caravan's rocking or the commotion from my parents' room, but at some point I must have drifted off. When I brought it up in the morning, my questioning came up against a wall of silence and I was left contemplating the mystery whilst eating my grapefruit.

Every time I look in the mirror there is a reminder of my holidays in Great Yarmouth, and it's not my glowing skin and sun-kissed hair, it's my teeth. I had been mucking about, as most six year olds do when they're on their holidays. The windswept beach was a no-go area, and with the potential for it to piss it down at a moment's notice we had stayed close to the caravan. I had climbed up onto the caravan hook, those horrible metal things that you attach to the back of your car, and had slipped off, banging my mouth so hard that I had to be rushed to hospital and have my gums sewn up. I can remember Dad scooping me up in his arms and Mum, pregnant with my brother Gary (all that caravan rocking had taken its toll), running behind me. I can't remember much more of that night, but I can remember it starting to rain (what a surprise!) and my parents anxiously trying to flag down a car to take me to hospital.

Once the drama was over, the doctor told Mum that when my adult teeth came through they would either come through black or crooked or both. My poor mother was beside herself. But although my teeth do look as though they're having a party, I always remind myself that it could have been so much worse: they could have been black stumps poking out my mouth. Thank God for small mercies.

My teeth have always been trouble to me, though. They're my Achilles' heel. I don't know if this is possible, but honestly, I've started resenting my own teeth. I know you need them to bite and chew, but they don't half piss me off. Impacted wisdom teeth, extractions, root canal work – I've suffered them all. I chipped one piece off a tooth when I was 12, when someone accidentally turned and whacked a fishing rod in my face.

'Look,' I said to my dentist, a lovely man called Lance, 'why don't we just cut to the chase and have them all out and fit dentures?'

He smiled sweetly. 'That won't be necessary.'

No, of course not. That's because he knows full well that if I do have dentures his profits will plummet. My crooked white teeth are his pension plan; whenever he sees them coming through the door he thinks, 'Holiday home!'

The saga of my ill-fated teeth continues. Only last month I was nursing a gaping hole in my gum where a tooth cracked when I was having a crown fitted. The only reason I needed to have the crown fitted in the first place was that after bypassing a Snickers and going for a 'healthy option' bag of apricots, I bit into one that hadn't been pitted and ended up cracking a tooth and killing the nerve. Then I had no choice but to have it extracted. However, Lance is planning to fit me a porcelain crown, an exact copy of my original tooth, he assures me – which I am dreading because when you have teeth as big as mine, it'll be like sucking on a urinal.

* * *

Back in Northampton, though, in the distant days of child-hood, home was a happy place. Mum eventually gave birth to Gary, and so when he was older I had a brother to play with. She had actually asked me the year before, when I was playing with my Evel Knievel figure in the garden, whether I would like a little brother. I can't remember what I said, but it looks like they went ahead with it anyway.

Even though everything seemed so warm and homely, I still managed to suffer, though, because I was so accident prone. I remember jumping out of bed on a Monday morning, excited because I had a whole brand new week of school. My family was having new carpets fitted and had taken up the old ones. In my eagerness to run downstairs, I caught my foot under the carpet gripper and ripped all my toenails out. I was in agony and instead of going to school and doing fun things, I had to lie on the settee watching *Pebble Mill at One* like a prisoner of war.

As with all kids, I was into He-Man and *Star Wars*, and any money I received would go to buy a figure that I could act out scenes with. Francesca across the road, who was my age, had great girls' toys, so we would often pool our resources and make up our own fantasy world. For nearly a year Barbie and Skeletor were co-habiting in Castle Grayskull without a care in the world. Our Castle Grayskull was actually a more feminine affair than usual. Under Francesca's watchful eye, it had a pink chest of drawers, pink curtains and a big pink double bed.

Contrary to what you might think, I scorned the pink frilliness of Barbie's world and chose to have 'wars' with soldiers. Fuelled by Saturday afternoon reruns of *Sinbad*, I would always have my sword and scabbard at the ready, and if I couldn't find those, a stick. Looking back, I wish that now I had a tenth of the energy that little Alan used to have. I was a bag of energy, full of beans, always making loads of noise, so much so that Mum cut the tongues out of my Hungry Hippos.

The only glitch in this boyish world that I threw myself into was the time I asked Mum to help me write a letter to *Jim'll Fix It* to ask if I could meet Wonder Woman. I knew her name was Lynda Carter, my mother's maiden name, and I prayed that she was a relative and that at a family wedding she would turn up, obviously dressed as Wonder Woman, and I could meet her and tell everyone I was related to Wonder Woman. Surprisingly enough, she never turned up – it seems Lynda cares more for her career than she does her own flesh and blood.

It was around my eighth birthday that I started having an unhealthy interest in birdwatching, too. For the next three or four birthdays, I asked for binoculars and books on birds – I even subscribed to a birdwatching magazine. Every month, I would become enthralled by the exotic birds that would grace the glossy front cover. Frustratingly, it would always be a flamingo or a frigate with its beautiful red plumage. This was particularly mean as well as misleading to the keen bird-watcher, as such cover stars were native to such tropical paradise as the Galapagos Islands and there was no way a landlocked ornithologist like myself would ever come across one. I would have to make do with the Canada geese and pied wagtails that I saw at Pitsford Reservoir.

One time we got a free tape of birdsong, that you played to get yourself acquainted with the different calls that you would hear when you were in your hide waiting to see your first bird. The twittering coming from the stereo speakers didn't really have much of an effect on me, but Big Puss went mental. His eyes as big as ball bearings, he stalked the stereo, ferociously intimidating, hungry for bird-meat. In the end, when he couldn't find a bird, he just jumped on me and bit me instead. He was ruthless, a tireless killer and also a sexual predator, and although he had been castrated he still liked to make love to inanimate objects. My teddy bears, my slippers. He would bite the head of my He-Man and grind mercilessly, making a horny purring sound like a next-door neighbour using a strimmer.

This was my first introduction to sex. Mum would come in and hit him with a tea-towel.

'What's he doing, Mum?'

'He's being dirty.'

So from then on, whenever Big Puss ground away on my teddies or sometimes even me, I would shout, 'Mum! Big Puss is being dirty! Big Puss is being dirty!' And Mum would come in with a tea-towel and shoo him away: 'Dirty cat! Dirty cat!'

I didn't know what being dirty was – I still don't think I do – but anyway that's when I first came across this thing 'being dirty', and I learnt it off a big horny ginger tom.

Like most families, the father thinks he rules the roost but it is the mother who is really in control. After my younger brother Gary and I had tired of pleading with our parents for a tortoise, we moved onto dogs. We wanted a pet dog. Dad instantly set out his stall: he wanted a 'big dog', a man-dog, a dog that if it was human would enjoy a pint and stare at the barmaid's arse as she bent down for the cheese and onion crisps. He must have felt pretty emasculated then when we came back with Minstral.

The only way I can describe Minstral is for you to imagine the kind of dog that Paris Hilton has poking out of her handbag at those Hollywood premières. Minstral was a gorgeous little mongrel a few months old with the most expressive face going. His mother had been a pedigree King Charles Cavalier Spaniel, the breeder told us snootily, but a dirty Jack Russell called 'Rusty' had sneaked through the cat flap and raped her. It seems the mother had brought shame upon his council house and wanted nothing to do with its bastard offspring, so we took it off his hands.

Contrary to what you might think, Dad and the bastard dog bonded and from that moment on they were inseparable. They would go to bed at the same time, rise at the same time and go for drives together, with Minstral sitting obediently in the passenger seat. The partnership got so intense that Mum thought the dog was resenting her. So much so that she phoned the vet to say that Minstral was giving her dirty looks. I was horrified. I envisaged the vet nodding sympathetically – 'Yes, Mrs Carr, that's right, Mrs Carr' – while trying to switch on 'speaker phone' so everyone in the clinic could listen to this 'weirdo woman' in a love triangle with a mongrel.

From that moment on, Minstral and Mum both battled for Dad's affection; it was a battle that would last the next thirteen years. At least Mum still had her figure; Minstral's had gone to pot, as every morning Dad would proudly walk him to the newsagent and feed him his body weight in Milky Ways. It's a classic case of an owner killing the dog with kindness, but his argument was that Minstral would look up with those little expectant eyes, and Dad just couldn't resist forcing what was to a dog the equivalent of a selection box down the poor creature's throat. The dog must have been good with the old expectant-eyes trick because when I did them to Dad (usually mid-cross-country run, pleading with him to stop) he just ignored me and made me touch another tree, while I was gagging for a Milky Way.

* * *

It's typical, really, that although I was hearing whispers at school that I was not like the other boys – and I don't think it was because of my birdwatching – the penny never dropped. A few times I had wondered what they meant by the catcalls, and of course now I know, oh yes, I know now very well what they meant. These cringeworthy moments hover in my memory glowing bright pink in neon shouting, 'Yoo hoo, over here – remember us.' Sometimes I was guilty of turning the most mundane tasks into ammunition for the bullies.

Every child loves ice cream, and I was no exception. Whenever the hypnotic melody of the ice-cream van would be heard in our cul-de-sac, time would freeze as every child would first run to their mum and dad and shout, 'Mum, ice-cream van – can we have one?' and then run to get their shoes. On one occasion, I couldn't find my shoes and blind panic set in, because I really wanted a 99. All I could find were Mum's knee-length zip-up leather boots. I thought, 'Sod it, I'll wear those.'

By the time I'd put them on the right feet, zipped them up and found a handbag to match (joke), I could hear the ice-cream van's engine starting up. I ran straight out of the front door to find my fears were confirmed – he was pulling away!

Kick-off!

As fast as I could, I chased the ice-cream van through my whole estate in high-heeled boots, shouting, 'Stop! Stop! I want a 99!'

It was only when I sat down on the kerb, slowly unzipped the boots and coquettishly sucked the flake, that I thought, 'God, you're sexy!' – no, I thought how ridiculous I must look. This was confirmed by the number of neighbours staring and kids giggling.

I knew they were thinking, 'That's Graham's son.'

* * *

Times changed, and when I was eight we stopped going to the freezing wasteland of Great Yarmouth for our holidays and started going on five-hour car journeys behind a string of caravans to Beverley Park in Torquay. That five-hour journey would sometimes take six if my violent car sickness kicked in and I had to vomit on the hard shoulder.

You can imagine the relief when we finally pulled up at Torquay and saw the sun and the crisp blue sky.

'They call this the English Riviera,' Mum said, turning round in her seat and smiling at me.

I was amazed. Unlike Great Yarmouth, it really did look like it did in the brochure. (In Great Yarmouth I think they'd superimposed a sun and toilet facilities afterwards.)

Now we were holidaying down south we were joined by an extra person – Nanny Tot. She should have been called Nanny Carr, but my Granddad Wilf was so tall he was nick-named Tot and it stuck. Nanny Tot didn't come to Great

Yarmouth with us, as she lived in Newcastle, so if she had wanted to get blown around and pissed on, she could just have gone to Whitley Bay, which was cheaper and nearer. When Nanny found out that we would be going to Devon and it would be free, she decided to tag along.

Nanny Tot was a lovely lady, but frugal to say the least. If she could get out of spending money she would do it. One mention of pocket money would have her diving for her panic button. Once, when I was a baby, she bought me a dress because it was cheaper than a pair of trousers. Gary insists that's where my 'trouble' started.

Every kid is excited when their Nan comes to stay, and we were no exception, but the excitement was doubled because we were going on holiday with ours – yeah! We would collect Nan from the National Express coach station ready for our journey onwards to sunny Devon. She would get off the coach and reach into her bag.

'Here you are, love. Here's something for you.'

It would be half a packet of Opal Fruits each – if we were lucky. Sometimes we didn't get them at all, because if Nanny Tot ever saw a disabled person or someone with learning difficulties, she would put her hand in her bag and whip out our sweets. I remember once in a café Nan going to give a paraplegic my uneaten chips. And if this wasn't embarrassing enough, Mum then told her off loudly, saying, 'They want to be treated as equal. They've got rights now.'

Nan's generosity with our sweets to less able-bodied people had a sliding scale of its own – a brain tumour: a whole box of Rowntree's pastilles; limb missing: Fry's chocolate cream; retarded: Bounty; while a stutter would equate to two segments of a Terry's chocolate orange.

Sadly, Nan's tightness actually affected her hearing.

'Can I have 50p to have a ride on the donkeys?' I begged.

She smiled sweetly and carried on with her crossword.

'Please, Nan!'

It was no good. She couldn't hear a thing. If Dad was buying us a fish and chip supper, though, her hearing would become so acute she would have put a bat to shame.

Despite the penny pinching, we did have a lovely time together. Mum and Dad would hit the campsite club and me, Nan and Gary would all sit and try and listen to the television over the noise of the rain pelting down the corrugated-iron roof.

If you were in an even-numbered caravan you were a royal and if you were in an odd-numbered caravan you were a rebel. Whenever you walked around the campsite and came across a redcoat he'd ask, 'What are you?'

'Rebel!' we'd all shout the first year, because we were in caravan 181.

The next year we found ourselves royals. 'What are you?'

'Royal!'

Honestly, who needs Disneyland when you can have this much fun?

Those holidays in Devon and eventually Cornwall were so idyllic. The sun always seemed to be shining and there was a lovely sense of peace about the place. Gary was getting older and becoming more fun and we were able to do things together.

For all the picture-perfect innocence, it soon became clear that something ominous was shifting inside me, as I discovered one afternoon whilst walking along the beach with my parents.

'Alan! Stop that. Stop doing that!' shouted my mother, pointing at me.

'What?'

I was subconsciously mincing along with my bucket in the crook of my arm like a handbag and twirling the spade around my fingers like a majorette.

'Hold it properly!' she insisted.

I personally thought I looked fabulous but I relented and held it 'properly'. Boring!

I often wonder whether my parents took it as an omen or whether it even registered, but looking back now I realise it was the thin end of the wedge.

The only argument I remember between my parents took place on holiday, though. It was quite serious. Dad had used Mum's really expensive shampoo and she was horrified.

'It's a waste on your head,' she retorted. 'You're bloody bald!'

It seems it was all right for Mohammed Ali to take the piss out of my father's lack of hair, but not my mother. He opened the caravan door and flung Mum's shampoo out so far that it cleared the enormous conifers adjacent to our caravan.

Mum cried out, 'Alan! Alan! Go and find my shampoo!'

Like a sniffer dog I was released onto the campsite in my pyjamas and slippers, searching for this bloody shampoo. I eventually found it outside the camp shop. It was lying in the car park next to two pensioners staring up at the sky, hoping that God would deliver them some expensive hair products too.

* * *

Dad's star was on the rise again. After keeping Nuneaton top of the League for a couple of seasons, he was spotted by Northampton Town Football club and he decided to leave the non-League and join a club that was actually in a division even if they were at the foot of that division, and basically bankrupt.

When your dad is manager of the football team of the town you are growing up in and the team are enjoying a particularly good season, even if you don't have the slightest interest in football, people presume you are good at it simply for sharing a surname. I didn't expect to jump over buildings and lasso criminals because I had a Carter in the family tree now, did I?

Simply being called Carr meant that I was genetically modified to be a world-class striker. So whenever I joined a new school and word got round that Alan Carr ('What? The really camp one with glasses and buck teeth?' – 'Yes that's him') was the son of Graham Carr, all the lads, even the tough ones, started hanging around me, inviting me round their houses for tea, asking if I wanted to share a cigarette, offering me a backie on their Grifters. My diary was fit to burst. For once in my life, I was in the midst of a social whirl. Well, let's just say, this was before they saw me on the pitch.

It didn't get me off to a good start. On Monday morning the PE teacher Jenko – he was Mr Jenkinson, but we could call him Jenko, and I would end up calling him a lot worse by the time I'd left that playing field, I can tell you – said, 'We have a celebrity's son with us today,' and then went and appointed me captain.

'Oh no, please, there's been a terrible mistake,' I wailed. 'I'd rather just be here on the sub bench.'

'I'm sure we'll all be pleasantly surprised,' boomed Jenko. They were surprised all right, just not in the way they intended. I lost it, whenever I did get the ball, I couldn't control it, I forgot which end I was meant to be shooting at, and instead of an almighty kick all I could muster was a toe-punt.

Dizzy, I turned round to face them, and they looked at me as if to say, 'This isn't what I ordered.' It was true; instead of being this athletic dynamo nutmegging the opposition, weaving with ease and scoring with flair, I was flailing up and down like Goldie Hawn in *Bird on a Wire*. I lasted five minutes and as punishment was made to collect the ball from the other side of the dual carriageway – which admittedly I had kicked over there, but not all the way over there, to be fair, it had ricocheted off a woman walking her dog.

I admit sometimes I brought the humiliation on myself, but more often than not it was induced by the PE teachers themselves. Jenko was all right, I suppose. I mean, he wasn't malicious, he just couldn't understand why some people were good at sports and others weren't. Jenko was the final one in a long line of unimpressed PE teachers.

I can cope with unimpressed, but it's the sadistic ones I find repulsive. It was during my years at the Middle School that I encountered the worst one of the lot. She was Mrs

O'Flaherty. God, I hated that woman, and I still do. She hated me, too. There was no love lost when I finally left. She covered for Science, and I remember getting one of my first ever migraines during her lesson. She refused to let me out and I had to sit through a lesson on poly-photosynthesis with a paralysed face and what felt like a tsunami of pain flooding around my brain. I hate it when people say migraines are just 'headaches but a bit worse', it really is like saying tuberculosis is a chesty cough – they bloody hurt.

Ooh! I detested that Mrs O'Flaherty. I can still remember those piggy eyes and her bowl haircut: she looked like Joan of Arc – after the fire. Every tennis lesson she partnered me with Matthew, who had learning difficulties, yes learning difficulties, so how was I supposed to improve? Oh, and don't think I didn't notice that everyone else had proper professional tennis rackets and proper professional tennis balls, while Matthew and I were given these rackets so large that I swear if we waved them about in the air enough we could have landed a Boeing 747.

To add insult to injury, our balls were made of sponge. All the other lads got to play outside, apart from us. Apparently, according to Mrs O'Flaherty, if she let Matthew and me play outside, our balls would blow away. So we had to stand in the school hall watching the other kids outside, listening enviously to the 'thwock' of professional rackets hitting professional balls over professional nets.

Poor old Matthew was simple, bless him. I know you can't say that nowadays but he was simple, he didn't know what was going on. But I did! That's what made it so frustrating. I tried to show him the difference between the others' tennis balls and our sponge balls, mainly by throwing them at his head – which is wrong, I know, but I get frustrated too, you know. How am I supposed to improve my backhand if I'm demoted to home-helping my opponent? It just wasn't fair.

Physical Education is the only lesson on the school syllabus where you don't get any help if you're no good at it. Physical it is, Education it ain't. No arm around your shoulder, no comforting word from a teacher, just a great big dollop of contempt and sarcasm. Can you imagine the headlines if little Susie in English couldn't spell scissors, and so was forced to do an extra lap of the library in her vest and pants and then have her arse whipped with a wet towel? The *Daily Mail* would have a field day. You can see why kids today don't want to do exercise and would rather sit at home playing martial arts games on their Nintendo. I wish I'd done that, too – not because I like martial arts, but because the next time Mrs O'Flaherty tried to humiliate me, in one swift *Crouching Tiger, Hidden Dragon* style I'd do a body slam, with a nipple twist, and finish it off with a scissor kick – that would show her! I'd be a hero, and all the fat kids would pick me up and carry me around on their morbidly obese shoulders.

My heart goes out to any kids who are, shall we say, athletically challenged. I understand 'Sport' now that I'm older; it's not so much to do with skill and finesse, it's about Fear. Sliding tackles, scrums, tobogganing, it's all about being fearless. I definitely wasn't fearless – no, I had Fear aplenty, Fear and Worry in abundance. One of the reasons for my Fear was the fact that I would read everything, read and read and read – it's true, 'Ignorance is bliss'. So when it finally came to starting a game of rugby, all the other boys were imagining running down the field (what's a rugby pitch called?) and scoring a magnificent try. Meanwhile, I would be remembering that article I read about the bloke who's a paraplegic due to a hooker falling on his neck. Oh no, not for me, thanks, you go on, boys, you knock yourselves out – how the hell are my glasses going to stay on with a cauliflower ear?

Whether it was me being a chicken-shit or some deeper Darwinian self-preservation thing kicking in, I feared the scrum and all it entailed. I remember Mum pulling my immaculate rugby kit from my bag and accusing me of playing truant. How dare she? I had played rugby. I'd run my little socks off up and down the field. I'd just avoided the muddy bits.

* * *

Overall, though, it takes more than a few isolated moments to dim a wonderful childhood. Yes, we had our ups and downs, but if you're expecting *Alan's Ashes* you're going to be bitterly disappointed. I haven't really had much scandal in my life either. Seriously, at one point I was thinking of getting an uncle to interfere with me just so I could add a bit of pathos.

And I grew up in one of the most boring towns in England.

Northampton is famous for shoes and, apart from the Express Lift Tower, a listed building that in certain lights looks like a concrete dildo, its main landmark is the Northampton

Boot and Shoe Museum, which we'd get dragged around every other year on a school trip. The museum contains a plaster copy of the shoe of one of the elephants that Hannibal used to climb over the Alps. Need I say more? Just imagine getting a guided tour of a massive Freeman, Hardy & Willis, only shitter.

'Excuse me,' I said, taking a replica of one of Marie Antoinette's shoes off the display and holding it out to the curator, 'do you have this in a six?'

'Alan Carr!' shouted the teacher. 'Put that back at once!'

With a weary sigh, I replaced the replica. I just wanted to add a bit of sparkle. Was that a crime?

Chapter Two

'YOU COULDN'T SCORE IN A BROTHEL!'

wish you were here ...

SEA SIDE TOWN

I'm not making excuses for my sporting failures, but a lot of the time my body let me down. Puberty had been unkind. Whereas it had come in the night and left the other boys with chiselled, stubbly chins and deep masculine voices, I'd been left with a huge pair of knockers and the voice of a pensioner – a female pensioner, at that. Breasts that I'd been constantly told were 'puppy fat' were becoming embarrassing. They were getting quite pendulous, and I was starting to get amorous looks from some of the older men when I was country dancing. It made me feel very self-conscious and it didn't help that our sports kit was red shorts, red socks and a white T-shirt that became see-through when sweaty. This, to me, was the worst-case scenario and if I ever had to run I would run with my arms across my chest, which was silly really as it only served to make my cleavage even more impressive.

And as for swimming, I didn't even have the security of a flimsy cotton white T-shirt to cover my bosom. I had to do it naked, except for a pair of dark green woollen swimming trunks, which ironically when they came in contact with water would weigh like lead and make you drop like a stone to the swimming-pool floor.

When you tell people that you had a swimming pool at your school, they raise an eyebrow and naturally assume you went to an idyllic Etonian establishment where it was pony riding, croquet and water polo before tea and scones on the lawn. Don't be fooled by the swimming pool; it was basically a concrete bunker attached to the school that was filled with so many chemicals your eyes would weep as you entered the building. The chemicals were so strong I swear that if you did more than two lengths you'd end up changing sex. All the boys including myself would stand there in their trunks, and even though it was a mixed group none of the girls would be in their bathing suits at all because – *quelle surprise* – they were due on. Every week, they would turn up and hand over a note which their 'mums' had written. 'Sharon, Kelly, Rachel, Caroline, Jenny cannot do swimming as it's their time of the month.' What? Every week?

The older boys would smirk, but I was none the wiser. I knew it had something to do with periods, but the woman on the telly went rollerskating, dog-walking and potholing, and she had a 'period'. All I knew was, I was standing there half naked trying to learn the butterfly and being giggled at by a group of allegedly menstruating young ladies.

People naturally assume I was the class clown – I was and I wasn't. The typical class clown is the lad that tells the jokes and the tough lads laugh and he doesn't get punched. That wasn't me, unless my jokes were really bad, because they used to punch me anyway. I was the one always playing the goat, mucking around. In Science when discussing the planets I was always the one asking the teacher, 'How big's Uranus?' Not particularly witty, I agree, but at twelve it would have the room in stitches, and the other children would look to me as if I were Dorothy Parker.

Even though I used comedy to make friends, I never really felt that I fitted in. I felt like an outsider, looking in, making jokes and comments that turned things on their head, which, writing this, strangely enough sounds like the job description of a stand-up comic. I never seemed to find anyone at school that I felt I had anything in common with, not just hobby-wise (Hey, lads, do you want to come behind the bike sheds and read an Agatha Christie?) but in everything. To me, they could have been another species, let alone another class. Plus, my best friend at the time, Jason, had come into school and took me to one side. 'My dad says I can't hang around with you any more.'

'Why not?'

'Because you're turning me gay!'

'I'm not gay,' I protested convincingly, I thought.

But Jason was adamant, our friendship was over. Apparently after hanging about with me all day at school, he had been coming home talking in an affected, camp manner, decorating sentences with over-pronounced 'ooh's' and raising his eyebrow at anything remotely worthy of innuendo. His dad definitely had nothing to worry about. Jason was very laddy, and I'm sure he must be married now with lots of kids. It goes without saying that you can't 'catch' homosexuality, but I'm afraid to say from personal experience 'camp' can spread quicker than bird flu if not kept at bay. I've reduced builders to simpering Danny La Rues in my time. It's all in the wrist, I guess.

Losing Jason as a friend was a real blow. We'd had a lot of fun times. Every weekend we would go into Northampton Town Centre and wander aimlessly around the Grosvenor Centre or Abington Park, generally mucking about, popping on the wigs in Debenhams or shouting out 'shoplifter' and pointing at an old person in BHS. I'm not proud of what we did, but it killed time.

We would usually end up at the ABC Cinema, this gigantic art-deco building that dominates the top of Abington Street. It's not a cinema any more – it's now the headquarters for the Jesus Army and, quite frankly, it's seen better days – but back then in the late Eighties it was the centrepiece of our Saturday afternoons. I saw everything there, *ET*, *Batman*, *Turner and Hooch*. It was during *Tango and Cash* that one audience member climbed up the curtains and swung daringly in front of Sylvester Stallone's face and had to be told to get down by the cinema manager.

With Jason doing his own thing, I started to dread the bell ringing for breaktimes and lunchtimes because it would normally mean walking around on my own. In class, you feel a bit like you belong, but time out of those lessons tended to make me feel a bit empty, with the breaks seeming to drag more than the actual lessons.

In my moping, I must be thankful for one blessing: I never went down the 'goth' route. Yes, I had been known to write poems expressing my angst, but I had never popped on some mascara and a black leather trench coat and hung around the library looking wistful. I might have been feeling sorry for myself, but I wasn't tacky.

* * *

It was only when I was on the cusp of adolescence that things started to happen. An identity started to manifest before my eyes, an identity that I wasn't particularly happy with.

Almost overnight words like blowjob, wank and cum were on everyone's lips, if you see what I mean. In the corridors you could almost smell the sex, which made a change from the toilets. All of sudden, no one was interested what Liam Gill did in Home Ec, we wanted to know what Tracey did with Darren after school in her back bedroom. Carnal lust swept through breaktime like a tropical breeze. I remember the controversy when one girl, Sharon Bell, had got a boyfriend who didn't go to school. He had a proper job at Homebase and would turn up in his tight white T-shirt revving his motorbike – how cool was that?

To the girls and me, he was the epitome of cool, but technically he was a paedophile. Soon every girl wanted a man with a proper job – sixteen-year-old boys weren't good enough any more. They wanted real men, and in that sense, not only were the lads in my class defunct, so was I. Suddenly girly talk and a boy who liked me for me was as cool as New Kids on the Block. As for the boys, they'd be talking about what they did with whom, where, when and how many times. They'd all laugh with bravado, and I'd laugh along, but on the inside thinking 'Ugh!'

Then it dawned on me, *my* role had changed. I wasn't the class clown any more; no, I was head eunuch in the middle of a debauched orgy. Stop, stop, I want to get off. This wasn't meant to happen; even Paul Simmons was telling people he'd kissed a girl. I mean, he had a long way to catch up with Steve

Templeton. He had been wanked off on the back of the bus on a school trip to the Northampton Boot and Shoe Museum, and Donna Dalton had said it was the biggest one she'd ever seen – she was only fifteen so hopefully she hadn't seen too many.

Panic gripped my body. I needed to act now, and my body went into what can only be described as a hormonal trolley dash. I needed to fuck a woman *now*, *now*, *now*, or at least to look like I was getting some kind of action, but sadly like the proverbial trolley dash my trolley wheels were buckled and I kept steering it towards the willy aisle. It just wasn't fair. It riles me when people say being gay is a choice. It really isn't. Why would anyone choose that? Your pants on the Science block roof – where can I sign up for that? You cannot describe to anyone the sheer terror and isolation you feel when adolescence finally dawns on you, and the path of girlfriend, wife, babies is as distant as Narnia. There is a definite feeling of uselessness and for me a sense of injustice. I remember thinking that it was like a curse, and asking what I had done to deserve this. I really didn't take it well at all.

I had had my moments. I had at one stage started fancying Maria from the board game 'Guess Who?' That long hair, that green beret, that sexy smile – yes, she was a fox. One night in Panache I had kissed a girl called Ruth. A short girl with green eye shadow, yum! It was a retro night and she had drunkenly come up to me during 'Come on Eileen'. I must admit I was tempted. Girls back then were like those big dippers you get at Alton Towers, terrifying but strangely alluring. The worrying thing was that once you actually got on the bloody ride you didn't know whether you'd like it or not, all you knew was you were stuck on it for the next five minutes. Ruth approached me drunkenly across the dance-floor, and my body slipped into fight or flight mode. I fought, but with my tongue. Her tongue tasted of Woodpecker Cider, which wasn't entirely unsatisfying. I lasted about twenty seconds, heard 'Baggy Trousers', made my excuses and left the dance-floor. I'd had a go, and you can't say fairer than that.

I think I was a let-down to my brother in that respect. I remember him asking me conspiratorially in his bedroom, 'How do you get a girl's bra off?'

'How would I know?' I retorted imperiously. 'Stanley knife?'

I think he realised there and then that we weren't going to have one of those laddish relationships, talking about birds and fast cars. So whilst I felt like I was cursed, I wasn't so self-centred as not to notice it affecting others in my family.

Although my brother and I are now the best of friends, the six-year difference between us made sure when we were growing up that we were never going to be bosom buddies. When I needed a friend to play with, he was a baby and technically useless, and when I reached adolescence the thought of hanging around with a seven-year-old made me go cold.

Like every teenager, the cry of 'Take your brother with you!' from your mother as you go to step out the house was the most depressing sound you could ever hear. How uncool was that? Hanging around with a seven-year-old. I would be well moody and offhand with him but he would get his own back in other ways. At fairgrounds I would have to accompany him on the baby rides only for him to start bawling halfway round and get taken off by my mother while I would have to stay on the stupid ride, going round and round looking like a simpleton.

There is a photo of me standing with the 'real' He-Man where Gary had chickened out and started bawling at the sight of He-Man's plastic face. 'Alan! You'll have to have your photo taken with He-Man. I'm not queuing for nothing,' Mum insisted, and there I am, standing next to an out-of-work actor in a He-Man outfit at Weston Favell Shopping Centre, both of us asking ourselves, 'What did we do to deserve this?'

Just when my self-esteem was at an all-time low, I was dealt a body blow, and it was called 'reality'. In Drama we had all been filmed on video performing various soliloquies and it was time to watch them back and get constructive criticism from our teacher. I sat down, all giggly, ready to watch myself with everyone, but I cannot tell you the shock that then shook my body.

That person on the screen wasn't me, there'd been a mistake, it was a grotesquely camp boy with a screeching voice and the most over-the-top mannerisms. He was the gayest boy I'd ever seen. I looked around at my fellow Drama students, hoping they would be just as shocked at this terrible mistake. Nothing. They just smiled back at me. Yes, the boy looked like me, but I wasn't like that, I didn't sound like that. This boy was as camp as Christmas.

Why wasn't anyone else phased by this 'possession'? Why hadn't anyone told me? I suppose they had, really. People hadn't been shouting 'Poof', 'Faggot' and 'Bender' for the last five years out of politeness. Without me knowing, I had been harbouring the world's worst secret. No urge for a girlfriend, Wonder Woman, wearing high heels to get an ice cream, fancying Face from the *A-Team*. Oh my God. It was staring me right in the face. Is this how I've been acting? Christ.

That horrible Drama video had a profound effect on me, and it left me feeling physically sick. I had looked myself in the eye and I didn't like what I saw one bit. I had had that moment of realisation that we all get, where the handsome brute in our heads that we think we look like doesn't actually match what's reflected in the mirror. Some people try to replicate the image they have of themselves in their head by having a make-over, going to the gym, highlights. I chose to give up. Forcing myself to be someone else just wasn't worth it, but I was furious nevertheless.

Typical! I had been the last person to know I was gay. What was my next move to be? I knew one thing for sure: there wasn't going to be a big 'outing' surprise at the kitchen table. I had planned to get everyone to the table and tell them, I had it all worked out. Dad would shout angrily, 'Is this some kind of sick joke?' and my mother would be quietly sobbing in the corner, but my guess was, they had probably passed this stage a long time ago without me, so mentioning my feelings and worries felt a bit like closing the door after the horse had bolted.

In fact the question 'Have you got a girlfriend?' had disappeared off the radar years back. Becoming a full-time gay with a capital G, all croptops and bleached hair, didn't interest me one bit, so I was sort of left wondering what to say and what to do. I chose not to say anything in the end, and still to this day my sexuality has not been mentioned, but with my non-existent love-life I think they've probably forgotten.

* * *

That summer a month didn't go by when I wasn't struck down with a migraine. We went to see the doctor, who said that it looked like I needed glasses. Relief spread across my mother's face – she had thought it was a brain tumour. Yes, I was over the moon; I only had to endure an eye test and not brain surgery, but the thought of having to wear glasses wasn't alleviating my body image crisis. To me, that was like sprinkling hundreds and thousands onto a dog turd.

My first pair of glasses were huge; the lenses were like two pub ashtrays welded onto a couple of pipe cleaners, and to make it worse the rims were bright red. The likeness to Christopher Biggins was uncanny. It broke my heart wearing glasses. I felt, not for the first time, that my body had betrayed me – don't you think I've got enough to be getting on with, without this? I was terrified, and after the optician had done all his tests he informed me that I had 'astigmatism'. I recoiled in horror. 'The wounds of Christ? In my eyes? Jesus never wore glasses!'

The optician put my mind at rest and told me it was astigmatism not stigmata. He told me that astigmatism is caused by the fact that the eyeball is shaped like a rugby ball. Typical! Yet again something sports-related kicking me when I'm down. Although the glasses were horrible, they were still better than the series of headaches that had plagued the last year at school; and besides I could actually see what was written on the board, which has to be a bonus in anyone's books.

I went by Weston Favell Upper School recently, and like most schools these days it resembles a prison. It's got this awful metal fence all the way around the sprawling fields, which does little to lessen the formidable exterior. The fence was put up after someone drove a car into the computer block. Going back and seeing those fields felt to me like I was revisiting a crime scene – all the times I'd run around and around those fields, whether it was cross-country running or playing rounders, all that dread and worry and sweat.

But my mood lifted when I looked beyond the fields and to the back of the school, where the English department stands. Wednesday afternoon was my favourite time of the week, because we had double English. The English teachers at the school instilled this love of reading for which I will be forever grateful. I'd always read, and I think anyone who wants to be somewhere else in life either goes down the video game route or the book route. The fantasy and mystery that can be lacking in your immediate surroundings can be found there, and for such a troubled soul as myself things seemed to make more sense between the pages of a book. The world seemed fairer, the characters more rounded, and then at the end good won over evil every time. Surely you can see its appeal.

I started out reading Agatha Christie and Sir Arthur Conan Doyle, which in turn made me want to be a detective. That's laughable when you think what modern-day policemen have to put up with – Miss Marple would shit herself. To think that I would walk over to a machete-wielding burglar with a crack pipe in his mouth.

'The slight indentation on your index finger shows you've had a stolen DVD in your hand over the last twenty-four hours. You're nicked.'

'It's a fair cop, guv'nor.'

I smile contentedly as he pops the machete down and hands himself over. No, I think Detective Inspector Carr would be horrified with what a real detective does.

I would always be reading and I'd always get an Agatha Christie for Christmas, ripping open the wrapping paper squealing with joy and running past the just-opened shin pads and football boots to start reading *Murder in the Vicarage* without delay.

I hope my literary tastes are more superior and highbrow now. Some of the books on the A-level curriculum are still up there on my list of favourite books, *Brighton Rock* and *The French Lieutenant's Woman*, for instance. Graham Greene is still one of my favourite authors. I loved reading, but the one thing I loved more than reading was reading out loud.

When the teacher would say, 'Today is Shakespeare. Would anyone like to read out loud?' while all the other kids in the class would all of a sudden find something totally fascinating to stare at on the floor, my hand would shoot up. My arm would ache in the socket hoping desperately to be the chosen one. But who did she pick? Philip Fucking Granger. Christ! He couldn't even read. Why choose him? I had a much better reading out loud voice. I could conjure up worlds and emotions with my voice alone. I would actually inhabit the characters on the page, bringing them to life. It was so unfair.

So we would have to sit there while Philip butchered the dialogue and spluttered over some of the easiest words in the English language. He might as well have done a shit on Hamlet's head. It was appalling. I had some satisfaction in hearing his boring voice drone on, though. On the playing fields he was always picked first and would never pick me, and here he was tripping up, getting disorientated, feeling self-conscious. English was my playing field and he'd just pulled a muscle.

One lesson I tried so hard to be good at was Art and Design. I loved performing in the school plays, I loved reading books, so to make up the trio and be a true creative force to be reckoned with I had to be able to paint well, sculpt well, create beautiful things. In other words be an artiste. Teachers would act differently to my scholarly shortcomings. Mrs O'Flaherty would sneer, Ms Dando would pity me, Mrs Wilson would be a bit more proactive with her criticism, particularly in my pottery lessons. With a cry of 'Start again!' she would violently bring her rolling pin down on my vase, my ash tray, my clown figurine, my tree, my mask – anything really that I'd made that lesson out of clay. They were shit, but aren't teachers meant to guide you and nurture you and not demolish your whole lesson's efforts with the swoop of a rolling pin in front of your peers?

What really got me was the way she never hid the fact that my work was shit. I remember her genuine disappointment when she opened the kiln to find Kelly Hubbert's sculpture, a beautiful, thought-provoking piece, cracked in a heap and my 'mouse in a shoe' monstrosity intact next to it.

'Why wasn't it yours?' she cried, with genuine grief, staring at me with accusatory eyes as if I'd tunnelled into the kiln personally and smashed up Kelly's masterpiece.

Despite this, I did like Mrs Wilson. She was a hippy with flame hair and would wear long flowing dresses and scarves and let us listen to music while we 'created'. She was a good person with a good heart, not like Mrs O'Flaherty who didn't have a heart, or feelings. They'd been cruelly removed when she'd had that dreadful bowl cut inflicted on her. Mrs Wilson had given up on my art, which frustrated me because I really wanted to be good at it, but some things you have to let go.

In Art and Design and PE, I became one of those kids that parents of the good pupils say 'holds the others back'. Artistically, I didn't have IT, whatever IT is. Yes, I was disappointed, but I was also realistic. Yes, they may be able to paint beautiful pictures and sculpt statues, but can they recite verses of Shakespeare and Keats off the top of their heads? I can't do that either, but you get my point. I was never jealous of the Kelly Hubberts in my class – though someone must have been because a few days before her deadline she had her artwork stolen from the class.

'There are some sick people out there,' Mrs Wilson told us. 'Now if they'd taken Alan's they would have been really sick in the head.'

I rest my case.

*   *   *

Dad's success as manager of Northampton Town Football Club had meant that we could move from the Moulton Leys Estate to the village of Overstone which, although quaint, was miles away from the school and didn't do much to assuage my feelings of separation. What friends I did make at school all lived miles away, and like every other teenager I always imagined that everyone else was having an amazing time and throwing wild parties while I was stuck in a shitty little village where the only exciting things to do were to water your hanging baskets and moan about ramblers. My parents totally understood this need to feel more integrated, and whenever there was a party at 'The Farm', they would faithfully drive me there. I must have had some friends because in my memory between the ages of 14 and 16 I always seemed to be going to parties, but then again there is a big difference between being lonely and feeling lonely.

The Farm was an outbuilding near Weston Favell Upper School that people would hire if they were having a party. From the age of 14 to 16, it seemed every Friday someone would be celebrating something, and so we'd put on our chinos and waistcoats and head on down to sip on a soft drink and listen to the sound of Yazz. The dance-floor was so uneven that when you jumped up as you did during 'The Only Way is Up', the floor would jolt, causing the stylus to veer off Yazz onto Big Fun. I don't think I ever got to hear the ending of that song.

Every parent booked The Farm apart from Michelle Douglas's, who booked out Danes Camp, which was a leisure centre with a swimming pool – as it said on the invite, it was going to be 'A Pool Party'. Everyone was so excited. Michelle told us that there would be a buffet near the pool, but if any food went in the pool it would have to be cleaned out, costing her parents an extra £200. As kids, we don't know we're born. The Farm was so tedious, week in – week out, and here we were being offered an amazing pool party with food, so how did we repay Michelle Douglas's parents? We grabbed armfuls of sausage rolls, cocktail sausages, those cheese and pineapple things and jumped in the pool – ensuring that the Douglases were in fact £200 out of pocket. Baps, sausage rolls, hot dogs, all bobbed past as we frolicked in the water. It was like swimming in an underwater Greggs.

Obviously, word got round the other parents about the Douglases pool/food fight party, and within weeks we were all back at The Farm. There was a menace there. It wasn't drink or cigarettes, and it definitely wasn't drugs, it was … the Bushwhackers. The Bushwhackers would bang on the windows while we were in there, and make threatening gestures and swear at us. Rumours that it was Michelle Douglas's parents furious about their daughter's pool party were quickly dispelled.

Only a few details were known about the Bushwhackers. They were allegedly from Northampton School for Boys, they had weapons and they could hide for hours in the long grass waiting for someone to come out of The Farm doors. They used to terrify us. Just one bang on the window with a stick would have had us all fleeing to the other end of the room, girls wailing and boys shouting whilst still running in the opposite direction. 'Come on then, I'll take you on.' I'm sure that whoever it was found it all terribly hilarious.

At one party they abducted Stacey Higgins. Everyone was in tears. Should we call the police? Should we venture outside and try to find her ourselves? We all waited by the window eagerly hoping to see what the Bushwhackers would do with this innocent girl's body. Then we spotted her – getting off with a spotty lad behind a wheelie bin. Stacey had used the Bushwhackers as a ruse to sneak out of The Farm and get a groping and a bit of tongue action. We were outraged at her defection.

The attacks by the Bushwhackers, although harrowing at the time, proved a timely distraction for me especially as the sounds of Stock, Aitken and Waterman began to slow and morph into power ballads, and everyone around me paired off to start dancing together. This to me was the death knell of the evening, the excruciating part. Why couldn't we just dance, dance, dance? I didn't really want to dance with the girls, but then I didn't really want to dance with the boys either, so it would leave me at a bit of a loose end, holding my coat at the edge of the dance-floor listening to the sounds of Richard Marx's 'Right Here Waiting'.

They never played Gloria Estefan's 'Don't Want to Lose You Now'. That song was so romantic and beautiful – I was such a big Gloria fan. I loved the *Cuts Both Ways* album and used to really crank up the dial when 'Oy Mi Canto' came on. I learnt that in English it means 'Hear My Voice' and I remember thinking, 'What a talent! There's not many pop stars these days who could sing so beautifully in two different languages.'

I went off Gloria when she suffered spinal injuries in that coach crash, not because she was nearly crippled or anything, it's because I realised she was shit.

It wasn't just our Gloria pumping out of my stereo, I was also a huge Prince fan. I bought everything, every biography about him, every album, even every awful film that he starred in, I was there on the day of release outside Our Price, full of excitement.

Let's get this clear, though. I never dressed up as him. I know some Prince fans go the whole hog and impersonate their idol, but I was getting enough stick at school without turning up on Mufti Day in a purple lace all-in-one body-stocking. I was mesmerised by Prince, the amount of times Mum would catch me miming to his songs and practising that bit where he jumps up and does the splits during 'House-quake'.

My father must have been beside himself: me, football-phobic, girlfriendless, camp and now the final insult – I choose to have a 5-foot transvestite as my Pop Idol. How could he not 'get' Prince? Well anyway he just didn't, and Prince was banned from the car even though I'd created a parent-friendly cassette of Prince's classic hits. My efforts were futile and instead we had to endure Chris Rea's *Road to Hell* on every journey, well, until he brought out *Auberge*. Whoopee-doo!

Ever since Dad had got Northampton promoted up from Division Four with a club record of 99 points and 103 goals and then to the heady climes of number six in Division Three, we as a family could afford to leave England and holiday abroad. Naturally, the chance of flying on a plane was so much more fantastic than the five-hour car journey behind a string of caravans to Beverley Park in Torquay.

Flying by plane meant you'd arrived, and in class you'd drop it into conversation that you would be going abroad, on a plane – yes, *you* heard – on a plane to Spain. The Spain that I had in my head was not the Spain that greeted my eyes when we pulled up at Fuengirola. I'm sure when it was finished being built it would look wonderful. It was to me a bit like Northampton-sur-Mer. Any Spanish culture had been trampled on by English bars promising 'English food' and 'English-speaking staff' for English customers. Of course this is the snob in me looking back with my fancy ways after sampling the cultural highlights of Barcelona and Madrid. Back then it was amazing. You got proper fish fingers and chips, and you could watch Del Boy on the telly – oh, this was so much better than Torquay.

Don't get me wrong, I'm not knocking Torbay or the neighbouring beauty spots of Paignton or Babbacombe. I have a lot of fond memories of those places, and I for one am over the moon that they are enjoying a revival of fortunes at present, it's just that we'd holidayed there at the same caravan park for the last five years.

My parents weren't the sort of people who waited for the designated school holidays, oh no, the Cobblers had their last game and then we were off – 'Cornwall here we come, lock up your pasties!' It was even known for Dad to take us out of school to go to the races. We were all in on it. I would not go to school, Dad would drive us to the race track and Mum would write the sick note. Due to her own experiences at school, my mother's inherent contempt for teachers would often surface in these sick notes. Sometimes she would just write 'Alan was ill', leaving me to do the dirty work and choose an appropriate illness, which would be hard for one day. One day off is too long for a headache, yet too short for ringworm.

Once there, the races were so exciting, especially if you got near the front, and the horses would thunder past you, leaving you windswept and breathless. I enjoyed visiting all the different racetracks. I loved the buzz of the winners' enclosures, and the flurry of the tic-tacking, but most exhilarating of all was being naughty and missing a whole day of school. Newmarket, Leicester, Ripon – by the age of 13, I'd visited them all. I couldn't read, but I'd visited them all.

I remember being at York races on a school day, studying the form, binoculars around my neck, and bumping into Mr Knott, a teacher at my school. I don't know who was more embarrassed, he or I. To be fair, he didn't have a leg to stand on. I was only jeopardising *my* education by being at the races – he was putting his whole class at risk. Tut tut. We soon got over our awkwardness, especially after I told him about a dead cert in the 2.15, 'Dancing Lady', odds-on favourite. He'd be a fool not to bet on it.

* * *

In the summer of 1990, Northampton Town Football Club had fallen out of love with my father and he got the sack. Northampton Town had been relegated back down to the

Fourth Division. My father's battle to keep them up in the Third Division, struggling with no money to buy new players, ended unsurprisingly in disappointment.

The problem with having a job in the public eye, as I am learning now, is that everyone knows your business and wants to let you know their opinion on your business whether you want to hear it or not. When Dad's sacking was on the front page of the *Chronicle and Echo*, the taunts of 'Your dad's shit' were replaced with 'Your dad's been sacked' – which is more of a statement than a put-down really, but each to their own. In fact they used to shout 'Your dad's shit' even when he was top of the Fourth Division, so in the end these insults proved more exasperating than anything.

One neighbour knocked on our door saying that she thought it was a shame that we would be moving so suddenly. She had mistakenly assumed that our house in Overstone had been bought by the club and that we would be evicted now Dad was unemployed. This woman hadn't said a word to us all through Dad's years of success but somehow Dad's sacking had awoken some kind of malice in her and she had come round to gloat. Cheeky bint.

However, much to our neighbour's disappointment, my father wasn't out of a job for long. Within days he was being wooed by Blackpool City Football Club and in a matter of weeks he was the new manager. Dad informed the family that we would be relocating up north to Blackpool. I would finish my schooling in seagull-shitting distance of the Golden Mile. I really had mixed feelings about this move. The excitement of living by the seaside, the Pleasure Beach just down the road, the dodgems, the Illuminations was undermined by a sense of 'Here we go again!' At least in Northampton it was better the devil you know. It was only the diehard bullies who still shouted 'Faggot!' and 'Poof!' – all the others had given up, bored that I never fought back. All they would get in retaliation was a 'tut' or at the most I'd twat them with my copy of *Murder on the Orient Express*.

The thought of joining a whole new school, friendless, looking as I did with this voice was simply terrifying. But Dad was unemployed, and so we had to go where the work was and that just happened to be the Vegas of the North – Blackpool.

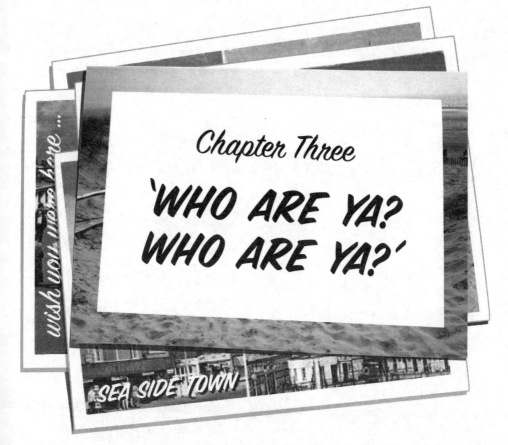

Chapter Three

'WHO ARE YA?
WHO ARE YA?'

wish you were here ...

SEA SIDE TOWN

Everyone has a place that seems to draw them back to it, whatever life choices they make, whatever they do. After a few years they can bet their bottom dollar they end up back there. My place is Blackpool. Like a piece of foil to a filling, I end up attached to it, which inevitably turns out to be a painful experience. Our move to Blackpool wasn't my first time up there: Gary, Mum, Nan and I had gone on a weekend break with Dad's friend Ted who, with some of his friends, drove us up in a minibus. The weekend was pretty uneventful. It was only a few years later, when Ted got arrested for running an unlicensed brothel in the next village and we recalled that all our fellow holidaymakers had been ropy women, that it dawned on us we'd had a weekend break with a minibus full of hookers.

It was a great weekend, to be fair. We had gone up to see the Christmas Illuminations. We had a fantastic view of them at the front of our hotel, and it was a real novelty to have the lights flashing outside our window. I suppose some of the girls would have been used to that.

The one thing that does spoil the whole Blackpool experience – apart from the architecture, food, cleanliness and quality of entertainment – is the weather. The wind is so merciless and bitter, it's almost frightening. We had a jolly Santa swinging outside our window one night; he was shaking so violently in the wind that I thought his sack was going to come through the window and electrocute Nan.

The other time I'd been there was with my mates, and they'd booked us all into Thompsons Hotel. While most Blackpool hotels have a selection of pamphlets on the front desk advertising the Winter Gardens or the Tower Ballroom, Thompsons has the latest North West STD figures and a sachet of complimentary lubricant. Apparently in the summer of 2004 gonorrhoea was more popular than Bobby Davro. The place was basically a knocking shop, with no locks on the door and the smell of sex permeating every nook and cranny and, believe me, there are a lot of crannies. At least we didn't have to be disturbed by the chambermaid in the morning asking if we needed teas or coffees; no, she could just refill the basket through the custom-made glory holes in the wall.

Of course, I was disgusted and outraged, but it's funny, isn't it, how after three bottles of wine and copious gins and tonics you get used to the minor design flaws and out-of-date curtains. That Sunday morning I woke up in Thompsons with the worst hangover I'd ever had. I didn't have my glasses on, but even through my myopic haze I could see that the man lying next to me had special needs. Then I felt someone turn over on my other side, a man who looked relatively 'normal'. Oh no! Please, dear God, please don't tell me I've had an orgy on a Sunshine Coach.

The helper reassured me that it had been only him and that the special needs man had his own room, but sometimes he couldn't sleep so he gets into bed with him. Although I couldn't remember anything at all, I was happyish with his story and didn't really want to pick it to pieces too much – yes, ignorance can be bliss. I thanked everyone involved, picked up my clothes and left Thompsons, got on a tram and went somewhere to have a wash.

* * *

Blackpool for me just throws up drama after drama, a bit like the sea does with sanitary products. It's a place that I just can't visit without 'something' happening to me. That 'something' happened again, recently. I was there filming a pilot for Channel 4, *The End of the Pier Show*, with the lovely Lionel Blair as my stooge. Working with Lionel Blair was an absolute scream – he is such a lovely man with a wicked sense of humour. I can honestly say I have never laughed so much on a show; if only the audience could have said the same.

Anyway, we persevered with the show, which was basically a music-hall/cabaret show at the end of Blackpool pier, and to be fair it went all right. So Lionel and I decided to have a celebratory glass of red wine in the bar at the end of the pier. Our drink was disturbed by a hunchbacked man advancing to our table saying, 'There's a man trying to kill himself. You've got to help him.' Why, when we were surrounded by life-guards and first-aiders, he came to the two campest men in Blackpool (and that's saying something) I will never know.

We followed the hunchback, and he was right. There was a man, shirtless, hanging off the end of the pier in a godawful blustery gale, wailing, 'I want to die! I want to die!' I instinctively thought the show wasn't that bad, but we decided to help nevertheless. I ran straight over; Lionel tap-danced. The man hadn't been in the audience (thank God, I thought – I might look confident, but my ego is as fragile as a porcelain figurine), he was mentally ill (hooray!).

Lionel dashed straight over and said, 'I'm Lionel Blair off the telly.' The man stopped mid-wail and looked up, totally bewildered. Then I popped my head over and said, 'Oh hello.' He looked dumbstruck, so while his brain tried to compute what Lionel Blair and Alan Carr were doing at 10 p.m. on the end of Blackpool Pier, we both pulled him off (not like that) and the police turned up and took him off our hands.

Did they give us a Community Action Trust Reward? No. Did we get any thanks off the man? No, all that Lionel and I were left with was a wonderful anecdote that we could hawk about at parties like the whores we are. We were even more buoyed up now; not only had we finished our pilot, we'd saved a man's life, so we went to Funny Girls and celebrated. We told the Drag Queen and asked for a dedication – Blondie's 'The Tide is High' – but the drag queen didn't get it. Ahh!

We spent the summer of 1990 up in Blackpool; we were totally supportive of our father and really wanted this move to work. But even he would admit the excitement at living by the seaside began to ebb away slowly, especially when we ended up living above a launderette. I don't think it ever stopped raining. The stacks of rain-soaked deckchairs looked a sorry sight, framed by the Golden Mile which through the rain looked the colour of baby poo. Plus the view outside the window of a flickering pelican crossing wasn't the illuminations that we'd been promised. The Chairman, Owen Oyston, sensed our disappointment and soon had us installed in a room at the Imperial Hotel, which sounds fabulous, but when you're 14 do you want to sleep with your family in the same room? It's Blackpool, not the fucking Blitz. However, we persevered with the weather, the cramped conditions, and everyone keeping schtum about the fact they weren't really enjoying this experience; this was Dad's job, and the family that sleeps together sticks together, if you see what I mean.

The job wasn't really going as Dad had expected either. The Blackpool fans, unlike the loyal Cobblers ones, didn't really take to him and he'd started receiving abuse. Abuse from people who've chosen to live in Blackpool – now I've heard everything. Sometimes it takes something totally unrelated to snap people out of a situation. Ours happened one morning with Dad coming through the hotel door, dripping wet, white as a sheet, holding Minstral in his arms like Superman did to Lois Lane.

'Why are you wet?' asked Mum. Minstral had fallen off the end of Blackpool pier and thankfully the tide had been in. Minstral in a panic was doing the doggie paddle (what else?) to get back to the shore, but instead due to the waves was getting pummelled against the sea defences. Dad dived in. Just like those people in the paper that you tut at for being so stupid who dive in to save their beloved pets and they end up dying whilst the pet swims quite happily to the other side thinking it's a game.

Yes, in a split second Dad turned into one of those have-a-go heroes. Minstral was saved and spent the rest of the day in shock lying meekly in his basket, although Mum was certain he was 'just being dramatic'. Surely the dog was too fatigued to be giving my mother dirty looks. This dramatic moment brought it all home to us, and we all agreed that none of us was enjoying this at all, and now even the dog agreed with us. We all decided that this was shit.

In November we were put out of our misery; Dad lost his job, and so we went back to Northampton. I'd never been so happy to see the place. We could tell we were getting close – we could see the Express Lifts Tower erect in the distance dominating the landscape like an extended middle finger.

* * *

After all the worry and the stress and ups and downs of Dad's career, the summer of 1992 was all about me. My GCSEs had finished and it was now time to choose where I wanted to take this sorry excuse of a life onwards. The different subjects floated around my head. Science and Football were automatically no-nos. One of the languages, perhaps, Religious Studies, Home Economics, I just couldn't decide. Maths had got so difficult with all the Pythagoras theorems and Pi signs; if I took it at A-level, I swear I'd have a stroke. I was none the wiser. I always think it's a shame that you get to do your A-levels at that age just when you're discovering the delightful distractions of going out, alcohol and partying. Believe me, when you're 16 and desperate to experience 'having a drink', even the dodgy nightlife of Northampton has a strange allure. I'd experienced being the other side of the bar when I was a glass collector at a singles night at Sywell Motel. It wasn't me. Being groped by menopausal women and answering crank calls from your own father asking if the 'Grab a Fanny/Dig up a Date' night was still on can get quite wearing, believe me.

I would often go drinking with my friend Carolyn. We had known each other since lower school, she being just another girl in my ever-expanding gang of ladies. Well, Carolyn and I would head down Bridge Street and drink 'K' cider. Just typing that letter makes me shiver. I don't know what was worse: the taste on the way down, or the taste on the way back up. Thankfully 'K' cider is no more. They used to cost a pound at 40's, the bar of choice for illegal underage drinkers, and looking back I still feel robbed.

Why do first-time drinkers always choose cider as their gateway drink? Is it because they think that the apples in the cider make up one of their five a day? I don't know, but I always drank cider. K, Strongbow, Woodpecker, anything. I can remember shitting myself in the Saddlers Arms after having three pints of Scrumpy. I was well pissed off because they were new flares. I use the word 'new' very loosely. Carolyn and I were going through that well-worn phase of becoming obsessed with the Seventies, the music, the fashion, the attitude, everything about it. So after getting high on the sounds of Chic, Parliament and Candi Staton in Carolyn's bedroom, we would scour the charity shops for funky clothes to emulate our soul sisters and brothers whilst doing the 'Wellie Road'.

The 'Wellie Road' – or to give it its full name, the Wellingborough Road – is basically a long road with pubs and bars on either side that leads into the town centre. It can get quite rough at the weekend, so why Carolyn and I chose to walk down it dressed as Shaft and Cleopatra Jones is beyond me. Of course, we thought we looked funky and superfly and that's why people were staring and pointing and shouting abuse. I realise now there's nothing superfly about smelling of musty piss or wearing clothes that have names like 'Elsie' and 'Wilf' sewn into the back of them. We were meant to look like we were from the Seventies, not *in* our seventies. Carolyn was and is a really pretty blonde girl, with these sparkling blue eyes and a curvaceous figure, and we would always play the same trick in all the pubs. She would go up to a man and say, 'Do you want to buy me and my friend a drink?' Of course he would buy two drinks waiting expectantly for another pretty blonde young lady to return from the toilet, but no, it would be me, in a sheepskin, smelling like a dead Alsatian. 'Thanks, mate,' I would smile cheesily as I took my first slurp of free scrumpy.

How I didn't get my head kicked in, I don't know – but then again, some of the men Carolyn picked were so paralytic, they thought I was a woman anyway. They probably thought I was a member of Boney M, popped in for a cider and black on the way to a Memphis recording session. Often we would end up at the Roadmender, which had only recently been revamped and reopened – by Roger Daltrey, no less. As you can imagine, we absolutely adored the monthly 'Carwash' nights. A whole night dedicated to the Sounds of the Seventies; we had the look, and now we had the music. It would always be worth hanging around to the end because more often than not a fight would break out and you would see grown men punching and kicking in Seventies' clothes, afros would go flying in the air, blood-spattered afghans littered the floor … It was like Sister Sledge had trod on a landmine. It was one of the funniest things you'd ever seen.

We thought naively that it was where we belonged, and we became quite protective about it; the Roadmender was for people like us. Those nights were pure madness, always ending up having an adventure, or waking up at some dodgy person's house. We'd each tell our parents that we were staying around the other one's house, so that gave us a free rein to make mischief and see where our Cuban heels took us.

Once I remember waking up one morning in a strange house with a Jack Russell sitting on my face. I know this sounds perverse but the house was so cold I let her sit on it for a bit longer; you can't beat a warm face. Worryingly, if the dog had sat a few inches down, I would have suffocated to death. Thankfully, the stench of K cider repelled her from my lips.

*　*　*

Although I loved the dressing up, the disco and the kebabs and chilli sauce that I would inevitably find plastered to the hem of my flares the next morning, I was itching to find people who danced my end of the ballroom, if you see what I mean. I wanted to see if there were any people in Northampton like me, so on a few weekends I would go out by myself, lie to my parents about staying at Carolyn's house and venture out, hungry to taste Northampton's gay scene myself, alone.

The only problem is there is no gay scene in Northampton, no bars, clubs or anything, so you would spend half your time trying to find clues and following camp men around town seeing where they were heading. A lot of the time they were going home and you would end up on a housing estate at ten o'clock at night none the wiser and sober as a judge. I remember thinking with my collars up as I slid from doorway to doorway, 'This must be what it was like to be in the Resistance.'

After weeks of intense research, I struck gold. There was one bar, Cabanas on Sheep Street, and every Thursday there was a poetry night which I took to be a positive sign. Come on, surely there were some gays at a poetry night. I turned up paralytic. I had been drinking heavily out of sheer terror of meeting a genuine homosexual in captivity. The bouncers refused to let me in because I was so drunk, which probably did me a favour, looking back. But I shuffled home dispirited – so near yet so far.

I returned to Cabanas in the following weeks and saw that it wasn't exclusively gay, but a mixed crowd. No, it wasn't Studio 54, I grant you, but it had a lovely relaxed vibe, and after the poetry the tables and chairs would be pulled back and everyone would dance to acid jazz. I felt really at home, it made such a change from the haze of Ben Sherman shirts and tight perms that crammed the pubs and bars on the Wellie Road.

Sadly Cabanas closed down shortly after, but in its place a proper gay club was built and the same crowd would turn up, and the partying would carry on as if nothing had happened. And I started to get lucky. I don't know whether because they fancied me or because I was fresh meat on the lazy Susan that was Northampton's gay scene.

At 17 I lost my virginity to a guy who took me back to his house. I was very drunk, so can't remember much; what I do remember isn't good. He had a hideous fern display on the wall and rugs on the floor that wouldn't look out of place in a nursing home. For a split second I thought, 'Oh my God! He's blind!' but alas he wasn't. Anyway, more to the point he was good looking which I suppose made up for at least some of the vile decor.

We started kissing in the hall and fell into the living room, me trying to unbuckle his trousers, and him trying to shoe-horn my Cuban heels off and peel back my sheepskin. He rushed over to pop on some music. He rushed back to me and we carried on kissing, only this time to the soundtrack of Celine Dion and Peabo Bryson's 'A Whole New World'. How am I supposed to maintain an erection with that racket banging on? Anyway, it was an experience, not the greatest but an experience nevertheless.

I was aroused from my slumber the next morning, with his arm around me. Then it hit me like a lightning bolt.

My parents are having their carpets laid!

In all the excitement I'd forgotten that my parents were away for the weekend and were having new carpets fitted. I had to let the man in! I jumped out of bed and shook him vigorously. 'I've got to go home. They're going to kill me.' He very kindly offered to drive me to my house, but I got the sneaky suspicion he just wanted me off the premises. We pulled up outside my parents' house.

'Do you want to see me–'

Before I could finish, I was launched from the car without even so much as a kiss, and in a puff of exhaust fumes he drove off. It was my first taste of the gay scene's entrenched fickleness – the bastard! Well, at least I wouldn't have to see those nasty ferns again.

* * *

Phew! I got my GCSE results and they were surprisingly good. I was overjoyed at the B I got for English. I got another B for Drama and Theatre Studies – another of my favourite lessons. One surprise – which was as much of a surprise back then as it is now – was my A for French. I really don't know how I got that. The oral exam was dreadful. I hadn't really learnt the chapter on 'la pharmacie', and when I was told I had to tell the doctor I had a sore throat, I whispered in a husky voice, 'J'ai une bouche rouge.'

Somewhere along the line I must have convinced myself that I was a competent French speaker, as for some reason I took that subject along with English and Drama and Theatre Studies for my A-Levels. French at A-level standard is so different to GCSE, and the difference hit me like a truck. All of a sudden we were bombarded with an array of different tenses. Pluperfect? Past historic? Past pluperfect? How many ways can you ask for a croissant? And really, as if anyone is going to hang around France long enough to learn all the different ways! Typical French, making out their language is soooo complex.

Learning those tenses was a real slog; it was a real shock to the system. At GCSE level I was happy saying, 'J'habite à Northampton,' and telling Madame Lebran to 'ouvrer' her 'fenêtre'. I didn't care what tense, just open your window, love, it's baking in here. If I'd known after all my hard work that I was only going to get a miserable E for the bloody subject at A-level, I wouldn't have bothered.

I had initially chosen History, but when I got a B for it at GCSE I naturally thought the A for French was Destiny leading me up the path onwards to a job abroad as an interpreter at the United Nations perhaps. My overactive imagination hyperventilating at the thought that there could be a life outside Northampton, other malls to shop at that weren't the Grosvenor Centre, other people who could be my friends, any little snippet that could offer a way out from this was grabbed with both hands and clutched to my breast. This French thing stimulated my mind; for one moment in my life I thought I might have a special talent for something. So without a second thought I turned my back on History, which in hindsight would have been much more fun, if the Suez Crisis and the Boer War could be classed as fun, and picked French.

A lot of the time it's the teachers that make the subject bearable. Mr Mulkern was one of those teachers that made it unbearable. He was a good teacher, I'm sure, but it's just the way he dressed with his drainpipe Farahs and threadbare leather jacket. You couldn't take him seriously, especially when in a documentary on the Holocaust you could see Goebbels wearing the exact same jacket.

Well, we were in bits, and before you knew it he would be spinning on his winklepickers like Michael Jackson in 'Billie Jean' to see where the snigger was coming from. He was so full of nervous energy, you could almost hear him crackle. I saw him on the last day and he asked how I'd done. I told him my results, and he said, 'Well done,' and threw his arms around me. I was rigid. I never knew he could be pleased for anyone, let alone give a public display of affection. When he pulled back, he seemed genuinely pleased, and in that moment I saw a connection with the bachelor, nervy teacher. Like me, he'd never had the opportunity to let his guard down and was just getting through it all on his nerves, desperate not to let anything slip, and with a swish of his Gestapo trenchcoat he goose-stepped out of my life.

For Physical Education I got a D, which is probably accurate. But one thing that does add insult to injury is the B I got for effort. So basically what the teachers were saying was, even when I tried really, really hard, I was still shit. Thanks! I should have just stayed at home. Looking down the marks, I see my only other Ds were Science and Art. The irony is I quite like science now. I'll watch anything about DNA, seismic plates, the moon, forensics, anything. It's so interesting, and that's what makes it so hard to associate it with the dreary subject they were teaching me at school. Slumped over a Bunsen burner wearing oversized goggles making sulphur, I'd rather listen to Chris Rea's 'Road to Hell', and if that doesn't make you drop off, here's a periodic table to really float your boat.

Probably one of the only lessons that sticks out from the grey mist that was science was the Biology lesson where we had to cut up a bull's eye and a spreadeagled frog. That was a lesson where I actually came alive – not because of the subject matter, but because Lucy Swann put a frog's leg down the back of my collar. I let out such a high-pitched shriek that I'm sure I shattered a test-tube somewhere in the lab. She had picked her victim right; you only get the chance to slip a frog's leg down your enemy's back once, so you've got to pick some-one who you know will make the loudest noise. And I deliv-ered. A giggling Lucy Swann got sent out (rightfully so) by our teacher Ms Dando – a lovely lady who deserved a better class – and was given a real good telling off. Lucy Swann told me later that Ms Dando had berated her for firstly abusing the frog's leg, and then picking on me, a 'sensitive boy', and that she could have done serious damage.

When it comes down to the task of picking what job you want to do when you're older, it can be very daunting. The perpetual fear that you are going to choose the wrong path and forever live the life of a lollypop lady is never far from your mind. This fear wasn't allayed much by Mrs Lees, the Careers Officer. In fact, the fear grew as she revealed to us in graphic detail all the joys that were awaiting us at the various depots and industrial estates in Northampton.

Visiting her was possibly one of the most disenchanting moments of my life. If you had no idea what you wanted to be, you would just fill in the multiple-choice form, and she would then feed it through the computer, and lo and behold, in ten minutes your ideal job would appear on a printout. The computer told me my ideal job was 'prison warden'. My heart sank. In the 'Likes' box, I must have ticked 'men' and 'confined spaces' a few too many times. Can you really see me pacing up and down a corridor shouting menacingly at lifers and serial killers, 'SHUT IT!' 'YEAH YOU 'EARD'. 'YOUR GOIN' DAHN'? No, neither could I. I was terrified – is that all life had to offer me? A big dangly set of keys and a grey polyester uniform.

I wasn't alone. The cleverest boy in the class got 'van driver'. At least in Broadmoor I would get to stretch my legs. Looking back, I don't know whether the computer was a deliberate ploy to get you to buck your ideas up before your A-levels or if it had been put on a Northampton default setting and was giving us an honest appraisal of the shite jobs available to us in the Rose of the Shires. Look, I didn't want to be an astronaut, but a data entry operative? Over my dead body! Little did I know that I would be doing data entry for Mr Dog Petfoods in a matter of years. It seems Mrs Lees would put Nostradamus to shame with her career predictions.

* * *

I'd performed a few plays and Christmas revues and although the terrible nerves that paralysed me before I went on marred the experience somewhat, it was the only thing I seemed to enjoy, apart from reading out loud, which is 'acting' really I suppose. My first ever play was *Animal Farm*, the George Orwell classic, not the one where the woman fucks a horse. Squealer was my name and my costume was a pink tracksuit, pink sticks for legs and a prosthetic pink snout, for an amateur production. The sets were stunning. My co-star, Napoleon, was Michael Underwood, who like me is also on the telly; he's a presenter on GMTV in the mornings and famously broke his ankle in *Dancing on Ice*. The wuss.

When it came to casting between him and me, he was always given the best roles, and rightfully so: he had the enthusiasm, the energy and, more importantly, a range. I was so excited about getting my first role in a play, I tried my pig costume on in the kitchen. Slipping on the tracksuit and then the pig's face, I was going to surprise my family in the front room. I burst through the door with a massive snort. It was a triumph! The whole family clapped at my transformation, commenting on my interpretation. Then I began to smell something. Minstral had shat himself in fear. On the beige carpet there was a foot-long skid mark where Minstral had yelped and followed through. I suppose just sitting there dozing off in his basket only to be awoken by a giant camp pig bursting through the door would be alarming to a human, let alone a mongrel. I made my mind up I would never surprise anyone ever again by dressing up as an animal and bursting into their lounge.

Animal Farm went well, and it was there that I got the bug for performing big time. I soon sniffed out any other productions that I could join or help out in. When you're at that level, no one cares that you haven't got a range, they're just pleased a boy wants to join the cast. Later that year I auditioned and got the part of Bottom in *A Midsummer Night's Dream*. I was excited and terrified in equal measures. I wouldn't be performing in front of parents, who were happy if you didn't walk into the furniture, but at a proper theatre, the Royal Theatre.

To my surprise, the show got rave reviews, and the *Chronicle and Echo* loved my Julian Claryesque portrayal of Bottom. Obviously, I didn't have the heart to tell them that I had no choice; believe me, my Macbeth would have been Julian Claryesque. Admittedly, some of the luvvies involved in amdram can do your head in with their affected mannerisms and teak performances, but underneath it all their hearts were in the right place and I enjoyed the camaraderie of putting on a show.

It's the same feeling I get when I work with Justin Lee Collins on *The Friday Night Project*, that feeling of mucking in, rehearsing, everyone bringing something to the table so we can put the best show on. As with most things, it's always the bits that go wrong that unite people. When you're doing an amateur production especially, the technical mishaps are plentiful.

We were midway through the play, up to the part when Bottom gets turned into an ass and Titania falls in love with him and kisses him, transforming him back into a man. So picture me, there in a trance lying in Titania's lap. She kisses me and goes to take my papier mâché donkey head off. Well, what we didn't know was that the costume woman had done the donkey's head elastic in a double bow so it wouldn't fall off. So as she was pulling it off it was pinging back on my face. The more she was tugging, the harder it pinged back. It didn't help that I was face down in her lap. From the back row it must have looked like the donkey was going down on her. 'What would Dame Maggie Smith do?' I thought. I had to snap the elastic myself. But theatre buffs needn't worry; I was

ME, TOPLESS ON WEYMOUTH BEACH

NO, I'M NOT LAUGHING AT MY MUM'S HAIR

'I WONDER WHAT POSITION HE'LL PLAY?'

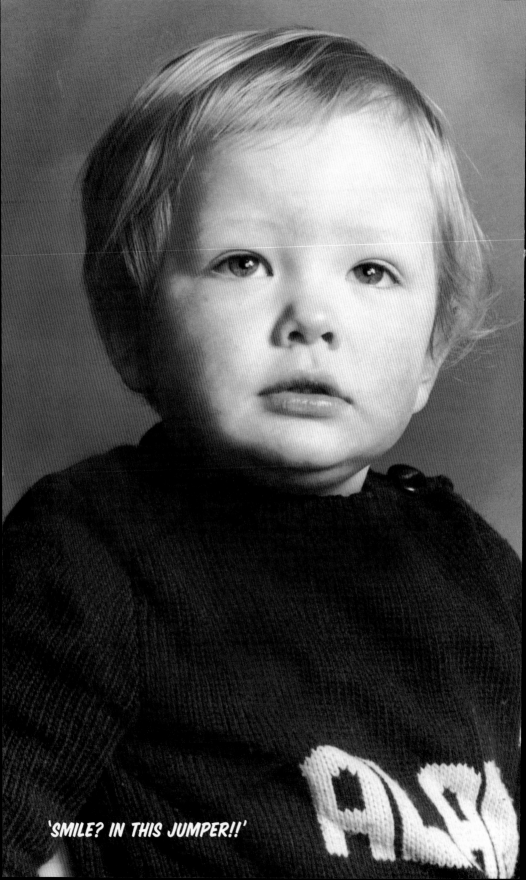

'SMILE? IN THIS JUMPER!!'

MINSTRAL - THE EARLY YEARS

ME AND BIG PUSS

NANNY TOT, ME, DAD AND THE OBLIGATORY FOOTBALL

AHHH! YOUNG LOVE

ME, NAN AND A SERIOUSLY
PISSED-OFF GARY

'STOP BEING CAMP – OR I'LL SHOOT'

LEGEND MEETS MOHAMMED ALI

ME WITH AN OUT-OF-WORK ACTOR

OUR BIRTHDAY PARTIES WERE KNOWN FOR THEIR EXTRAVAGANCE

BUTTER WOULDN'T MELT

PISSED!

MY POLYESTER HELL

MY TEETH, WITH ME IN
THE BACKGROUND

THE TOOTH FAIRY HAD HAD A DOUBLE SHIFT THAT DAY

'PLEASE BE AN AGATHA CHRISTIE!!!!!'

only out of my Julian Claryesque character for a split second, you'll be pleased to know.

The Royal Theatre is a very atmospheric place, and probably one of the few places in Northampton that you could honestly say had an atmosphere. I was excited to perform there and also a little bit intrigued, as a few years before on a school trip I had seen my one and only ghost. I saw a grey lady in the Royal Theatre foyer, and it was a ghost. She was hovering and everything; for about three seconds this grey, smoky apparition just wafted past me. It was a strange feeling really; I thought I would be scared, but I wasn't. Don't get me wrong, I don't want to see another one. Apparently many performers have seen this woman, and some have reportedly heard her wail, but then that's understandable, trapped between life and death and forced to walk the streets of Northampton for all of eternity. At least if you're a poltergeist you get to throw things.

The 'grey lady' wasn't my only run in with the paranormal. I'd started mucking around with an ouija board. My friend Michelle had found it in her attic and eerily it had had wax on it where obviously the previous residents had sat around playing it by candlelight. Well, let's just say that they were a lot braver than I was.

We started playing it, joking at first, then it started moving by itself. Of course, we thought the other one was pushing it, but we weren't. It freaked us out. However, when Mum called to pick me up from Michelle's house we told her what we were doing. Now, Mum's pretty cool with this; she used to play on the ouija when she was a kid and had had some really weird experiences. Mum popped down her handbag and put her finger on the glass. Jesus, it started whizzing around the board, spelling out names, places, telling us about themselves. Mum definitely wasn't pushing the glass. This was confirmed when one spirit called Lee refused to say goodbye and called Mum 'a slut'. Mum said, 'Maybe we should put the board away and go home.' I agreed. Neither Michelle nor my mother nor I ever played the board again. If we wanted to hear those kind of words, we'd shop at Aldi.

When it came to me taking my A-levels, I don't know what I was more excited about – taking French, English or Drama or not having to take PE or Home Economics, because believe me that had been a real pain in the arse. Some bright spark had put Home Economics and PE on the same day, Monday. So every Monday I'd turn up at Weston Favell Upper School with more bags than Mariah Carey; one a Tupperware box full of ingredients and the other my PE kit. Sometimes I'd wedge the two in the same bag and after a whole day of trundling from one class to the next, something would have fallen out of its pot and I'd have the humiliation of doing star jumps in shorts laced with a runny egg and bicarbonate of soda.

At the time my A-levels dragged, but in retrospect they seem to have gone in the blink of an eye. But in that blink a lot of things had changed. I had made progress and smoothed out a lot of my creases. I was starting to fit into my skin more; the sight and sound of me on film wasn't making me feel so nauseous and, once the hormones that had hijacked my body at adolescence had calmed down, I actually started to like myself.

Choosing a university wasn't the hardship I thought it would be. I had had so many rejections, there wasn't an actual choice as such. I was stuck in a 'like it or lump it' situation. The only university to offer me a place was Middlesex. It wasn't ideal, to be honest. I was a bit pissed off that Oxford and Cambridge hadn't come knocking. In my head I had pictured myself riding a pushbike side-saddle across the cobbles, debating with my fellow students or punting on the river with people called Jemima and Crispin. Alas, I accepted Middlesex University's offer mainly because of its geography – the campus was based in North London. At last this was my escape. I would see life there, I could feel part of something, and at least it wasn't Northampton.

As with everyone else, there were still things that needed work: my sexuality still hung around my neck like an albatross; in fact, it was not only hanging there, it had started to smell. Frustratingly, the longer it hung there, the more it dawned on me that perhaps it wasn't a phase that I would simply grow out of. I also noticed that some of the boys in their transition to men were becoming quite handsome. Whether it was more definition in their cheekbones or that few inches taller, it was like I'd had a bottle of wine – people seemed to be getting better looking. I hoped one day that my cheekbones would emerge triumphant from my puppy fat.

I'm still waiting.

Chapter Four

PLAYING AWAY FROM HOME

SEA SIDE TOWN

wish you were here ...

At last it was time to go to London. When I turned up in the city I was 18 and desperate for adventure. So I was a bit disappointed to stay in halls of residence for the first year. Naively, I wanted a house in Camden near the market or High Street Kensington with trendy, bohemian London types, not to stay in a brick purpose-built block of flats on the Cricklewood border. Although a disappointment at first I'm so glad I did end up in halls because that was where I met some of my best and closest friends. Mum was in tears at the gate as we arrived at the halls that Sunday. I had a duvet under my arm and a potted plant ready for my new room. We'd gone to 'Food Giant' across the road and stocked up on soups, ready meals, basically anything with 'just add boiling water' on the front.

Once I'd popped my aspidistra on the windowsill and had a sip of my Oxtail Cup-a-Soup, it finally sank in. Wow! I was living alone in London. I couldn't believe it. This was living. My life had just begun. OK, it was Cricklewood. OK, I was doing a course that was taking me in a totally different direction to where I wanted to go. OK, so I couldn't afford to leave Cricklewood to enjoy this amazing London life, but it was life.

But anyway, I left my new room to meet my fellow thesps. The bloke opposite was called Michael Chicken (that was his real name). A lovely but strange man, he would often eat cat biscuits and had a sign saying 'Astoroth' on his door. I think it was something to do with Dungeons and Dragons. He showed me a photo of when he'd scrawled 'Revenge' in his arm, but he had carved 'Revenje'. Later that year he gave me the shock of my life. I was awoken from a power nap by Michael standing over me, dressed as the 'Crow' and saying Mum was on the phone downstairs. (Now I know how Minstral felt with the pig costume.) He was a sweet guy, but altogether a bit strange. Usually if your surname is Chicken, you like to keep a low profile, but not Michael, oh no.

The next person I met on my course was a big girl called Helen. She was nice enough but we never really gelled as mates. The last time I saw her, she was trying to remove a one-pence piece lodged in her face that someone had thrown at her during the Middlesex University slave auction. Ironically, it was a penny more than anyone had bid for her.

As you can imagine, seeing these two hardly filled me with joy. I rechecked my university prospectus to see if it in fact read 'Circus Studies', but no it definitely had 'Theatre Studies' emblazoned on the front. The prospect of spending three years with them seemed quite daunting. After I'd unpacked, we met some other first years. In a desperate attempt to bond and make the best of a bad situation, we went to a local pub. After being asked in the first pub to donate to the IRA, we decided to move on to the next one where Vicki, a bookish girl who lived downstairs, told us that this was the pub where gay psychopath serial killer Dennis Nilsen picked up his first victim. The omens for this course weren't looking good at all.

My saving grace came the next day when the girl next door knocked to introduce herself. It was Catherine. We had a bit of small talk, mainly about the strange man called Chicken sitting in our kitchen in an off-white muscle top eating cat biscuits. I asked her where she came from, and she replied, 'Kettering.' That probably means nothing to you, but it's a town just ten miles from my house in Northampton, and it was music to my ears. Well, we instantly bonded, united by our contempt for life growing up in the Rose of the Shires. As it turned out, we had gone to the same nightclubs. We both dubbed Reflections 'Rejections' – see, I was witty even back then. As it happened, we also had a smattering of mutual friends. It was the beginning of a wonderful friendship that is still going today.

Catherine wasn't doing Drama or Theatre Studies; she was doing French International Business, and it must have been frustrating for her living among these Drama students. She would often spend hours slumped over a hulking great French business dictionary trying to find the right words, doing yet another essay till the early hours of the morning, and we'd come in 'exhausted' after doing two hours of breathing exercises and movement. I don't think she realised how tiring it is being a tree.

The Drama and Theatre Studies course was based at this rather run-down mansion at the top of Golders Green Hill. It had been Anna Pavlova's old house. Her dying wish was that her house should be used by the council as a centre for creativity and arts. Looking back at some of the shit we came out with, I'm sure she's pirouetting in her grave. But the house was very conducive to being a centre of creativity. It had wonderful grounds, a lake and two performance spaces – I won't say theatres, because that will build your hopes up. You could imagine how beautiful the house must have been in its prime – the tall ceilings, the staircases, the air of quiet contemplation in the large study, adorned with oil paintings and murals before a load of excitable Drama students burst through the doors. What a fall from grace. Even the large mirror in the rehearsal room that Anna Pavlova would practise in front of had a massive crack through it by the time we'd finished there. A fat girl had fallen against it in a dance class. The final insult.

I was still envious of the Acting course over at Trent Park. We were hearing stories that they were doing all these dynamic, challenging dramas, and were working nine to five every day. That was exactly the thing I secretly wanted to do, but sadly I wasn't talented enough for it. I kidded myself that I enjoyed making things out of papier mâché and wire-wooling the gussets of leotards. Although the course wasn't to my satisfaction, I threw myself into London life. Ivy House's location was a wonderful spot, right at the top of Golders Green Park. It was the perfect antidote to the grey of Northampton's industrial estates. There was the park on your doorstep. A short walk up the hill, you had the pub Jack Straw's Castle, and then the magical Heath spread out before you. Hampstead Heath's reputation has been sullied a bit of late. When you mention the wonderful walks and impressive scenery, people look at you suspiciously; but there is something mystical about that heath, especially at one o' clock in the morning when you're looking for your bearded collie in the undergrowth.

It does sound poncey, but after doing two hours of stretching and vocal warming, meandering across the Heath with a copy of Ibsen (unopened) under your arm, you couldn't help feeling like an artiste, even if you didn't have the range to back it up.

As it turned out, the two hours of breathing exercises on the Monday and the two hours of designing theatre sets on the Thursday were the entire course for the first few months. A few students left, stating that it wasn't intense enough, but I loved it. After the intensity of A-levels and the weariness of life in Northampton, I felt reborn. We lived like tourists. We had an amazing amount of free time to see the sights, and we visited all the museums, shopped at Camden Market, pottered around Portobello Road, and went to all the cool clubs, after a few hiccups in the first week. We naively believed the hype about these neon super-clubs in Leicester Square like Equinox and the Hippodrome. But we took one look at the Japanese tourists doing the conga to Ace of Base and turned on our heels. We were young and in London – we only did the really cool clubs. We only went in the week, mind, when it was a pound a drink. We never even ventured there at the weekends, when the drinks could cost as much as £3.00. *£3.00!!* Oh, the outrage.

At the weekend we went over to Food Giant and bought this lovely champagne with a plastic cork, Château Belnor, for 98p. It was always welcome at Cricklewood Halls. The Drama students would crank up the stereo and dance the night away, while the Business students complained about the noise and asked us to turn it down as they couldn't concentrate on their French dictionaries. I don't know what was in Château Belnor, but it would bring out the worst in us. I don't know if it was the bubbles or the slight whiff of poppers that emanated from the cork-hole. I remember Matt, who was always so sensitive and gentle, banging violently on Thannos's door and threatening to deck him when Greece gave us 'nul points' in the Eurovision Song Contest.

I remember thinking what a loser everyone else was, and that I was so lucky to be a creative type and not one of those boring Business students who don't know how to have a good time. Of course, all those Business students had the last laugh when the Theatre students graduated. We'd all be waiting for the Pertemps minibus to pick us up in a layby to take us to some godforsaken industrial estate, while they'd be driving past in their sports cars making deals and having power lunches. Obviously, they'd be on Brut and Laurent Perrier at these power lunches, and I'd have a Château Belnor poking out of my Tupperware box. But that was the future. That was a whole three years away; c'mon, let your hair down!

In a way, I was helping to seal my own fate. I was getting incredibly lazy. I didn't go to London's Glittering West End at all to watch the hot new plays by the hottest new playwrights. That would mean giving up a night of drinking. I didn't even put on plays in my spare time to get myself an Equity card. I was blasé about life in London, and anyway, I wanted to be at the front of the stage, not behind it, which is shameful. Even though we only worked a four-hour week, to our shame we never read the plays we were supposed to. We'd turn up oblivious to who was in it, what happened and why. Instead, we would sit down with a packet of Hob Nobs and watch daytime telly. Besides, when we weren't focusing on stage sets, sound and directing, the acting modules of the course (which were minimal at best) would concentrate on such styles as Kabuki theatre or August Boal's Invisible Theatre. I just wanted to be in *Hollyoaks*.

* * *

Not surprisingly, as I was such a social butterfly, my social outgoings were becoming enormous, and my evening journeys to Food Giant for Château Belnor were becoming more and more frequent. The guilt of doing absolutely nothing in term-time began to jar with my conscience. Mum would ring up asking what I'd been up to, and I didn't have a clue. I'd start making things up just to throw her off the scent, but you could tell in her voice she wasn't falling for it. I couldn't act to my own mother let alone an audience of theatregoers, but she was right to be cynical: I wasn't doing anything. After a while, doing nothing became exhausting, and I thought that it would be best if I got a job. At least then I'd have some money. My flatmate Karen was working part-time at Tesco Brent Cross and said that there were jobs going – would I be interested? At £4.80 an hour the money was good, plus it was double time on a Sunday. I was very tempted to say the least.

Look who it is!

I went to see the store manager, Carol, a woman with dyed red hair and a pinched expression. The photo of her, near the store entrance, welcoming the customers in to 'her store', was sadly, like the food in the discount aisle, past its use-by date. It had been airbrushed within an inch of her life. It was Dorian Gray in reverse. She took me behind the scenes of the shop floor and quizzed me.

'What attracts you to working at Tesco Brent Cross?' she asked with a straight face.

'Er, I love pushing trolleys around a car park in tight grey poly-cotton trousers?'

I got the job. Result! And with a '10% off' loyalty card, I felt like the King of Brent Cross.

The money came in very handy, and I quite liked sitting there gossiping with the customers, scanning their shopping and learning all the different food codes – 7710 for bananas, 10 for a clove of garlic and 3245 for Braeburns. It was fun – well, for about ten minutes it was fun, then it really began to drag. That was before Tesco turned into the monster that we all know today. I'm sure it was a monster back then, but its fangs weren't quite as sharp and its grip over the high street wasn't quite so tight.

Tesco was intent on pushing the ideal of 'customer service', the belief that the customer is always right, even if said customer is mentally ill. I used to dread Tuesdays, because that would be the day Stan would come to shop. Stan, for some reason, had taken a shine to me, not in a fruity gay sense, but in an OAP/youngster-type capacity. The problem was that he only had one arm, and every time he wanted something off the shelf he would have to put the basket down, take the product off the shelf, pop it in the basket and then pick up his basket and carry on. As you can imagine, this got very tedious for him, but we couldn't allow a one-armed pensioner to push a trolley unaided around a superstore.

So every Tuesday I would hold the basket, and he would point with his one good arm, and I would take the product off the shelf and pop it in his basket. This would carry on every week. At one point, I was thinking of sellotaping five fish fingers to the end of a baguette and somehow strapping it to him and a basket to give him a makeshift arm – anything just to leave me in peace. On the front of the horrible grey polyester uniform we were forced to wear we had to pin an oversized badge proclaiming: 'Here to Help'. I was glad it was oversized because the more polyester it covered, the better. Because you were wearing the badge, customers assumed you were an oracle.

'What aisle is the desiccated coconut?'

'How long do you cook a butternut squash?'

'What would you have with a pan-fried red mullet?'

'Where can I find the Holy Grail?' Enough already!

Some people obviously misread the 'Here to Help' as 'Hello, I'm your bitch!' That especially applied when the princesses descended from Golders Green in their 4 x 4s, clicking their fingers and stamping their feet at me. I remember one woman wafting her hands in the air, which I think symbolised 'Pack my bags and take them to the car'. I started packing. I don't know what came over me, but I saw she had bought her son a Thomas the Tank Engine birthday cake. So without her knowing, I packed that at the bottom and forced a six-pack of Pedigree Chum down on it. I squashed it down good and proper and smiled subserviently as I took it to her 4 x 4. I wish I had been at that kid's party when his mum brought out the cake and the kid started screaming because Thomas had a cleft palette and an imprint of a Labrador on his forehead.

Some of my duties would be more mundane, like collecting the trolleys in the Tesco car park, taking back customers' returns and repricing the food that was coming up to its sell-by date. Sometimes things could get exciting, like when we had a shoplifter or a thief. When a crook used a stolen card fraudulently, a name would pop up on the screen and you would have to ask a supervisor if he could have a word with Mr —. This was a code word for 'Call the cops'. At that point, knowing we were on to him, the card fraudster would usually just dash for the door, followed by the security guard.

I was also there when the foot-and-mouth crisis gripped the country and the meat aisles were jammed with unwanted beef. No one would touch it. It got so bad, the bosses asked us to appease the customers by saying that our meat was perfectly fine to eat and that you could trust Tesco. I would frequently tell them that Tesco beef was the best in the country, only for them to say tartly, 'I don't think I'm going to endanger my family's life with your beef, thank you very much,' and then pop lasagne, chilli con carne and moussaka onto the conveyor belt. What did they think it was made of? Pick 'n' mix?

One day when I turned up for work we were all taken to the cafeteria and told about this brand new innovation, the

Clubcard. For every pound you spent at Tesco, you would get a point on your Clubcard, which could later be redeemed. I thought it sounded like a shit idea, but what do I know?

'This Clubcard needs to be promoted,' said Carol Reed, the store manager, 'and we need some fun and outgoing people to promote it. We need someone who will make our customers go, "Wow!"' I watched as Carol's eyes scanned the room: Jacqui with the lazy eye, Ganesh with his minimal English, Phyllis with the wart, and the rest of the team who looked like extras on *Shameless*.

Her eyes fell on me. 'Alan! You do Drama. Will you come on board?'

'Will it get me off the tills?' I replied.

'Yes.'

'Count me in, Carol!'

The next thing I know, I'm standing on the Brent Cross petrol station forecourt with a blue Clubcard sash around me asking people if they would like to have a Clubcard. I wasn't over the moon about the sash, but the previous idea had been to dress me up as a waiter, approaching customers with a tray bearing – yes, you guessed it – a Clubcard. Brent Cross is pretty rough at night, and we would often get gangs of lads shoplifting or intimidating the staff. So I was a little bit worried, standing there like Miss World on a petrol station forecourt. Overall, though, it was a welcome respite from working on the till, and at least I got to stretch my legs away from the beady eyes of Carol. I can't help thinking that I had a part to play in the success of the Tesco Clubcard. I really excelled myself in those days, going up to unsuspecting Tesco customers and getting them to sign up. Thanks to my hard sell on that forecourt, the Clubcard was truly the talk of the town.

It was a particularly grim night. I was standing there on the forecourt with my sash nestled between my breasts, that damn puppy fat still clinging on for dear life. What I thought was the glow of two orange headlights caught my eye. As it turned out, it was Dale Winton, coming out of his red sports car parked behind me. I turned on my heel and said, 'Dale, can I interest you in a Clubcard?'

'It's OK, darling. I've got one.'

He was lovely then as he is now. I haven't ever mentioned that first encounter to him, but I was so starstruck. He was the first celebrity I'd seen since I'd moved down to London. Yes, I'd seen Geoff Capes at Overstone Solarium, but this was London, where they all lived. Celebrities are like buses: you wait for one and then two come along at once. Who do you reckon I saw the next day? Dr Fox! Yes, *the* Dr Fox. He was with a pretty woman, and I remember his fox cufflinks winking in the glare of artificial light that bathed the shop floor. I was thinking, 'Please, please! Come through my checkout!' Frustratingly, he went to the next checkout along. I felt like a lover spurned, and I was itching to leave my till and ask him whether he wanted a Clubcard. I knew I was part of something, a phenomenon.

The phenomena kept on coming. I was also working at Tesco Brent Cross when it became the flagship 24-hour store. Impressed? I know, I know, at times my life seemed to imitate Forrest Gump, but whereas he was present at all history's momentous occasions I was at all the shitty ones. BBC News was there and everything, and I had put my name down to work through the night. It was such a monumentally historic event that only a select few would be chosen. After much consideration, I got to work on Checkout 12. There was I, Alan Carr, working at the first ever 24-hour supermarket in the United Kingdom.

Of course, once all the excitement had died down and all the checkout people, including myself, realised that it was just an ordinary shift (obviously), the rest of the night felt like wading through treacle. Tesco Value Treacle, at that. A few curious shoppers turned up to see what the fuss was about, but mainly it was drunks and stoners with the munchies. It was left to the staff to tell the winos, 'Yes, the supermarket is 24-hour, but the alcohol licence only lasts to 11 o'clock and if you want alcohol you'll just have to burn off some Benylin. It's in Aisle 5, next to the sanitary towels.'

It was my last-ever night shift, and it really was a drag. It was popular with the people who needed money fast. They could work through the night. One checkout girl used to take speed at the beginning of her shift because she was trying to save up for a car. No, the 24-hour shift was too much for me, and I returned to my usual daylight hours. I left at 10.00 p.m., just as all the shelf-stackers emerged onto the floor in their grey tracksuits, those mysterious, mute, nocturnal people who disappear when the sun comes up.

Middlesex University made its money by taking in plane-loads of rich foreign students. Let's face it, they weren't going to make any money from the talent, so there was always a fresh influx of victims. I remember one poor Chinese girl. She had just waved her parents off and turned around to walk into her room, when out of nowhere she was drenched head to feet with a washing-up bowl of potato peelings that Matt had lobbed at Melissa, but missed. They didn't even apologise, they just laughed. I know it's horrible, but food fights were the order of the day. Someone would flick a kidney bean at someone's head to provoke a reaction, then it would be flicked back twice as hard, and before long one poor innocent would be sitting there wearing a plate of Rogan Josh as a brooch. Looking back, I feel such a moron. It was hilarious at the time, but the other students must have looked at us with such contempt, and rightfully so. That old adage is true, though: the devil makes work for idle hands.

You must be thinking, 'Why is he bothering telling us about food fights?' The honest answer is that we had more food fights than we actually did work. You were more likely to have a shepherd's pie catapulted through your window than open up a theory book. We were useless scum, we were the students that people talk about in the *Daily Mail*, spongers, always down the pub, doing little or no work. A food fight was the highlight of the day, but to be fair the source of our food didn't help: Food Giant. It's probably a blessing that most of the food ended up on the walls. I remember buying a pack of fish fingers for 59 pence. It had on the box, 'May contain less than 15% fish.' That's big breadcrumbs, I thought.

We were annoying, and we were bored. It seems that not only were we content to ruin our own prospects, we had to bring the others down with us as well. One irritating Japanese girl, Business student probably, always used to have her power ballads blaring out through her windows. Celine, Bonnie Tyler, Whitney, which, as you can imagine, can grate after a while. We spied on her through her window and saw that she had the same stereo as Finn, a fellow Drama student. So we lined ourselves up on the stairs opposite and with his remote control started operating her stereo through the window. You should have seen her face as we changed CD track, turned it down, turned it up, froze Bonnie mid 'Holding Out for a Hero', and turned on Kerrang FM. It was harassment, but it was funny harassment. Her bemused face was a picture. It took her ten minutes to realise it was us, and we were supposed to be the thickos!

* * *

If I'm honest, the novelty of doing nothing all week soon wore off and the shifts at Tesco weren't doing anything to alleviate the tedium. So when we finally got to perform some plays we thought all our Christmases had come early. The plays we performed encapsulated all the different theatrical genres. One semester it would be the absurdist play, *The Maids*, by Jean Genet, Shakespeare's *Measure for Measure* and Edward Bond's *Saved*, which featured possibly one of my worst performances ever. *Saved* was part of the political theatre genre. As I am possibly the least political person there is, I knew there would be problems. It had been banned by the Lord Chamberlain in the Sixties and had quickly gained notoriety, mainly because the play contains a graphic scene where the protagonist stones a baby to death.

I was as shocked as the next person to be given the part of Len. Obviously, playing against type can offer an actor a chance to show the true gamut of his emotions. However, as I had to stone a baby to death in this role, I really didn't know where to begin. In my opinion, it was the worst piece of casting in the history of theatre since Cliff Richard stepped onto the moors in *Heathcliff the Musical*. I only got the part because the director had had a row with the lead and out of spite gave him the role of the long-suffering husband who had to spend all his scenes behind a newspaper, tutting. How easy is that? I had to kill a baby. I don't know whether it was naivety or arrogance that made me accept the part, but I did. I had to play an impressionable young man with a dark side. I remember thinking, 'I can't do brooding.' I don't think I'd ever been brooding. I could look arsey, but something told me that wouldn't be good enough.

The play started out on the wrong foot. I had to come on intoxicated and have intercourse on the sofa with Pam, who was played by my flatmate and fellow Drama student, Julia. Apart from Ruth with the green eyeshadow, I'd never kissed a girl before, let alone touched a breast, so I really had to concentrate. Whilst caressing her nipples I didn't look lustful; I just looked like I was retuning a video. As I slipped my hand up her blouse and tried to unhook the bra (I knew the hook was at the back – I'd seen it on *On the Buses*), I grunted like a wild animal, admittedly one with its leg caught in a snare.

After sex, I had to get up arrogantly and light up a cigarette. Personally, I can't stand smoking, and this fucking play
was beginning to get on my tits. Smoke a cigarette, stone a
baby, touch a tit – all I needed was to swim with a couple of
Great Whites in a tank and I'd have faced all my fears. It was
supposed to look like a post-coital cigarette, but the director
complained that the way I was holding it was too reminiscent
of Bet Lynch opening up at the Rovers Return. The problem
was, as I didn't smoke it didn't look natural. There is a way,
admittedly cool, that smokers handle the cigarette and
matches with aplomb. But I couldn't stop shaking when it
came to light the damn thing. I wasn't nervous, it was the
thought of touching another pair of breasts in the matinée.

It wasn't only my fault. The supporting cast was just as
out of place. Miscues, badly positioned props, wrong lines. I
remember in the pivotal scene where I bumped into a gang of
lads in a park and was slowly brutalised, Melissa, who played
my mother, walked on set with a teapot and shouted, 'It's on
the table!' That was a reference to the next scene, where I
popped around for dinner. After her awkward realisation,
Melissa slowly sidestepped off, watched by a tittering audience.

The night before, it was me who messed up. I was seated
at the dinner table and said, 'That looks delicious,' before
she'd actually put the trifle and custard on the table. What a
complete disaster! And this was before I had to stone that
bloody baby.

Finally, that dreaded scene came. I was alone in the park,
and the baby was upturned in its pram, crying. It was down to

me to deliver this important and iconic scene with gusto and brooding introspection. I slowly picked up the pebbles and began to throw them. All those hours of motivation and rehearsals could not mask the fact that I throw like a girl. To be honest, the audience were on the edge of their seats mainly because of the fear of getting stoned. I kept missing the pram, and it was a miracle that I didn't wipe out a St John's Ambulance person. The pebbles started pinging off the walls, and some of the women in the audience had started covering their faces with their handbags. Not one hit the bloody baby. If this had been real life, the baby would have survived scratch-free and gone on to do its GCSE.

The whole thing was a complete embarrassment, and quite rightfully I got my worst ever mark for that production. But it taught me a lesson: stick to what you're good at. If you have got the range, then you can play against type, good for you. But I think my forte is light-hearted, comedic roles. Maybe I should leave infanticide to the experts.

Chapter Five

GOING DOWN IN THE BOX

Unlike some of the richer students, who went back home to chill out and relax, I had to work in the university holidays. My family didn't really know any businessmen or managers who could get their eldest son a job temping in an office. My father's social circle only extended to warehouse foremen and forklift drivers. So more often than not, I would find myself in some dreary depot in a hard hat and steel toe-capped boots. Because Dad was held in such high esteem, they would bend over backwards to get me a job – the bastards.

I had never been happy with the recommendations that the career's adviser had given me at Weston Favell Upper School, but she had never warned me that jobs like this existed. Really boring, mundane, wrist-slittingly dull jobs. My first job was for Laxton's at Brackmills Industrial Estate. I'd saved up and bought myself a yellow Mini which, sadly, didn't help change anyone's perception of me. In fact, driving through Overstone on a summer's day, I heard one of the kids shout, 'Look, it's Mr Bean!'

I loved that car, and it broke my heart when it had to be sold for scrap two years later. You always have a soft spot for your first car, even if it has let you down on numerous occasions. The bonnet would often fly up as I passed the 70 miles per hour marker. It would be terrifying to know that any minute your windscreen would be obscured by a piece of banana-coloured metal. The heater didn't work, and the car didn't have a radio. So I would put my ghetto-blaster on the passenger seat and pop cassettes in and sing along, which wasn't the safest thing to do, I admit.

Every morning, I'd defrost my car and head off to my job at Laxton's. The first week, I was packing boxes with video recorders. I was absolutely terrified. How could this effeminate student cope with being flung into this world of machismo and ribaldry? These workers hated students at the best of times, but I was the worst kind of student. I was a Drama student. I thought the best thing was to become mute. As soon as I opened my mouth, the game would be up. I had to get more masculine. I had to become one of them. It was my toughest role since Len. This had to work. I had to create a whole new identity, one that would be believable and one that I could dip into, if I needed a get-out clause. This alter ego would have a steady girlfriend whom I would mention at various times in the conversation – that might throw them off the scent. I just hoped they never saw my yellow Mini parked outside.

We started at 6.15 a.m. I'd been told I was taking over from the night shift. I went into the staff canteen, which was basically a room with one of those revolving food dispensers. What I at first thought was frosted glass was in fact the fumes from twenty-five years of passive smoking smeared on the window. When looked through, the nicotine-stained glass gave the canteen a sepia glow, as if it were from yesteryear, a

Victorian workhouse perhaps. But this warming, nostalgic feel was shattered as soon as I inhaled the smell and saw the hardcore pornography on the television. I couldn't take my eyes off a shaven-headed woman moaning in ecstasy as she was being masturbated over by a gang of men.

Before I could say anything, one old man turned to me and said of the bald woman being masturbated over, 'That'll make her hair grow.'

I nodded and went, 'Not half!'

That made everyone look, not because it was said in a camp voice – believe me, I deliberately butched up – but because I sounded like someone from a *Carry On* film. I couldn't have said what I wanted to say – 'Actually, I think this kind of smut degrades women and puts the suffragette movement back thirty years, if you ask me,' or alternatively, 'Don't you hate it when that happens?'

I could see it was going to be a verbal minefield, this warehouse malarkey. I was going to have to be very careful. I just sat there mute. I didn't want to get involved in any conversations, so I read and re-read the ingredients on my Ribena carton. Citric Acid and Sodium Benzoate – hmm!

What really pissed me off was that I had a brand-new P.D. James in my bag, but I guessed that was going to have to stay where it was. Well, at least until the men in the porno had come; then maybe I could get some peace and quiet.

It's a fact, factory workers resent students because they would waltz in every Christmas, Easter and summer holiday, laugh, joke about, take the piss out of the workers and then waltz off back again to their halls of residence, telling their friends about the ghastly people they were forced to work with – and I was no exception. The trouble is, I was the only student there because Dad was friends with the foreman. To be fair, he was doing me a favour employing me in the first place. A lot of the time, I would be on my own. There were so many occasions when I just wanted to exchange a look or roll my eyes at someone. When I got home, my parents wouldn't understand what I'd seen that day, and I would be left frustratingly subdued.

My Drama student alter ego didn't stay under wraps for long. You'd always get some mouthy foreman pre-warning his work colleagues, 'I've got that Graham Carr's son coming next week.'

Of course, all their ears would prick up, and then he'd deal the fatal blow: 'He's a Drama student.' I knew he'd told them because, a few mornings in, they would start.

'So,' they would say, looking over at their colleagues' faces, 'I hear you tread the boards. What programmes would I have seen you in?'

Of course, typically, not seeing the trap and relishing the chance to talk about something that wasn't vagina-based, I would start talking away.

'Yes, I would like to do television, but theatre is my first love ...' This would be interrupted by a giant howl, and I would think, 'Damn! They got me when I was weak – the buggers.'

Then as the day progressed, I could see the shift changes. New workers and lorry drivers would come in, and although I couldn't hear, I knew they were talking about me because they would nod in my direction, do a mincey walk and then all laugh.

I couldn't help feeling that if I had some of my university friends working with me, it would be a bit of a morale boost. I craved someone to see this surreal factory double life I was living. The minutes dragged, and there was always an endless supply of videos to be put in boxes. There was no sense of satisfaction (could you ever be satisfied packing boxes?) because, just as the last video was placed in its box, some unsmiling worker would deliver a whole forklift truck more of them. Your heart would sink, and your eyes would look to the clock with its motionless hands and think, 'Someone's taken the batteries out of that thing, surely.'

My only saviour was the radio. In Northampton, we had Northants 96.6 blaring out from two speakers that would reverberate through the warehouse. At first, the cheeky banter and cheesy Nineties tunes would be quite uplifting, but then the resentment would start to creep in. Why am I stuck in this dump? Why aren't I a DJ? I wouldn't mind being like the travel girl and going up in the helicopter telling everyone about the traffic – anything but packing boxes. It got so bad, I actually got excited when I was moved from packing the boxes to unpacking the boxes. Boxes, boxes, boxes, I was doing everything with boxes, everything but climbing inside one, stamping a faraway postcode on it and hoping a kind lorry driver would take me away from this cardboard hell.

Now, chatting with women and having a good old gossip is my forte. There aren't many women's hearts that I can't melt with my cheeky, bespectacled face and witty repartee. But oh no, not these ladies. Talking to these women was like talking to Dad. They talked about women's bits and scratched their crotches more than the men did. One of them, Sue, could give as good as she got when it came to the catcalls and sexist remarks.

On the first day, I asked her to help lift a pallet. As she bent over, she went, 'Ooh! I've touched cloth.' I didn't think that was the right moment to ask Sue what finishing school she went to.

I remember walking to my Mini at home time. Sue had decided to cycle to work, and the men had gaffer-taped a huge dildo to her saddle.

'I bet you'll enjoy riding home tonight,' shouted Doug, the resident sex pest.

'It won't touch the side, what with the size of my c**t!' Sue replied wittily.

Everyone laughed, apart from me. I fled to my Mini as if it was a panic room, got inside and quickly shut all the doors. I could see Sue in the wing mirror pretending to fellate the dildo. What is this place? I didn't want to know any more. I just put my foot down and drove out of the industrial estate.

Factory work after a while slowly numbs you to the outside world. Admittedly, with the fortnightly stints at Christmas and Easter, the light at the end of the tunnel was never more than a weekend away, but during the summer holidays you could be entrenched for up to eight or nine weeks. You slowly started becoming brainwashed into their way of life. It was just little things, like siding with the perms when a temp started (probably a student), getting to know the name of the tuck-van lady and, worse, start sharing information with her. I would find myself having a chat with her about her family, and worse still, making jokes with her. I had become one of them. I used to sit there scowling at this rough woman with the dyed hair and a sovereign on every finger. Now I was laughing with her, complimenting her on her hair and asking her if the rings were real brass.

Factory life is strange, and petty things take on huge significance. People cling to inanimate objects. I remember being scolded for using Sue's tape gun, the gun you use to gaffer-tape the box into which you put the videos. I had picked it up without realising that written on the reverse in black marker was 'Sue's. Hands off!'

One of the temps who joined after me made the mistake of sitting in the wrong chair during the break.

'I wouldn't sit there if I was you,' said Colin, not taking his eyes off the porn. 'That's Ken's seat.'

The temp sheepishly collected his coat and moved to another seat. Everyone smirked and shook their head knowingly, as the temp tried to find a seat that Ken didn't treasure so highly.

It isn't just the tools you work with that you develop an attachment to. While I was in the factory, I started developing crushes on my workmates. These people, who outside of the factory I wouldn't even look at twice, were in those grey dreary shifts my knights in shining armour. The way their paunches hung over their loosely fitting dungarees seemed enchanting, while the cheap earrings dangling from their cauliflower ears were utterly spellbinding and just added to the whole, irresistible package. It was as if my heart was creating this lust to divert me from the world-weariness that was slowly seeping through the rest of my body. It was trying to stoke some passion in a colourless world.

It was only when I said 'Phwoar!' at a fat French pony-tailed lorry driver as he lifted a pallet off the lorry that I realised I had to stop these flights of fancy, and soon. The man looked like Captain Hook, for Christ's sake.

* * *

When I returned to Middlesex after these stints, I felt like a lifer who had been released from gaol. A sense of redemption came over me every time I clocked out for the last time. I promised myself that I would use my time at university wisely and read all the plays and be more enthusiastic about Ibsen and Steinberg.

As soon as I returned to the halls of residence in Cricklewood, Matthew, Ben, Jo, Melissa and Catherine and I went straight to the pub to catch up on all the gossip, each one desperate to get their stories of degrading jobs out first. Melissa even beat me to it for the worst temping job. She had been working at a catalogue returns factory in her home town of Peterborough. Her job was to take out the cardboard gusset from the returned swimwear and replace it with a new one for the next unsuspecting customer. Believe me, that isn't the kind of job where you say to your foreman, 'Don't worry, I'll work through my lunch.'

Naively, I thought that these totally dreary jobs were confined to when you were a student. I honestly thought that with a BA Hons in Theatre Studies I would be made for life. Businessmen would go, 'Oh my God, this Alan Carr guy, he can do political theatre and operate a gib. He's hired!' My timing was impeccable. I was becoming part of the generation where everybody has a degree, and their value, particularly in Drama and Theatre Studies, was not even worth the paper it was written on. Everyone had a bloody degree. It was like they were giving them away free with the Sunday papers.

The really bright young things were the ones who studied a trade like plumbing and joinery. They would be the ones in the fancy cars and the homes with the electric gates, not me. I'm not saying I made the wrong choice. Plumbing and joinery didn't even flicker on my occupational radar – oh God, no, joiner was up there with bomb disposal unit and WWF wrestler. I just didn't know what I wanted. I still don't think I do. My stints at the factory were a wake-up call – this dreary existence could be your life, if you don't pull your finger out. What are you going to do? I started to panic. The three years had flown by, and I had no idea what I was going to do, or what in fact I wanted to do. I was staring into the future, jobless, skill-less and useless.

I needed a miracle – or a sugar daddy?

My options were few and things were getting desperate. Hence the thought that I might even be able to toy with the idea of befriending a lonely old heir who would finance my acting ambitions in exchange for a kiss and a cuddle – no sex, that's extra. Sex, now that you mention it, proved as disappointing as the job prospects. University hadn't turned into this sexual wonderland that everyone had promised. In fact, it was one of my more barren periods sexually. Mum had told me not to get any girls pregnant. That might seem laughable, but to be honest, there was more chance of that than of me finding a gentleman caller.

The first year was wasted for me, as I pretended to everyone that I wasn't gay – yes, I know! I strenuously denied it because I didn't want to be so easily read. I wanted to be complex. It went hand in hand with my wish to be an actor and, I guess, to be deep and more than that hideously camp, gurning gargoyle I'd seen on the video. The decision to lie about my sexuality still makes me cringe, and my only explanation can be that, deep down, I thought the new start at university could be a chance to reboot and literally become a changed man. Isn't that typical of me, though? Most people choose university to reveal their true colours and showcase the person they had always kept hidden deep down inside of them, but were denied at school. I, on the other hand, chose to become someone light years away from the real me and steal the identity of a streetwise, fanny-loving heterosexual with a passing interest in theatre – well, you couldn't say I wasn't complex. As you can imagine, it was like telling the tide to go back.

By the spring of 1997, I was living in Hendon with two fellow Drama students in a little flat above Captain Fish on the Hendon Way. It was convenient for its proximity to Brent Cross Shopping Centre, but really dire for airing your washing. If you hung it out the back, it came in stinking of haddock. If you hung it out the front, it would come in smelling of exhaust pipe. So we would have to resort to having the clothes drip around us in the flat, praying that we didn't get a shadow on our lungs from each other's panties.

There was a lot of excitement at the college, as an exchange student programme was offered. We could swap with Drama students in American cities such as New York and Miami. Although I was living above a chip shop, I decided to stay put. But a few of our students went over there and immersed themselves in the American way of life – one girl, Sally, a bit too much. She came back with a new nose. Later that year, we had to honour our side of the bargain, and a whole batch of American students, Patty, Paige, Carol Ann, Mary Beth, etc., came over here. They were lovely, and their enthusiasm was catching. This sudden rush of new blood into our tired social scene also did us the world of good. We had new people to talk to and, more importantly, to take the piss out of.

As it happened, two of the students developed a crush on me, Anne and Chad. Now, I never believe anyone fancies me, basically because they don't. So when both of them started to make eyes at me, I thought it was a bet. Why would they be interested in me? I couldn't work it out. All I knew was that it was starting to get embarrassing. They really, really fancied me. No one had ever done that before. It was as if they had been hypnotised; when they heard the magic words 'Hello, I'm Alan', they would turn into lustful, horny nymphomaniacs, intent on removing my clothes.

One night, after having a few too many glasses of wine, Anne straddled me in the Horse and Jockey, demanding that I fuck her. I refused, and she started to ride me like a bucking bronco. I'd never seen the like before. I didn't know where to look. I was so embarrassed, especially since the landlord had only just relented and lifted the ban after 'Anna Pavlova-gate', where I had danced like Salome with a net curtain over my head, knocking over a table of drinks. But that's another story.

The even stranger thing was that Anne and Chad were both actually attractive. This was a first for me, good-looking people showing an interest. If all the mingers came forward and sold their stories, it would look like I'd had a gangbang in a circus. If I had ever pulled someone nice, it was usually after a very big drunken session, and the morning after they often wouldn't hold back their contempt for the bespectacled, buck-toothed person lying next to them.

Obviously, the camp voice resounding from under the covers – 'Oooh, love, you wouldn't mind popping on the kettle?' – would destroy what little passion still lingered. Usually, I wouldn't get my cup of tea. I'd just get told to put my clothes on and be escorted out of the flat with a blanket on my head, like a paedophile heading off to Crown Court. You wouldn't even sully the occasion by asking if they'd like to see you again. You'd get the gist. If the tea isn't forthcoming and they've phoned a taxi before you've even woken up, then the chance of a civil ceremony can seem very distant.

Chad was a thick-set, Jewish American who had a heart of gold, but an insatiable lust for me. I'm not much of a sexual person. Sex is a bit like 'Cash in the Attic' – I can take it or leave it – but he was like a crazed nymphomaniac. He had a soft romantic side, too. He was staying in a hostel with all the other Americans, and I remember once that, except for Chad, they had all gone on a two-day trip to some northern theatre. He had the dormitory to himself. So he put all the mattresses on the floor and set up rows and rows of candles and flowers all over this huge cavernous room. It was so romantic, and such a wonderful surprise as I walked through the hostel door. I couldn't believe it. We had a lovely night – well, once I'd stopped worrying about the obvious fire hazard and memorised my escape route in case a mattress did go up like a Christmas tree.

But then for every romantic interlude, there would be a sex-crazed session. He was insatiable and sometimes he would try to drag me into bushes for sex. He'd also follow me into a toilet and try to pull me into a cubicle. The man was an animal. I'm not into all that, but the more I resisted, the more lustful he became. He probably thought I was playing mind games, whipping him into a frenzy, then letting him have his way with me at the last moment. But I wasn't. I genuinely did want to finish my crossword – and, no, I will not count to ten and follow you into that portaloo. My life became a nightmare.

Don't get me wrong, some people would love to have that kind of dynamism in a relationship they would relish the fact that you don't know when and where you'll be having sex. But my nerves are shot at the best of times, so the last thing I need is the equivalent of Cato on Viagra, jumping out of a wardrobe with a raging hard-on. Yes, I loved having a boyfriend, but there were three people in that relationship: me, him and his penis.

* * *

In the final year at Middlesex I chose the Stand-up Comedy module. That was not because I liked comedy or wanted to be a comedian, but because all my friends had chosen it, and we got to go away on a long weekend to Tenby for a comedy bonding session. It sounded like a lot of fun, and the end of the course was looming. I think in the back of our minds we knew that this would probably be the last time we would all be together. Excitedly, we all bundled into the minibus and left Ivy House for Tenby.

Tenby is a really picturesque part of South Wales, its pretty houses and dramatic coastline framed by the hills. When we visited, it was so quaint and unspoilt. We stayed on a lovely farm which belonged to the comedy tutor, Huw Thomas, who ran the comedy night, 'Downstairs at the King's Head', in Crouch End, where we would be performing these comedy routines the following week. With its two barns, one for the girls and one for the boys, and its surrounding land which ran down to the seashore, the farm encouraged the liberating feeling of getting back to nature. We let that sense of freedom wash over us and the grime of North London soon became a distant memory.

We made a fire on the beach out of some branches that we found. We bought some beers and sat around reminiscing and telling stories. Huw would gently nudge each of us to tell a funny story, and in turn everyone would nervously tell an anecdote. The alcohol loosened us up, and the warmth of the fire seemed to draw us out of ourselves. Before long, the stories and jokes came gushing out. Huw had cunningly showed us what we needed to recreate next week at the busy pub in London: intimacy, confidence, empathy, and, of course, the capacity to be fucking hilarious.

It was a lovely evening, and I remember having a wonderful sense of fulfilment as I made my way back to the boys' barn. I lay in bed and thought about the next week. What would happen? Would I get booed off? Would I bring the house down? These thoughts were thrust right out of my mind when a hand was clamped over my mouth and another hand went down my pants. Terrified, I tried to scream. It was only when I heard Chad say, 'Get in my sleeping bag,' that I at least started to breathe.

'Get off me,' I hissed. 'How long have you been waiting here?'

'Thirty minutes,' came the reply.

As it happens, Chad had slunk across the room whilst the others had been asleep and clung to the bottom of my bunk bed, like Robert De Niro gripping the axle of that car in *Cape Fear*, and waited. I told him to get back into his bed, and he sulked off. This was getting too much.

The next day we honed our stand-up skills. Instead of the cosy warmth of the fire on the shore, the venue was a third barn, which had been made up like a comedy club. There were tables and a microphone on the stage. We still had beers to take the edge off it. We all tried our newly prepared jokes and hoped that people laughed. As you can imagine, it was a mixed bag. Some went down well, some died a death. But overall, we were all gunning for each other.

All I knew from those two nights was that this comedy lark was terrifying. The fear that takes over your body and turns your stomach inside out was unbearable. Through the years of doing comedy gigs up and down the country, I have learnt to control it and harness the nerves. Now I use it to get excited and focused, a positive energy, you might say. Thankfully, nowadays it is very rare for me to get those knee-trembling nerves and heart palpitations. But when it comes, it comes, and it's an acute reminder of those early comedy gigs when you couldn't eat all day, even the smell of food turning your stomach. The fear seized you as you were standing in the wings, making a silent prayer to God and saying, 'I would rather do anything than go out on that stage tonight. Screw this comedy lark. Why do I want to be a comedian, anyway? Why don't I just go and get myself a boring shit job instead?' Then I'd stop myself and go, 'Oh, I have! I'm packing shampoo bottles tomorrow at eight.'

The next week at 'Downstairs at the King's Head' we were all set to perform our comedy routines. That morning I'd woken myself up at 7.30, after having the worst anxiety dream ever. In the dream, I'd gone on stage and no words came out of my mouth. They just stuck in my throat. I had lost my voice and the crowd had started booing. People had started to walk out. Hoping that it was not a premonition, I made myself a cup of tea and a couple of slices of comedy and sat down on the comedy and watched a bit of comedy on the comedy. Please stop thinking about this fucking comedy routine, I pleaded to my already overcharged brain. The whole day just froze. It would stay frozen until I went on stage and said the magic words:

'Hello, I'm Alan Carr.'

When we finally arrived at the Kings Head at six, we were led 'Downstairs', and the nerves went up a notch. I thought, 'So this is where I'm going to die.'

'Downstairs at the King's Head' has all been done up now, but back then in 1997 it was dark and gloomy, almost bunker-like. It wasn't conducive to comedy at all, in my opinion. We went through the running order. I was in the second half – oh great, more time to fret. By this time the nerves that had tormented my stomach all day had travelled up my windpipe and were persecuting my throat. I would have gagged if I'd had anything to eat all day. So it was more of a dry heave as we were shown our dressing room and the toilet, which, looking back, was handy really.

I can't remember how I bided my time before my performance that night – oh yes I can, I shat myself. Not literally, you understand, but I might as well have with the wind I was producing – oh goodness, it's an affliction that haunts me to this day. Royal Variety Performance, *Friday Night Project*, Hammersmith Apollo, my wind has no discrimination when it comes to the classy venues; it just pops out and lingers, a bit like the Grey Lady at the Royal in Northampton.

As it progressed, the night became too much for my nerves; every step of the comedy night sent my anxieties up to the next gut-wrenching level. When Huw shouted, 'The doors are open,' that would crank my nerves up. Then hearing the voices of the punters – another crank up. The opening of the second half, gulp, and then finally, 'Ladies and gentleman, Alan Carr' – I passed out.

Well, I didn't pass out, but I couldn't tell you what I said, what I did, if they laughed. I went into tunnel vision. All I know is that after the ending of every joke, the knot in my stomach loosened. After what seemed like a couple of seconds, I heard myself through the dream saying, 'I've been Alan Carr, goodnight,' and then, thankfully, applause stirred me from this strange half-slumber I'd been living in. Apparently, I'd brought the house down. People were patting me on the back, allegedly I'd had everyone in stitches. A huge wave of relief washed all the nerves away, and I just slumped in the corner feeling the last spark of nervous energy leave my tingling body. I remember thinking I never wanted to do that again.

But I did.

Chapter Six

MISSING
CHANCES

The next day at Ivy House, people were saying that I should do comedy professionally and that I was a natural at it.

'Thanks, but no thanks,' I politely replied.

Yes, the adulation and all the positive comments were lovely – ask any comedian, you cannot beat the euphoria you get when you've stormed a comedy gig, it is the most exhilarating feeling in the world. However, the nerves that had ravaged my body were too much. I simply couldn't muster up that energy to perform every night. When would I eat? When would I sleep? I vowed I would never go through the strain of performing comedy again, and I stuck to my word for four years. 'Besides,' I would tell my fellow students, 'I'd rather continue with my acting. I enjoy that.' They would nod sympathetically, remembering my Len and the baby-stoning incident.

The end of the course was simply a matter of weeks away, and desperation mixed with panic is a lethal cocktail – especially when you are about to make important life decisions. Whilst we had been drinking, mucking around, joking and winding people up for three years, some of the more proactive students had sensibly earned their Equity cards, put on shows, travelled Europe and joined theatre companies.

I hadn't done any of this. I was just assuming something would happen, I don't know what exactly, but something. All of a sudden, it was like being back at The Farm. One minute everyone is dancing with you to 'Baggy Trousers', the next it changes to a slow dance, you're on your own, and all around you people are waltzing off with careers, smirking at you, a knowing look in their eye, mouthing 'ha ha'.

I was obviously worried because I approached one of my tutors, David Owen-Bell, about the future. He sat me down, and we talked about the best way to find acting work. He advised me to get my photos done professionally and create a CV to send to the casting agents illustrating my height, weight, accents, dialects and additional skills.

'Skills?' I said.

'You know, horse-riding, swimming, fencing,' he replied.

'I don't really have any of those skills.'

'OK. What about accents? Dialects, maybe?'

'I can do Scouse.'

'Marvellous. Pop it down. Any others?'

'Brummie.'

'Wonderful. You see.'

'Scottish as well.'

'Brilliant. Now here's a list of addresses of some of my theatrical connections. Print out your CV, send a photo and don't forget to mention my name.'

I left his office much happier and more positive. At least my CV looked like I hadn't drifted aimlessly through the last three years in a haze of alco-pops and had acquired some form of a thespian education.

Missing chances

But the feeling of enlightenment and hope faded as my conscience began to awaken. Yes, I could do a Scouse accent, but only if the line was, 'Grrrrrreeeet, I'm 'avin' an 'Arvey Brrrrrriiistol Crrrrrreeeeeaaaaamm.' As for my Birmingham and Scottish accents, they were 'Alright Bab' and 'There's bin a muurrrrrrder', respectively. If the part required any more lines, then I would be exposed as a fraud, and if my character was anything more than a one-dimensional stereotype I would be for the high jump. Nevertheless, I sent the CV off (I'd added horse-riding and tap and jazz for my dancing disciplines – you never know, it might open some doors) with my photo and hoped that I would never ever get an audition and have to admit that I was a charlatan.

Needless to say, rejection followed rejection. Apparently, the acting world had no need for a horse-riding Scouser. It wasn't just the acting community that had turned its back on me. David Owen-Bell had put a modelling agency down as one of his contacts by mistake and I had the complete discomfort of having the rejection letter drop on my doormat two days later. I was horrified. The rejection letter was sweet, saying at that moment they weren't taking on any more models, but I really do dread to think what they made out of my flimsy curriculum vitae and accompanying black and white photo of me looking moody/constipated.

As my time at Ivy House entered its swansong, my situation became desperate. This wasn't it, surely? With menial work and hard labour seeming the only option, my life stretched ahead of me like a plate of dry toast.

Did I start to audition? Did I look into post-grad courses? Did I brush up on my accents?

No, I went to Camden Market to have my palm read by a gypsy fortune-teller.

At the time, it seemed like the only sensible thing to do. I went on 14 June 1997, my 21st birthday, as a birthday treat. My friend Kieran, whose birthday is the day after, came too. As it happens, we had two very different experiences. I went in first and, disappointingly, the gypsy woman wasn't what I expected – no scarf around her head, no misty crystal ball to peer into. In fact, she looked like one of Mum's friends. I thought, 'Here we go, what a waste of money.'

'Hello', I said.

'You're very theatrical,' she replied, 'and you are doing something dramatic, yes?'

Look, love, even David Blunkett could tell I wasn't on a welding course. I bit my tongue.

The gypsy carried on with her gay stereotypes. 'You're close to your mother, you don't like sports, you're the first on the dance floor, you like quiche.'

Strangely enough, as the session continued, she began to say things that were spookily accurate. She mentioned my dog by name – 'Minstral' – and said he was half Jack Russell. True. She said I was seeing someone American. True. Then she said something strange; she said that after today I wouldn't see him again. That was actually true; the bastard went back to America the day after my birthday without telling me, and I didn't see him again until this year when just by chance I bumped into him in Times Square in New York. Surprisingly, Chad didn't try to drag me into the doorway of Radio City Hall and shag me, so I've either got ropier-looking or he'd been neutered.

These little half-truths and educated guesswork gushed out of the gypsy's mouth, some spot on, some way off-course. In the middle of such predictions as 'You'll find love with someone beginning with S just before your 30th birthday' and 'Steer clear of anyone called Tony,' she told me that my future was in stand-up, and that I would make my money writing and performing comedy.

I remember shaking my head. I physically could not go through the stress of performing night in, night out, shitting my life away in pub toilets and swallowing sick. However, she was adamant.

I was unconvinced, and said, 'No, I don't think so.'

Seeing my horror at the thought of it, she insisted, 'You will!' but added enigmatically, 'But it won't be as you, you'll play a character.'

That, I suppose, is open to interpretation, but anyway I didn't take much notice of it because there was no way I would be doing stand-up anyway, was there?

I looked at my watch and saw the half hour had flown by. I waited outside while Kieran went in and had her palms read. Then we reconvened in a coffee shop and talked about our respective futures. I was disappointed. She hadn't mentioned an acting career or winning a BAFTA, and waiting till 30 to find love seemed ludicrous and impossibly old – I'm now 32 and still waiting.

Kieran came out from her session downcast. It seems my predictions were fabulous compared to hers. The fortune-teller had told her people would come from far and wide to hear her sing. You don't know Kieran, but her singing voice is worse than mine, and that is saying something. To top it off, she had been told that in the not too distant future she would be taking a journey in a white vehicle. Lovely. An ambulance!

So we headed off for a few birthday drinks, with me confused and Kieran a little downhearted. There's nothing like a prediction that you are about to be hospitalised to really get the party started.

* * *

I ended up with a 2.1 from Middlesex University. The graduation ceremony was at Wembley Conference Centre, and we all turned up with our mortarboards and gowns. But just like the course, the graduation ceremony seemed to drift aimlessly. No one took it seriously and no one saw it as an amazing end to an era. There was still no hope of a job, but then again I hadn't even tried to look for one. The lucky break that I had hoped would come and save the day hadn't materialised and I was stuck.

After having three hazy, slumbersome years at my disposal, I found now that I didn't even have a minute to decide what path to choose. All I knew was that, as soon as the ink on my last essay was dry, I had to find work, and quick. I couldn't be arsed with even more rejection letters and living in London was (and is) so expensive. So I moved back to Northampton and, thanks to Dad's amazing Northamptonian work connections, I got a job in a paint-spraying factory, wiping the grease off gearboxes before they were sprayed.

I guess I chickened out. I didn't really give this acting lark a go, to be honest. As always with me, that mixture of apathy and outright pessimism made me falter at the first hurdle. I wanted a great acting job, I wanted acclaim, I wanted my own trailer, I wanted a Lifetime Achievement BAFTA, and I wanted it all now. Not because I thought I was great, but because I couldn't be bothered to wait for them. I'm not one of those artistic creatures who will persevere for years, sleeping on people's floors, wiping down tables in a run-down caff, just to get that one amazing role. Oh no, I'd been poor for three years and it wasn't really me; I just wanted to get some money, pay off my debts and live a normal life. Unlike most of my peers, I couldn't wait to shed my student skin. I wasn't scared of moving on.

Interestingly enough, I bumped into one of the old Ivy House students at Heathrow Airport only this year. I instantly recognised her from her dreads and tie-dye. There is something tragic about seeing white people the wrong side of 30 with dreads.

'Hello, love. Where are you off to?'

'India. Stilt-walking in a festival,' came the reply.

I remember thinking, 'Of course you are. What else would you be doing? Not changing any stereotypes, that's for sure.' And so she headed off all bubbly, probably to have a chickpea curry, or realign her chakras near the baggage reclaim. You just know she's ten years away from a breakdown.

Ironically, I couldn't stay for the whole ceremony at Wembley Conference Centre because I'd only got the morning off from my job, and those gearboxes weren't going to degrease themselves. My dirty fingernails and the faint whiff of turps – the only things betraying my grotty day job. As I had to dash off, I missed out on having a drink with my friends. But after spending three years with them intensively on a course that at most occupied us for a day a week, we got the gist. We were ready for the next phase, whatever that was going to be. One thing I knew was that it was going to be grim.

Therefore, the words of our tutors as they stood on the podium talking about how we were the future – 'Watch out, future employers, Middlesex students are coming to get ya!' – felt hollow to my ears. I anxiously kept looking at my watch – not in a 'C'mon, world, let me at 'em' way, but more in a 'C'mon, my foreman is going to be furious if I'm not there to cover that afternoon shift' way. Anyway, that ideological 'we can make a difference' shit seems to be more relevant to a middle-class upbringing. It's only the privileged that have got the time and resources to make that change. When you're skint, you're too busy keeping the boat afloat to try to rock it.

So after a photoshoot of us all throwing our mortarboards in the air next to a giant roundabout, me and my parents made our excuses and headed back to Northampton. I could not wait to earn my first post-university wage. At least the money I earned didn't have to be spent on extortionate rent, photocopying or books that you wouldn't use as a coaster, let alone read.

* * *

Missing chances

I don't know whether it was an omen, but my Mini's engine burst into flames on the way to work in the first week. I don't know whether it was the thought of returning to an industrial estate or something automotive-related, but my beautiful yellow Mini 'Agnetha' just couldn't go on and gave up.

I stood with her as she was consumed by flames on the side of the A14. I felt guilty because I had promised her a new life, a car parking space at a posh city centre office-block or a studio flat, not another factory forecourt. It was the last I saw of Agnetha before she was taken away by a scrap merchant. She had been my first car, and we had shared some wonderful experiences together. It had taken me ages to pass my test and Agnetha had been a £500 treat to myself for my perseverance.

There is only one other man that I know who has taken just as long to pass their test as me, and that man is Justin Lee Collins. Four times – and that was before they brought in the ridiculously simple theory part. Not only did it take four times, it took three instructors. Driving instructors and I don't mix. I don't know whether it's their humourless stare or their pernickety attention to details, but they rub me up the wrong way. I didn't want anyone to bend the rules for me, just cut me some slack. The first instructor was horrid and we didn't last long. He used to talk to me as if I was a piece of dirt on his shoe. I don't care how badly you drive there's no excuse for calling someone a c***.

I moved on to Lance, and he didn't last long either, this time, not because of me, but because he was leaving the country, which was a shame as he was one of the good guys. His honesty was enchanting, especially when he rang up to tell me that he couldn't make the lesson that day as he had an attack of the shits, something that I never failed to forget as I sat in the driving seat of his Renault.

The last one, Len, was the worst, but ironically it was with him that I passed. I couldn't believe my luck when I saw this spitting image of Charlie from *On the Buses* sitting in the driving seat, scowling and smoking a Berkley Menthol. Why couldn't I have a good-looking one? Carolyn's driving instructor had taken her on drives to restaurants and paid for her to have dinner with him, but this one looked a right arsehole. Let's get one thing straight – I could drive, that had been established in the first few weeks. It was just the damn parallel parking and reversing around corners that threw the spanner in the works and dragged out what should have lasted a couple of months into the best part of a year.

I couldn't get it. The image in the rear-view mirror just didn't correlate with my hand that was white and gripping the steering wheel. It didn't help that Len had such a short fuse. On the dashboard, he would show me by using his fag packet as the car and reversing it around a cassette box, but by the time his explanation had finished, the fag packet would be in tatters and I would be close to tears. To be fair to me, it didn't help that they took you to drive around some of the roughest council estates in Northampton to learn the rules of the road. Apart from the usual hazards, you would have to be on the lookout for overturned trolleys, broken bottles and Staffordshire cross terriers running out in front of you.

You would think that spending so much time with Len a friendship would blossom, but that wasn't the case. We only had contempt for each other, he for my driving, and I for his sad little existence. On the day of my test I came out of the house wearing my contact lenses. I was certain that my glasses were the root of my driving trouble; the feeble excuse that they were causing an unnecessary blind spot prompted me to act.

'Where are your specs?' he said.

'I'm wearing my contact lenses,' I replied.

He tutted and muttered under his breath, 'Vanity, vanity, vanity.'

I cast one eye over his beige slip-ons and his teeth that looked like a brown Stonehenge and put the key in the ignition. I was going to make sure that this was going to be our final drive together, Len.

When I arrived back at the test centre, Len was chain-smoking. I got out and deliberately looked sad. He tutted, and then I screeched, 'I've passed!' Months of contempt and abuse fizzled out in front of our eyes and we hugged. Neither of us could believe it. I had been a little bit out on the reverse parking, but not enough to get me failed. I had been a bit more focused this time; the erratic driving had been replaced by carefully controlled movement. It had killed me at points. A low-flying pigeon had dipped in front of the windscreen, and where previously I would have screamed and driven the car into a shop window to avoid killing it, this time I applied the brake and took control.

It was the happiest day of my life. No more expensive lessons, no more reversing, and no more Len.

'Things are looking up,' I told Len.

'Yes Alan, they definitely are,' he said, as he pressed his beige slip-on to the pedal and we drove back to Overstone.

* * *

With Agnetha gone, and daily 6.30 a.m. pick-ups in the temps' minibus becoming a permanent fixture, I started to resign myself to this existence. Even as the minibus snaked its way around Northampton's various council estates collecting more and more miserable temps, for some strange reason it didn't dawn on me that my life was spiralling out of control. Nor did I understand that the longer I did these jobs, the more they were having potentially devastating effects on my CV.

Don't get me wrong, gearbox degreasing was an integral part in the well-oiled machine that was paint-spraying. I had to wipe the grease off carefully with a cloth that I would soak in a massive vat of methylated spirits. Once the metal part was clean of any grease, the sprayers would coat it with paint. Then I would hang it up in a kiln, so it would dry and set. Take it off four hours later and – voilà! – a nice new painted piece of metal. Don't ask me what they were for – I didn't know and I didn't care. All I knew was that they were something to do with cars.

The novelty of earning money and living with my parents was beginning to wear off, and 'professional Alan' was starting to reminisce about 'student Alan'. The temps' minibus was picking 'professional Alan' up at the same time as 'student Alan' would normally be stumbling through the door from a hard night's clubbing. The only positive thing about the job was that you were your own boss, you went at your own speed and didn't have to talk to anyone. It was only when the bell went that you'd have a cup of tea with the sprayers, and have a chat about, more often that not, spraying.

Working all day with an open vat of meths without a mask was having strange effects on me, I realised. Like most of Britain's workforce, I would turn up bored and tired at the beginning of the day, but by the end I was happy. No, not just happy, hysterical, and not just because home time was nearing. I would start giggling at the most mundane things and dancing at all the tunes that boomed out of the stereo, filling the cobwebbed corners of the factory. The Pet Shop Boys' 'Go West' was the anthem of the summer and was never off Northants 96.6 and, believe me, that song wasn't lost in my little outlet. I would be laughing hysterically, dancing away, pointing west and singing along with all my heart, while my brain was being reduced to mush, ravaged by the toxic fumes. Everyone left the factory shattered, but I always seemed to leave the place buzzing, only to endure the worst comedown with Mum and Dad over tea hours later wondering why I had a splitting headache and had lost the will to live.

Days turned to weeks, weeks turned to months, and nothing had really happened in my life – of course nothing had happened, you'd chosen to degrease gearboxes for a living, you dickhead! It wasn't *The Apprentice*. I was feeling really low, nostalgia and meths had clouded my vision, and in a bolt from the blue it hit me: university isn't going to interrupt this hell, this is your new life now! If I went on a game show my occupation would be 'degreaser'. My introduction would be:

'My name's Alan Carr, I'm 21, and I wish I were dead.' I was becoming a statistic. I'd started socialising with the other workers, been invited to the Christmas party, barbecues, you name it. For the first time in my life I was one of the boys, and I didn't like it.

'I've had enough,' shouted Cracker as he burst through the canteen door. It was a bit too early for histrionics, but no one was going to tell him. He marched past the poster of Linda Lusardi, grabbed a chair and told us what he had had enough of. He'd found out that his wife was having an affair with the landlord of the local pub, the Wellington. Cracker had always informed me about his marital shenanigans, whether I wanted to hear them or not. Bored of telling everyone else in the factory, he must have seen me dancing the jig, off my face from the fumes of methylated spirits and gurning, and thought, 'I'll tell him about my troubles. He seems like he could put an upbeat twist on my predicament.' I'd always smiled and nodded and agreed with whatever he had said, avoiding the tattooed fist that he would often waft in my face as he described what he'd do if he ever found the man who had been pumping his wife. After finding the culprit, he had a plan to get revenge on the accused and, as you can imagine, it wasn't psychological mind games.

'I've got balaclavas and baseball bats,' he shouted aggressively.

I started looking at Linda Lusardi.

'Who wants to smash up the Wellington after work with me?'

Most of the men got excited and said, 'Yeah, Cracker, count us in!'

There was a pause, and then he asked, 'And you, Alan?'

Well, I nearly spat my tea out. After I realised that this wasn't some sick joke, I replied, 'Oh yes, count me in,' raising my mug of tea courageously.

What was I supposed to do? I'd never been in a fight before, let alone instigated one. How do you smash up a pub? Do you go for the top row? Piss in the pool table pockets? And, let's be honest, in a police line-up I'd stick out like a sore thumb, firstly because of the voice and secondly because I was the only one wearing a pair of glasses over a balaclava.

My already awful day had been made worse by the thought of terrorising some poor, admittedly adulterous pub landlord. As it happened, Cracker couldn't wait till home time and smashed up the pub alone in his lunch break. He came back with a bloodied nose, but a smile on his face – job done. All the lads were furious – 'You should have waited for us.' I mumbled something along the lines of, 'Damn! I was looking forward to that …' I trailed off at the end of the sentence, just in case he got a second wind.

Chapter Seven

'IT'S NICE TO KNOW YOU'RE HERE – F*** OFF!'

Things couldn't carry on like this. The meths quite literally were doing my head in. The company was diabolical and the prospects were grim, to say the least. Plus, some of the men had started to guess my sexual orientation. One man who was urinating on a pile of palettes waved his penis at me and shouted, 'Bet you've never seen one as big as this before!' He was right, but this really wasn't the time or the place. Boy, you can tell you're in a dead-end job when the highlight of your day is being flashed at by a work colleague. Something had to give.

Why is it that with a shit job the minutes drag, yet the years fly by, and before you know it you're not the new boy, but one of the fixtures and fittings? I needed to push myself. My other friends had made progress. My upper school buddy Michael Underwood had started hosting *The Ministry of Mayhem* on ITV Saturday mornings, and it awoke something in me. It showed me a life that might have been, if I'd been braver and more focused. This niggled me. Everyone seemed to be moving on, yet I was stuck. I could tell my family were embarrassed about my job because when people would ask how I was doing they would say that I'd died.

You can see how people get stuck in a rut. I couldn't afford to leave Northampton, and where would I go if I did leave? London? I knew from experience that it's impossible to live in London if you don't earn a fortune, and in a weird way it would look like a step back. Then out of the blue I got a phone call from Catherine who had recently returned from her French Business School. Catherine was pissed off and, like me, instantly bored.

We met up and wanted an adventure. We decided to go travelling. We would save up and go around the world. We thought, 'Yes, we're skint, but you might as well be skint and tanned and on a beach with a mojito in your hand.' That makes sense, I'm sure you'll agree, so we started saving.

I decided to leave my gearbox-degreasing job and get a more office-based occupation that was more 'me'. Smart slacks, a tie, photocopier – yes, it was feeling better already. I joined the temping agency Manpower, and soon I was being sent all over the county performing menial office tasks for very little reward or satisfaction. Obviously, due to my lack of (any) skills, it was mainly data entry or reception work that I would be prostituting myself for, at £4.40 an hour.

Data entry, for those of you who haven't had the pleasure of doing it, is where you sit at a desk and are given a pile of statistics or names, which you have to enter into the company's database. That's it. No filing. No water-cooler moments chatting with your colleagues. No bonding. Just entering data. Temping in an office is no different to temping in a factory; you are ignored because you are a temp, you are persona non grata. People talk through you, and when they're making a cup of tea they don't ask if you'd like one. I've lost track of the number of times a tin of Celebrations has bypassed me.

What didn't help was that I was doing data entry for Mr Dog, the old name for Cesar Dog Food. Mr Dog had set up a competition. To win a caravan or whatever the prize was, the dog-owner/mug had to send in their dog's name, breed and birthday, so Mr Dog could send the beloved pooch a card on its birthday. That's what I did from nine to five for a month. 'Pippa, Bearded Collie, 1989', 'Mr Tibbs, Chihuahua, 1993', 'Sue, Alsatian, 1987'. Some people had up to ten dogs, so imagine if they won the caravan. It didn't bear thinking about. So my existence as a professional data entry-er continued: Inland Revenue, Barclaycard Fraud, British Gas. The only thing keeping me going would be the holiday brochures which I'd read in my breaks. In just a few months, Catherine and I would be off around the world for a year.

*   *   *

I was desperate to make as much money as possible, so I became a driver's mate for Wicks' Conservatories at the weekends. A driver's mate accompanied a lorry driver on a long journey, keeping him company, map reading. More intriguing, though, was the fact that if you slept with him overnight you got an extra £100. Now I was like you; when I heard I had to sleep with the driver, I was horrified. I don't mind doing a bit of map reading or taking the cellophane off his sandwiches, but I'm not giving over my body on the M25.

After I'd stopped dry heaving, the man in the agency told me that because Wicks' delivered their conservatories the length and breadth of the country, I would have to sleep in a lay-by on the outskirts of London overnight and then carry on to Devon and Cornwall with a hopefully replenished and refreshed driver. The thought of £100 titillated me, and I accepted it. I could live like a king in Thailand on that and, you never know, the driver might be one of those big, burly ones, with thick arms and stubble who holds me tight in the lay-by as the other drivers rush past the window.

But no, he was a skinny thing with a hairstyle like a King Charles Cavalier Spaniel. Yes, he was minging, bald with two strands of hair that hung down either side of his sorry little grey face like cheap curtains. His breath stank: every time he spoke it was as if someone had opened the door of a portaloo.

Never mind, I thought, he could have a great sense of humour, and the miles would fly by as we laughed our way through the various counties, unable to read the map because of the tears in our eyes. No, he was deadly dull, but what's worse is, he thought he had a sense of humour. Ten minutes into the journey, he wound down his window and shouted to a field of pigs, 'Where's your uniform?' God.

Jim and I just didn't get along. We'd got off on the wrong foot because I had turned up in jeans. Hadn't I been told it was shirt and tie? Shirt and tie? For delivering conservatories?

'Jeans don't look right.'

'Well, neither does your hair, but you don't see me complaining.'

148

To top it all, he deliberately sped up and drove his lorry into a flock of low-flying seagulls, killing the back one. So I had the remains of a squashed gull in my face for the best part of the M1. If there's one thing that I am worse at than football, it's map-reading. I admit it, I don't get it, the symbols, the lines, the key. What does it all mean? Plus, this was before SatNav, so it was really just me and a map, and the number of times I directed him up a B road to find that a 2-tonne truck or whatever it weighed wasn't allowed to go over a hump-backed bridge ... Every time I would make an innocent mistake he would start kicking off about his bonus; he got an extra pound added to his wages if he got there within 30 minutes. Apparently, being directed the wrong way down a one-way street by me affected his bonus.

'I don't want to lose my pound,' he grunted.

'Look, I'll give you the sodding pound. Just let me find out what these red-coloured roads are.'

Once we had finally arrived at the houses and carried the conservatory from the back of the lorry, we were asked whether we'd want a cup of tea. As we all know, they were just being polite, but not only did Jim say 'Yes', he said 'Yes' every time. So Jim and I and the owners of the house would all be standing there in awkward silence nursing a cup of tea in their kitchen. Apart from Jim, none of us wanted to be there. How much small talk can you make about conservatories?

Well, that fateful time of the day approached. Night fell, and I knew what that meant – I had to sleep with Jim. How do these prostitutes do it? It terrified me having to sleep with Jim, and I knew him – it wasn't even 'sleeping' sleeping, you know. We pulled into this lay-by, and I started unpacking my sleeping bag. I went to use the toilets, brushed my teeth, and started thinking that this so wasn't worth a hundred quid. Jim undressed and swallowed a tablet – I prayed it wasn't Viagra – and said, 'Night night.'

'Night night, Jim,' I replied.

I really don't know who had the most sleep – I, who was uneasy sleeping in a trucker's cabin with all these cars whizzing past, or Jim, sleeping next to an effeminate temp wearing a velvet eye-mask and Vics on his chest.

* * *

I didn't get any more work being a driver's mate. I don't know whether that was Wicks' doing or that there genuinely weren't any more jobs. However, in my grey little temp world it was 'busy, busy, busy'. In fact, a new temporary receptionist job at Horiba Instruments on Moulton Park Industrial Estate had come in, and Manpower thought I'd be perfect. Horiba Instruments dealt in Carbon Dioxide Emission Testing Machines, and scientists would ring the receptionist from all over the world asking for specific parts and advice. The receptionist would then redirect them to the appropriate engineer, so yes, as Manpower had said, I would be perfect for it.

I turned up at Kyoto Close – apparently Dr Horiba was so into his homeland, he named a cul-de-sac on a Northampton industrial estate after it. I wonder what Dr Horiba would have thought, as his Rolls Royce pulled around the corner and he saw the burnt-out car in the forecourt and the gypsies' horses neighing around the adjacent fields. I kept thinking 'Kyoto must be a shit-hole.'

I turned up on the first day, and told the woman from Horiba that I was from Manpower. After looking me up and down and muttering something about 'Trade Descriptions Act', she showed me to my desk in the foyer. It was just me and a potted plant. My job would be to welcome people to Horiba Instruments, answer the phone and open the post. Of course, like the time a few years back when I'd been collecting glasses and working at the Singles Bar at Sywell Motel, Dad decided to start his crank phone calls. So for the first few weeks I had to endure phone calls from a 'Japanese' man with very poor English, usually with ridiculous names. That wasn't really fair for me, because I was already struggling to operate the busy switchboard, plus there were genuine Japanese scientists ringing up with genuinely ridiculous names.

I remember one called Dr Fukishammy, a name that would have been perfect for Dad's wind-up, but was, I'm afraid, a bona fide doctor on Horiba's payroll. The job was pretty mundane, but the people were great, particularly Andrea, the managing director's PA. She would pop all the purchase orders and invoices in the right in-boxes after I'd messed up again. To this day, I still do not know what a 'purchase order' is. Nevertheless, I continued to work there, answering the phone, filing, typing, but ultimately dreaming of Mexico, the newly decided first destination for our round-the-world trip.

It's strange commenting on these tedious jobs from the comfort of where I am now. In hindsight, they seem quite funny in their own little mundane way – the gossip, the petty rules, the ridiculous office hierarchy. But I wouldn't be doing myself justice if I didn't mention how miserable and depressed I was at the time. To have one dead-end job is unlucky, but to have one dead-end job after another really starts to affect your self-esteem. You do feel that you're just a statistic.

You would walk around town and bump into people who you went to school with, all suited and booted, going to jobs where they brokered deals, had power lunches and made decisions. The only decision I ever made was whether it was 'family bereavement' or 'the shits' when I decided to pull a sickie. You can see why these people find *X-Factor* or *Big Brother* attractive, can't you? There are so many grim jobs out there that any welcome respite from the drab existence of a nine-to-five factory job must be tempting, even if it means spending twelve weeks locked in a house with freaks. I'm not too proud to say that I would have gladly joined them – I had nothing to lose.

Socially, it wasn't looking too good, either. My three years down in London had shaken off what remaining friends I had, so I had no one to go out with, Believe me, I wasn't asking any of my colleagues if they wanted a swift half at the Rat and Parrot. Even my good old friend and drinking partner had gone. Poor old Carolyn had been struck down with MS, had virtually gone blind overnight and had relocated to Worthing to be near her family. That terrible disease had struck at one of the nicest and best friends I had ever had. It really shows, you never know what's in store, and it puts into perspective my witterings about a couple of crappy jobs.

Before she moved down south, Carolyn and I partied hard. Even though she was blind, it never stopped her giving it large. She would always get into the thick of it. Her not being able to see was never a hindrance; in fact, we used to be in such states, sometimes I think Carolyn saw more than I did. Whether it was on the dance-floor of a club or at an illegal rave in some dilapidated barn, we would enjoy ourselves. Admittedly, sometimes I lost her, but thankfully I always found her again – although once it was only because I'd found her white stick, brown and bent, wedged in the mud pointing towards the disabled toilets, where she was vomiting. It's not the classiest thing you'll read on these pages, but going out with Carolyn and me was never classy – fun, but never classy.

* * *

The magical day 7 June 1999, that day which I'd anticipated for what seemed an age, finally dawned. Not only was it Prince's birthday, it was also the day Catherine and I were about to start our round-the-world trip. After two years of dreariness following university, my life was about to begin again. My life was about to have a good old shot of adventure. We looked the part, we'd both treated ourselves to brand new sandals, and with the money that the people of Horiba gave me in a whip-round I bought a brand spanking new rucksack.

Dad drove us down to Heathrow, and as we pulled up at Departures I was surprised to see my father crying. That, of course, made me start crying, and then Catherine started, too. It was strange seeing him cry. I'd only ever seen him cry over *Noel Edmond's Christmas Presents* on Christmas morning. Every year he would be genuinely amazed when the people's families weren't in Sydney, Australia, but actually backstage, ready to come through the doors and surprise the awaiting family in the studio. The family would cry, Noel would cry, Dad would cry.

But this time he was crying about me leaving for a year. I gave him a big hug and told him not to worry. I didn't dare tell him how worried I was. I put on a brave face and didn't let it show that I was about to embark on a journey into the wilderness, a journey that would take me across the hostile plains of the Chiapas, the forests of Malaysia and the deserts of Australia. Would my body be ready for this undertaking? Yes, it would, and without much bother, really.

It's only when you get to these 'exotic' places that you realise that they're on such well-trodden tourism routes, you feel a bit stupid for picking somewhere so utterly predictable. The travelling infrastructure is so well-oiled that sometimes you wish you could go a bit off the beaten track, and you end up tagging along with Quentin and Pippa, chartered accountants from Surrey trying to find themselves. Great! No, I'm afraid my fears of finding myself alone in a jungle trying to kill an orang-utan for food were well off the mark. These days you're more likely to find the golden arches or a Tesco Metro squatting in the jungle than a tribe of indigenous cannibals. It's a shame really, not because of commercialism – I just have a soft spot for cannibals.

Obviously, this awakening was awaiting me on the other side of the Atlantic, but I was green and excited/nervous. Anyway, whatever happened, I wasn't clocking in at Horiba Instruments at 8.45 a.m. the next day, so who gives a shit?

The flight took eight hours and, like all my favourite plane journeys, it was uneventful. I didn't really want to spend all year saving up for this round-the-world trip only to go into the side of a mountain. No, the journey was fine, albeit a little cramped. But it was the height of luxury compared to what we had in store.

According to our *Rough Guide*, our hotel was near to La Plaza de la Constitución in the middle of Mexico City. Plaza de la Constitución or El Zócalo is one of the largest squares in the world. It is used for concerts, artistic celebrations, civic duties or, as it was on 7 June 1999, a demonstration where all the poor of Mexico City descend on the Zócalo to complain to the government about their poverty-stricken lives. You will not believe what greeted our tired eyes as we came up the subway. The Zócalo had been transformed into a shanty town. I say 'transformed', but I don't know what it looked like previously – although I never saw chickens, women screaming and gangs of Mexicans banging makeshift drums out of bins in any of the travel information.

The only tip we had been given was not to look like a tourist. So there we were, standing in what can only be described as a riot, with a rucksack on, reading a *Rough Guide* and holding a camera. The only other thing that was pastier than our skin was the dead chicken that this 18-stone Mexican woman was waving around her head. It was pretty scary, but eventually we found the road we needed for our hotel and made a quick exit.

We decided to leave Mexico City and head down south to Oaxaca. Some surfers had advised us to get out of Mexico City and make for the coast, so that's what we did. Looking back, I regret not spending more time in that city, with its striking architecture and its ruins, but the night before had shaken us up. Besides, I had seen a corpse in a doorway that morning on the way out for a croissant, and that really made my mind up. We'd been there a day and the only Mexicans we'd seen were either rioting or dead. We made it to the bus station and began our six-hour bus journey to Oaxaca.

The first thing that hit us was the massive shanty town embedded in the side of this hilltop. As you saw the corrugated-iron roof and cramped conditions, it made you think that it was a bit like being on this bus, only on the hill they weren't swerving in and out of Volkswagens and being driven by a man off his face on tequila. I don't care what you say, the scenery between Mexico and Oaxaca is boring. Cactus after cactus after cactus whizzing past my window, and then a few hills for six hours. Things must have been bad because I started reminiscing about the M6, with its delightfully coloured orange bollards and charming eateries like Little Chef. As the television wasn't working, the driver popped on the Vengaboys album, and that was that. 'The Vengaboys are coming and everybody's grooving …' on a loop for six hours, and all there is to look at is fucking cacti. I left Northampton for this?

All our fears seeped away as we arrived at this beautiful Zócalo in Oaxaca, dominated by a magnificent cathedral that itself was framed against the Sierra Madre del Sur mountains. On the top of these stood Monte Alban, these huge magnificent Zapotec ruins. The Zapotecs apparently never made as big an impact as their Inca cousins, so in fact they were a bit like a prehistoric Dannii Minogue, but don't let that put you off. They are really impressive, these huge stones that some poor sod must have had to carry up the hillside from the valley down below thousands of years before. It is genuinely an eerie place, especially when you walk up the southern platform which was used for human sacrifice. As you stand there looking out across the valley, you wonder for how many people that would have been the last thing they ever saw. Brutal, yet beautiful. This was the Mexico I had waited for.

As we continued our journey through Mexico, we quickly found out that a six-hour bus journey was relatively swift. We were soon experiencing eighteen-hour journeys, weaving up and down mountains. Sometimes we were so high up, we were driving through clouds. In fact, we were getting quite used to the travelling. I don't know whether we had resigned ourselves to it or the scenery had improved, but it seemed the deeper into Mexico we ventured, the more vibrant and lush our surroundings became. Women selling guava and mangoes, tiny churches teetering on the edge of a cliff, waterfalls, and not a cactus in sight.

Everything was going so well. We'd had a week of exploring. Yes, the travelling had been a drag, but we were getting the gist – there are mammoth bus journeys, but at the end you're rewarded with a little gem of a town or city. However, I wasn't counting on getting 'Montezuma's Revenge'. Now when I mention 'Montezuma's Revenge', I'm not talking about the video game for the Commodore 64, I'm talking about severe diarrhoea. 'Montezuma's Revenge' is a 'humorous' name. It's especially hilarious when you've shat yourself on an Inca ruin. It's a myth to do with the Aztec god cursing the invading Spanish, but it's technically a bacterial infection you get from eating the food that's been washed in their water. Obviously when I was sober, I was vigilant about not having salads or ice cubes. But after a couple of 60p bottles of Corona, you get the munchies in a Mexican village and reading the label isn't that high on the list of priorities.

It wasn't too long before, thankfully, we went to a beautiful island, Isla Mujeres, a few miles off the Yucatán Peninsula in the Caribbean Sea. Maybe I'm a philistine; you can see all the history and ruins you want, but until you've popped on your Speedos, swung in a hammock and sipped a daiquiri your holiday hasn't really started. Oh, just me then. Seeing that blindingly white sand and that turquoise sea was such a blessed relief. The last fortnight had been enjoyable, but it hadn't been easy. Now we were in paradise. Whether it was my body slipping into holiday mode or the skip full of Imodium I'd been taking, my bowels had quietened down substantially.

We carried on our journey down the coast staying at more and more cabanas, beginning our metamorphosis into proper tourists. Our skins turning a lovely golden brown, sarongs replacing our shorts and our insides toughened up so much we were eating the local food off the stalls in the street. There was even no more screaming if a lizard jumped out from behind a cactus, well, maybe just a little gasp.

More beautiful beaches, more ruins and more bus journeys awaited us. The morning we were set for Acapulco we had overslept, and when we had reached the bus station the only two seats they had left were at the back next to the toilets. I didn't think this would be a problem. I'd sat next to the toilets on school trips and on a National Express – how bad could they be? Fucking awful! They reeked. As we walked down the aisle, people were holding their noses and waving anything they could find to try and generate some air that wasn't in fact rancid. It was dreadful.

Thankfully, the bus started quickly, and we were off on our way to Acapulco. The air conditioning on the bus wasn't helping things in the least, and to make it worse, every time the bus went around a corner the toilet door would fly open and happy-slap us with its stench. I was gagging at this point and trying to find a gap in the window insulation where I could get some fresh, healthy air. As the bus trundled up a mountainside, the toilet door flew open nearly every few minutes. It became too much, I couldn't take any more. I was so nauseous, I slammed it shut out of pure frustration. With a huge 'clang', the door remained shut, and the aroma seemed, thank God, to have abated for the time being. The back of the bus could take a deep breath, literally, take a deep breath.

We thought nothing more of it until a Mexican man from the front of the bus came to use the toilet. He grabbed the handle to pull it down. Nothing. He tried again. It didn't budge. He pulled a bit harder – yes, it was jammed. Then he looked at me and pointed aggressively at the toilet door. Did I look like I had 'Toilet attendant' written on my forehead?

Obviously, I didn't say this to him, as he looked scary. He was gesturing to me that I had broken the toilet. That's gratitude. I didn't see anyone complaining when I had deadened the smell. I had gone from bus hero to bus villain in the space of fifteen minutes. What was I supposed to do? Buy a Glade plug-in?

By then, a couple of other Mexicans got involved, talking in Spanish, then looking at me and scowling. I looked away. It wasn't my fault that we were one hour into a twelve-hour bus journey without a working toilet. They managed to force the lock and – 'Open sesame!' – the door flew open, offering up its eggy treasures for the whole of the back of bus. We would just have to make do with the smell for the next eleven hours. Not only did we now get the smell when we went round a bend, we got the sight of a Mexican sitting on the toilet as well.

Acapulco was a bit like one of those ageing rock stars: they're famous, but you don't know what for, and even if you did, it all happened in the Seventies. By my reckoning, Acapulco needed a makeover and quick. As always with Mexico, they could try to be hip and 'with it', but they always seemed to get upstaged by their heritage. In Acapulco's case, it wasn't the bars or hotels, it was La Quebrada that stole the show. La Quebrada, made famous by the Elvis film *Fun in Acapulco*, is where these fearless men dive 136 metres off the top of the cliff into a sea. But if you ask me, if they really wanted to be fearless they should try to stroke one of the cats there.

These bronzed, lean, Speedo-wearing men would kiss the statue of the Madonna, lucky bitch, nestled on top of the cliff, and then dramatically leap into the sea. One error and they would be dashed against the rocks and banished to a watery grave. It was all very exciting. Some people claim it's only for the tourists – yeah right, as if these men are going to throw themselves off for a laugh. It was during this marvellous spectacle that Montezuma took his revenge on Catherine, but this time both ends.

So poor old Catherine was not looking so well at all. She was feeling weak and exhausted, exactly as I had done all those weeks ago. As we sat there, disheartened and looking at each other across the ripped linoleum, a noise began to fill the room, a noise that I'd heard so many times before in Mexico, a noise that filled me with dread. Oh no, it couldn't be. Oh yes, it was. It was the fucking Vengaboys! 'Boom! Boom! Boom! Boom! I want you in my room. Let's spend the night together.' A so-called 'party' cruise ship was circling the bay and, like some tramp's projectile vomit, that song had seeped out, to everyone's inconvenience.

The Vengaboys' music was becoming like the fabled Black Dog. Wherever it appeared, bad luck and carnage would soon follow. Catherine began to vomit again, not knowing whether it was caused by Montezuma or the Vengaboys' B-side. I made up my mind we were leaving Mexico. I was sick of being ill. I was sick of being on a bus. The amount of money Catherine and I had spent on buying new underwear meant that, at the rate we were going, we would have blown our budget by Tuesday week. So the next day I bought two plane tickets to fly us to the border. This was a big step because I used my Visa card, a card I had promised to use only in an emergency. I returned to Catherine and told her the good news. Don't get me wrong, I had a wonderful time. Mexico is an amazing place, but as you've read over the previous pages, you pay with your bowels. I can only assume it's like being tagged: your options are limited, you feel trapped, and you are forced to stay in one place at one time – which, in my case, was near a toilet.

I guess I wasn't the hardcore traveller that I thought I was. I'll admit it, Montezuma won, my arse lost, but, hey, onwards and upwards. As soon as we crossed that border into California we both breathed a sigh of relief. I don't know whether it was psychosomatic, but our stomachs seemed to feel better, the air seemed clearer, and we headed into America with a regained sense of optimism.

* * *

The contrast between Mexican and American life is so stark. Yes, boundaries are everywhere – whether they are emotional or social – but the physical one that lies between California and Mexico takes some beating. The poor, run-down Tijuana and the urbane cosmopolitan San Diego feel they should be continents apart and not just a few miles. I'm not going to get too much on my 'Make Poverty History' soapbox. The US gets criticised for being bigger and better, but that's fine with me; as long as the Americans give good customer service, I ain't complaining.

California went like a dream. The food was great, the weather was divine and the people were to die for. Admittedly, their friendly attitude can be quite unnerving to a cynical Brit.

I was in a mall (shop) holding up some pants (trousers), and a passing shop assistant said, 'Hey, you look good.' I automatically scanned her face for sarcasm. None. Hmm! What was her game? 'You'll look hot in those. Trust me.'

It was a revelation. I've never had anyone say I was 'hot' before, well, apart from that man in Yates Wine Bar, but then again he was playing 'Pull the Pig'. It was just the shot of positivity that I was looking for, and do you know what? I bought the pants (trousers). She was right: they were awesome (wonderful) because they showed off my ass (bottom) and weiner (penis). I know it's not trendy, but I love Americans.

We got a Greyhound bus up to San Francisco, a destination I was so excited to visit. When we arrived, it didn't disappoint; it was everything I'd expected it to be. It was so fresh and open and one of those places that you could just walk and walk and walk. One thing that I found really strange was the sight of those Mexican pan pipers that seem to be in every town centre the world over. San Diego, San Francisco, they even have them in Northampton. What? They make Starbucks look like a cottage industry. But, bizarrely, we never saw a single one the whole time we were in Mexico. I never heard a single pipe being blown or any Mexican say 'Hey Roberto! Let's make some lift music with zee pipes.' No, it seems the Mexicans didn't want to piss off their own kind, oh no, they would irritate the rest of us in protest at being persecuted all those years ago. And where would they do it? In shopping centres. They know we like to shop. Very cunning, those Mexicans.

When I tell people I've been to San Francisco, they automatically raise an eyebrow and go, 'Oh yes?', naturally assuming that I popped into a sauna and partook in a down and dirty rampant sexathon for four days. I'm afraid the opposite is true. I found the Castro, the big gay area, a bit full on to be honest. San Francisco is big on leather biker bars which, as you can probably tell, isn't really me. Obviously, I went to have a look – for research purposes, of course – but the bars terrified me. God knows what a heterosexual would feel. Approaching these bars that had names like 'The Stud', 'The Cock' and 'Daddy's', I felt a lump come to my throat – and it wasn't the kind of lump I was hoping for. Personally I like my gay bars to be a bit more subtle and have a bit of mystery, and besides, we were running out of money, I couldn't afford a sandwich let alone a pair of bumless trousers to go partying in.

In saying that, we always seemed to have enough money for drink. Strange, isn't it? Your face could be pressed up against the glass of a restaurant window like some urchin salivating at all the people eating, yet when it came to drinks I was as flush as Rockefeller. My Visa card was taking some battering, I'm afraid. This card, which at the beginning of the trip was for emergencies only, was now bearing the brunt of mine and Catherine's drink problem. But then again, after a hard day taking in all the sights, in some respects a gin and tonic with ice and a slice could be seen as an emergency.

* * *

I was wary about returning to Sydney. I'd had an awful time the first time I'd gone. I had visited Carolyn with her new boyfriend in this dodgy cockroach-ridden youth hostel.

'It's nice to know you're here – F*** off!'

Whenever you turn up in a strange city, accommodation is top of your list. If you're a poor backpacker in Sydney, there's only one place to head to, and that's King's Cross. This sleazy part of Sydney is like its London namesake, seedy and grubby and full of prozzies. Our hostel was right at the other end of King's Cross. That meant walking past the neon migraine which was the titty-bars with their menacing, puffed-up door staff trying to lure you in.

Our hostel was friendly and clean, with a lovely roof terrace where you could look down on King's Cross and see people being mugged, prostitutes getting arrested and drunk aboriginals shitting. But when the sun is shining and you've got a beer in your hand, you could be in paradise.

Accommodation was sorted. Now all I needed was a job. I bought myself a couple of shirts from David Jones, the department store. These were the cheapest shirts you've ever seen, they were one step up from tea-towels. 100% polyester – just ideal for a workday in a city that often reaches the late 30s Celsius, don't you think? Let's hope the offices aren't too confined. The trousers were also cheap, my shoes were these disgusting black slip-ons whose soles were so slippy, you could do Torvill and Dean's Bolero down the street without lifting a leg.

I went round all the temping agencies in the Sydney area with my CV. It's refreshing to know that a 2.1 in Drama and Theatre Studies is just as useless on the other side of the world as it is here. Employers are keen to use us Brits over there, not because we're hard-working or enthusiastic, but because they don't have to give us benefits like sickness or holiday pay. So it was nice to know that even my pitiful CV would come good at some point. However, it was the same message from each agency – 'No work at the moment. Come back next week.'

I needed work, and I needed it fast. It just so happened, as I was walking down George Street, the main thoroughfare in Sydney, Catherine spotted a friend across the road. This friend turned out to be Sarah, a girl Catherine had known in Kettering a few years back and had lost touch with. It's ridiculous really that the backpacker trail is so well worn that you are more likely to bump into an old friend on it than in your own high street. Sarah was here with her girlfriend Cherry. At that point I did not realise that Sarah and Cherry would become two of my best friends, but let's not spoil the story by getting over-sentimental just yet. I asked Sarah if she knew of any work going.

My first mistake was to say 'I'll do anything.' She was working at a restaurant called Café 191, and they needed a 'dishpig' ASAP. Sarah informed me that a 'dishpig' was polite Australian slang for a washer-upper and that Café 191 was on Oxford Street – slap-bang in the middle of Australia's gay scene. Oh, what with the excitement of finally earning some cash and the chance of maybe finding a possible holiday romance, I accepted and told her I'd meet her there at half seven.

Café 191 was a very swish, modern, cosmopolitan establishment where the gay glitterati dropped in for cocktails and people-watched before swanning off to a club or a private members bar. Not that I saw any of this because I was round the back, sweating profusely while scrubbing at a wok with a scourer. The gay world has a hierarchy, and never was that more in evidence than at Café 191: lesbians and ugly gays out the back and pretty boys and muscle Marys at the front. I wouldn't have minded, but some of these gays were retarded, mincing around taking the wrong orders, ignoring the ugly customers and serving the good-looking ones first. Huh, maybe if I'd had streaks in my hair I might have been able to fraternise with the customers, too. Instead, the only time I was spotted on the restaurant floor was when my pink marigolds would come through the serving hatch to collect the tray of dirty plates and dishes.

Any mystique I'd conjure up with those marigolds would be destroyed at midnight when my true identity would be revealed as I took all the kitchen waste out the back and popped it in a giant tin bin, situated conveniently next to the entrance of Sydney's premiere gay nightclub. Sarah was right, I was meeting lots of gay people; they were scowling in their minuscule muscle vests while I was standing with a binliner and half of Café 191's menu down my pinny. Surely one of these men would slip their phone number down the front of my apron? Alas, no.

Despite all this, Sarah and I had a right laugh, especially when the owner grabbed a pot from the top of the cupboard and a rat jumped down the front of his ruffled top. And you think I can scream! As always, it's the grim occasions that bond people, and among the drama and stress of the kitchen the seeds of our friendship were sewn. I was introduced to her girlfriend, Cherry, who was working in a fish-and-chip shop under Sydney Harbour Bridge. She was just as lovely as Sarah, and we were relieved that we weren't the only ones enduring a mundane job in the name of travel. I lasted a couple more months at Café 191, but then thankfully my CV finally bore fruit. I got a job at HIH Insurance in an administrative role. It seems those polyester shirts I bought were going to come in useful after all.

HIH Insurance was one of the biggest insurance companies in Australia, and my role was to collect all the claims that came through by fax and accredit them to the right department. Yes, that was my job plain and simple, but at least I didn't have the chance of getting Hepatitis B from emptying a bin. The form was simple: name, address, what is the injury? Where on your body is it? One form that still makes me laugh was from this farmer who worked driving a tractor in the Outback:

What is the injury? Piles
Where on the body is it? Where do you fucking think?

The job was pretty tedious, but the people were great. I have such an affection for Australians; they just get our sense of humour, don't they? Whether it's the amount of sunshine or the sense of space that just makes them so optimistic and cheery, I don't know, but my time there just seemed to be filled with laughing and getting pissed. I soon befriended one of the doctors there, Janet Hay. She was my partner in crime, and we would always go socialising together. Because she was high up at the firm, she would always get me into the staff dos and work lunches that humble temps like myself wouldn't normally be invited to.

I remember being so wrecked at a works do that I blacked out after being hit on the head with a chicken wing – don't ask. I woke up under the table. Janet, just as pissed as I was, tried to hail me a cab, but no one would stop. And so I decided to go home on the City Circle, their underground system. I gave her a kiss and made my way back. Finally, I got home after a succession of people had looked discouragingly at this pissed-up Brit nodding off on the train. It was only when I looked in the mirror and saw that someone had drawn a swastika on my forehead that I realised they'd stitched me up good and proper. You can imagine the cheer I got when I turned up for work hung over the next morning. With a cheeky Nazi salute, I returned to my filing.

The Backpacker Hostel was becoming a drag. It was becoming impossible to have a lie in due to the continual drone of the tannoy waking everyone up at eight o'clock with its offers of cheap manual labour. 'Road sweeper needed, $10 an hour' or 'Bricklayer wanted'. I listened out for 'Actor needed for Hollywood blockbuster. Must be camp and have buck teeth', but it never came, so I just rolled over and went back to sleep.

We decided to find a house of our own, somewhere new and fresh where the bathrooms weren't communal and you weren't continually being asked if you wanted pussy when you stepped out of the front door. We needed an upgrade. Besides, I was working in insurance – I had a reputation to uphold. Catherine and I had made friends with three Irish guys, and we all decided to move in together. The rent would be cheaper, plus we all got along – indeed, you might say that we got along too well. Catherine and Aaron are now married. In fact, it was me who brought them together – oh yes, I can be a right little cupid when I want to be. I should sort myself out sometime.

Aaron had come into the kitchen that morning, and both Catherine and I had gone 'Woof!', our codename for any men that we fancied – subtle, I know. I was making breakfast and, unbeknownst to me, the tea-towel had caught fire on the ring heating up the beans. Suddenly the flames started burning my hand, and I began screaming and waving this tea-towel like an Olympic gymnast. I threw it on the floor, and one of the Irish lads stamped on it for me, saving me from being burnt to death. That broke the ice, and we invited them to join us for breakfast and over the smell of burning tea-towel our friendship began.

We ended up taking a house in Darlinghurst, a pretty, lovely suburb that was a short walk to Rushcutters Bay and Paddington, the place to be seen. Paddington could be found at the other end of Oxford Street and it would be strange walking down there at night, passing by all the trendy wine bars and chi-chi boutiques. Then as you got to Oxford Street, you'd see dodgy-looking drag queens and doped-up rent boys standing in doorways, or what I saw one night, a drag queen hitting a policeman over the head with a baguette.

We couldn't have picked a better spot. At the end of the road there was a place called the Albery. They had Gay Bingo there, which was an absolute scream. 'Two fat dykes – 88,' squawked the drag queen, Clare De Lune. 'One and eight – eighteen and never been fisted.' You never got that at Mecca

Bingo, but then again you weren't playing for dildos and a set of love-eggs. I know this is blasphemous, but I got sick of the gay scene. It was too image-conscious at times. There didn't seem to be anybody around like me – normal. They were either drag queens or these ripped, veiny, muscle-bound guys who resembled a Lion Bar that's been left by a fire.

One of the highlights of my life was seeing in the Millennium in Australia. We saw it in at Rose Bay, a really picturesque spot with its moored yachts and park. But its main appeal is the perfect panoramic view you get of Sydney Harbour Bridge and the Opera House. I always smile inwardly when someone says how their New Year or Millennium celebrations are always a letdown. Don't get me wrong, mine usually are, but that Millennium year was a triumph. We had this spectacular view with the most amazing firework display that lasted for what seemed another millennium. Then we danced the night away with Tom Cruise and Nicole Kidman, who were together back then in the early 2000s. When I say 'partied', they did it on their yacht, which was rumoured to be floating about 100 metres away from us on the water, and we congaed on our bit of dry land.

In the end, we gatecrashed a house party that was happening in the salubrious area of Potts Point. Free champagne and cocktails were the order of the day, and it rounded off our celebrations nicely, if not a bit chaotically. At one point I saw Catherine emerge from a bush where she'd obviously passed out. I couldn't help laughing because she had two footprints on her chest. Someone had obviously trodden on her as she lay on the floor, and she'd been so gone she hadn't noticed. That's my girl.

After all the fun, it was hard to get back into the swing of it. I was getting bored. I felt like I was stagnating, not just in the house, but in Australia. Plus, after an expedition up the Gold Coast failed to materialise, Sarah and Cherry found themselves homeless and ended up living with us for a couple of weeks, bringing the total to one heterosexual girl, three heterosexual Irishmen, one homosexual man and two lesbians sharing a tiny two-bedroomed terraced house. As you can imagine, the atmosphere in that front room became as stifling as the Sydney air itself.

While standing by the fax machine waiting for yet more people to complain about their injuries, I decided that it was time to move on before I started to resent Sydney. It had been a fabulous experience, but it was time to leave the party. The only problem was, I hadn't saved any money for the rest of the trip. I was skint, broke, penniless, and I had the rest of my trip to do. Obviously, looking at my bank balance, there was no way I could continue around Australia as planned. I would have to cut straight to Malaysia and Thailand and hope that living there was as cheap as everyone was raving about.

Catherine was lucky; she was able to cash in some bonds, so she could afford to do the rest of Australia and New Zealand. But I couldn't ring my parents up and ask for money so I could go round New Zealand, they'd laugh in my face. Dreadful as it sounded, it looked as if we had to go our separate ways, which was heartbreaking. We'd started this fantastic journey together, and it felt only natural that we should end it together, but, alas, it wasn't to be. So we made our tearful goodbyes, and I travelled alone off to Asia.

* * *

I had been in touch with Carolyn by email throughout my journey. Whereas I had had one of my best years, Carolyn had had possibly one of her worst, not only adapting to a life without sight, but enduring the painful treatments that came with it to try to save the little sight that remained. When I knew that my planned trip was being shortened, I asked if she wanted to join me in Singapore and work our way up through the islands for a month. She said yes, and I knew I wouldn't be alone much longer.

The backpacker trail up through Malaysia and Thailand is so well ploughed that it's never too hard to make friends, so Carolyn and I weren't on our own for too long. We stayed in Kuala Lumpur at a grubby youth hostel in Chinatown. Lying in the nylon sheets made my skin crawl. Carolyn and I made our way around the town. Apparently Kuala Lumpur was a haven for bargain-hunters. As I wandered along looking in the shop windows, I saw something that was so graphic it felt like a punch to the stomach. The image that winded me so was a beggar who was not only blind, but also had no eyeballs. It was as if the whole ball had been scooped out, leaving two empty craters.

I felt sick and ran away, the image was too much. I'm ashamed to say, I left Carolyn there. Shielding my eyes so I couldn't see his face, I tried to drag her away from the beggar.

I could see her calling out 'Alan!' Alan!' I was dreading that she would turn around to the beggar and say, 'Have you seen my friend Alan?' and he would reply in Kuala Lumpur-ese, 'Are you taking the piss?'

We drifted up through to the Thai islands of Koh Phangan and Koh Samui. The Leonardo DiCaprio film, *The Beach*, had just come out in the cinemas. We'd seen it, and it had fired up our imagination, and we couldn't wait to experience it for ourselves. I loved the laid-back atmosphere on those beaches and have very fond memories of swinging in a hammock. I just hope the locals haven't built up the area too much and replaced that wonderful serene ambiance with the stiffness of an all-inclusive resort.

I could kick myself now but then, strange as it sounds, I realised you can get beached out. Honest to God, I can hear myself now complaining that I was getting sick of the beaches. Stupid, I know, but the continual landscape of white sand and turquoise seas can get – dare I say it? – monotonous. Months later, when I had my headset on and was tapping away at my data entry, these thoughts would come back to haunt me. What I wouldn't give for a sip of a mojito in the afternoon sun!

So I gradually made my way up through Thailand to my final destination, Bangkok. It was sweet with its floating markets and yes, more temples. I bought the obligatory knock-offs, the Diesel T-shirts and designer bags and wallets. I thought they were fantastic bargains, only to wear them and watch them fall apart piece by piece. The bag was the worst; first the buckle came off, then the lining came away, until I was left just walking around with a leather strap over my shoulder.

Of course, I had to visit Patpong. This is the infamous district of Bangkok where a huddle of grubby bars put on the kind of entertainment you wouldn't see at the Palladium. Basically, you can see women firing ping-pong balls without using their hands, if you see what I mean. We went along to the seedy bars and watched agog. I know it's awful exploitation, but they did put on a good show. One woman had the hardest-working fanny in show business. She fired darts that popped balloons above my head, she blew candles out, smoked a cigarette and, her *pièce de résistance*, she played 'Frère Jacques' with a mouth organ. Believe me, Bangkok really has got talent. I couldn't think of a better way to see off Bangkok, and the next day with these dirty images fresh in my head we decided to return to England.

Believe it or not, I couldn't wait to get home. The little plane that was on the screen hovering across the Urals could not hover quickly enough. I started imagining the joy at seeing my parents, finally earning good money, and the chance at last to get some kind of a career up and running. I could see England getting tantalisingly close, and to welcome us back the sun was beaming its little heart out. Then the plane dipped below the clouds and the sun's rays evaporated, quickly replaced by thick slate-grey rain-clouds and the concrete vista that is Heathrow Airport. The terminals were grinning up at me like a row of rotten teeth. While I'd been away, someone had bled all the colour out of England. Even the green of the fields seemed strangely muted. It was like the rest of the world had kept all the colours for themselves. More to the point, nothing had changed. The only thing that had changed was Vanessa Feltz. When I left the previous June, she was fat, and now she was slim! Is that all that had happened?

I got back to the house. It was strange not having Minstral run excitedly to the door and greet me. Minstral sadly hadn't lived long enough to see my return. Before I left I had asked Mum specifically not to tell me if anything happened to the pets while I was away. She had agreed.

'What could you do on the other side of the world?' she had said. 'It would only spoil your holiday, wouldn't it?'

So in Thailand, seeing an empty telephone booth, I'd rung her up, groggy with sun and beer.

'Hello Mum. How are you?'

'MINSTRAL'S DEAD! HE'S DEAD! MINSTRAL'S DEAD!' wailed my mother like a banshee. 'GONE FOREVER!'

I'm not sure which part of 'it would spoil my holiday' she had failed to understand, but how could I be angry with a woman beside herself with canine grief? I started crying too, which wasn't ideal as there was a string of hippy backpackers tapping their feet behind me and impatiently looking at their watches. This wasn't the time or the place to have a break-down. I put the phone down, walked across onto the beach and cried all the way back to my cabana.

Anyway, once the various anecdotes had done the rounds and I'd shown off my tan, the real misery of my situation began to emerge. Just like before, I was still skint and living in Northampton. But this time I had the glorious sunny memories of the past year poking and prodding me, taunting my unfortunate situation. Please God, I couldn't go back to work at Moulton Park Industrial Estate, could I? Not after my amazing adventure. Then someone threw me a lifeline.

I got a phone call from Sarah and Cherry. They were back in England and were renting a house in Manchester. They had a spare room – would I like to take it?

Well, what do you think I said?

Chapter Eight

CHANGING ENDS

SEA SIDE TOWN

wish you were here ...

Manchester, oh Manchester! I didn't realise this wonderful vibrant place, my home for the next seven years, would turn out to be so pivotal in my comedy career. Obviously, comedy was the last thing on my mind when I stepped off the National Express coach near Piccadilly Gardens. It was raining when I got off, and if my memory serves me well it never stopped raining for the next seven years. Anyway, to me, Manchester was just another destination on my round-the-world trip. Yes, there were no Buddhist temples or tropical beaches, but then again it wasn't Moulton Park Industrial Estate. After a big group hug, Sarah and Cherry showed me my room at Rusholme Place in Rusholme, South Manchester, and I instantly felt at home. Typical, isn't it? I go around the world trying to find myself, exploring my own personality, looking for the real me, and where do I go and 'find me'? On the Curry Mile.

It was great living there. The Sangam Indian Restaurant was at the end of the road, and every Friday night would be curry night. Town was in walking distance, and if you were really bored, visit the Whitworth Art Gallery across the road, which in my opinion had the sorriest collection of art you've ever seen. It looks like the kind of stuff you'd get on Tony Hart's gallery.

Life was great. The jobs were just as shit as in Northampton, but at least here I had the social life to counterbalance the tedium. Every weekend we would grab the Manchester clubbing scene by the scruff of the neck and not let go till Monday morning.

Word must have got round about how great Manchester's nightlife was because every weekend our friends, some good, some bad, some wanted, some unwanted, would descend upon our spare room. It seems in the first six months we must have taken in every waif and stray. Each Sunday morning there always seemed to be someone new to bring a cup of tea and marmite on toast in for. Our house became a halfway house, friends in between jobs, girls who had fallen out with their boyfriends, boyfriends who had fallen out with their boyfriends. We even ended up looking after a friend Ian while he convalesced. After having an operation on his spleen he decided in his wisdom to have some fun and went on a Waltzer in Preston City Centre; after about five spins, the squeals became screams as his stitches popped out one by one, so for a week he took our spare bed – all part of the service.

One bonus was that Manchester had a Gay Pride weekend which as you can imagine was a revelation to me. Northampton had never had a Gay Pride; obviously, what they did have didn't fill anyone with pride. It wasn't floats and parades, it was a stall in Abington Park and two lesbians pushing a wheelbarrow down the high street. It was a start, I suppose, but Manchester delivered, a whole weekend dedicated to hedonism and being gay. I'd missed Mardi Gras by a week when I lived in Sydney but up here in the North West I was going to grab it and not let go.

Changing ends

One night I went to during Pride was 'Treat in the Street', which was an extra special club night mainly because the council had opened up Granada Studios and the set of *Coronation Street* was dressed for a rave-up. It was meant to be a mixed night, but can you see any self-respecting homosexual missing the chance of dancing on those hallowed cobbles? The sight was hilarious but very surreal, especially towards the end of the evening when it descended into human carnage. People vomiting outside Steve McDonald's, men snogging up against Audrey's salon windows and a paralytic girl getting fingered outside Roy's Rolls – it was all part of the rich tapestry that was 'Treat in the Street'.

I ended up chatting with a pre-op transsexual called Annette in the Rovers' Return. 'Tits and a dick, that's me,' she growled. It wasn't just once that I checked my drink hadn't been spiked. They never did Treat in the Street again, and frankly I'm not surprised.

* * *

After the madness of these nights, I had the grimness of my job to drag me back down to earth with a bump. Even the Manchester job market didn't have much time for an out-of-work Drama and Theatre Studies postgraduate. The crappy temp jobs rolled on and on, one day cold-calling some poor sod who'd just got in from work, the next day churning out cheque amounts for HSBC. One place I was at for quite a while was the telecommunications company Cable & Wireless – or 'Unable and Clueless' as the staff so wittily dubbed it.

Cable & Wireless, in all their wisdom, decided to build their headquarters in the middle of Europe's biggest council estate, Wythenshawe. So every morning we would get on the 43a bus from Rusholme and journey into deepest darkest Wythenshawe. I don't know why I bothered washing my clothes because by the time we'd taken the 45-minute bus journey and arrived at the Cable & Wireless foyer I was so badly stinking of skunk, I was high as a kite and smelt like a Rastafarian's ashtray.

Because I had a degree, I was immediately upgraded from answering the phones to sorting out meeting rooms and booking all the executives' travel arrangements. Not only was I organising trains and cars, on some big jobs I was even booking flights, yes, flights. Finally, I was getting a job with responsibility. Then I got some even better news. Will, my superior, asked if I would like to be promoted to Facilities Manager. If I said yes, he could start me off on £13,000 a year. 'Oh my God,' I thought, 'that's nearly a grand a month after tax!'

Things at last were looking up, and I accepted the job and the rise that came with it. I was on top of the world and told Mum that I was a manager and that I would be supervising all the Cable & Wireless facilities. Mum excitedly told Dad, and word got round that Alan wasn't a loser and that in fact he was holding down a managerial position. The shine came off my job somewhat when one of the top executives came in and complained about the state of the urinals in the downstairs bathrooms. I carried on sorting out the facilities paperwork, not envying the person who would have to deal with that little mess.

Changing ends

'Who here is the Facilities Manager?' I jolted upright. Then the penny dropped. I had been a victim of the poxy rebranding that's endemic these days in the office workplace. The 'facilities' were the 'toilets' and the 'manager' was the 'attendant'. I was a toilet attendant. I wasn't even one of those in Northampton. I looked at Will, who looked back sheepishly. When we had discussed 'Facilities', he had mentioned overhead projectors, board rubbers, the occasional making of tea, not popping on a janitor's coat and swilling out a trough. I had been duped good and proper.

My job didn't get any better because we had what can only be described as a 'phantom shitter'. Someone at Cable & Wireless was going around shitting in the corridors. I do not know to this day whether they just squatted there and did it, or they brought them in prepared and using a set of tongs plopped them in the corridor and fled the scene of the shite. They could have easily smuggled it in on the 34a bus, because I'm sure the stench of the marijuana would have masked any faeces that they were carrying. The phantom shitter was becoming a pain. I would be up to my neck in hiring out some office equipment to another site, only to hear, 'There's a turd on level 3. We need the Facilities Manager now.'

* * *

I never found out who the phantom shitter was, but I want to thank them because they helped me to make my mind up that I was better than this. Checking toilets, picking up excrement, surviving the bus journey through Wythenshawe, I'd had enough, and all the time I could still hear the waves of Bondi Beach lapping against my subconscious. I could still be there. This wasn't living.

I went to see Vanessa, my recruitment agent, and she said that there were job vacancies going at Barclaycard in the centre of Manchester for £13,000 p.a. Yet again, I was mesmerised by the amount. I'd never earned so much in my life. Plus, Vanessa had said the longer I stayed there, the more the wages would increase. In seven years' time I could be up to twenty grand a year – it didn't bear thinking about. I was tempted, so much so that I accepted.

Call centres are dreary places. If you think it's frustrating hanging on the line waiting to speak to a human being, you try working there. At least when I worked in a factory I could take my broom and lose myself among the shelving. But sitting there with my Janet Jackson headset, being monitored every second, being abused by rude people and not being able to move made me feel like a galley slave rowing towards the island Barclaycard called 'Profit Margin'. I remember turning up to work and being told that Barclaycard had made an amazing £6 billion profit or whatever it was. The big cheese had sent us a letter saying 'Well done' and, because of our hard work, we were going to get – a muffin! Yep, you heard, a muffin. Either a blackberry one or a chocolate chip one – not both, said Mary, who pushed the trolley around. What had the executives done with the rest of the £5,999,999,999 profit, because this stale old muffin wasn't really what I'd expected?

The one thing I learnt from working in the call centre is that people are rude and people are stupid – and sometimes they're both. If they are, they're given a credit card and told to ring us up. Surprisingly, though, it was always the vicars or the reverends who were the rudest. It became a bit of a joke; whenever Rev or Vic popped up on the screen, you knew you were going to get some nasty man of the cloth being vile and abusive. No wonder congregations are at an all-time low, I remember thinking. Some of the queries bordered on the ridiculous. One customer had bought a DVD with his Barclaycard at a souk in Tunisia and – surprise, surprise – when he got it home it didn't work. Well I never, sir. Who'd have thought it? I had to restrain myself from saying, 'I've got some magic beans. Would you like to buy some?'

The £13,000 a year wage that had so whetted my appetite was beginning to make me feel short-changed. Any spare money I had was spent on booze because it was the only thing that made the pain go away. It wasn't just me. Morale had hit rock-bottom. As you can imagine, call centres in general were getting a bad press. It was rumoured that Barclaycard was going to move all its call centres to Bangalore and that we would all be facing redundancies. Everyone in the office seemed upset, but I couldn't wait. Barclaycard tried its best to boost morale. We would have a dress-down Friday, competitions, nights out. Barclaycard would do anything to lift our spirits – nothing, it seems, was out of bounds, however surreal it felt at the time.

We were all sitting there, wishing we were dead – as you do – when on the board which tells you how many customers are in the queue in bright red letters appeared the words 'Mexican Wave – NOW!' So all through the office we did a

Mexican wave, still with our headsets on, still talking to an abusive customer oblivious to the fact that we'd all stood up and were waving our arms like a wind turbine. This, apparently, was to inject a little bit of *joie de vivre* into proceedings.

It didn't work.

Every couple of months we would all be taken into an anteroom to discuss our progress with one of the managers. These discussions would be full of banal office-speak – think 'outside the box', try to 'touch base' with your supervisor as often as you can.

'Do you know what's wrong with some members of this team, Alan?'

'No, I don't.'

'There are too many people listening to W.I.I. FM.'

'Eh?'

'What's In It For Me?'

What a load of S.H.I.T.! I thought.

As always when you're in a rubbish job, you tend to make friends more easily, especially at lunchtimes or breaktimes when you just need a smile or a conversation that isn't debt-related. David, who sat opposite me, became a good friend, and as our friendship evolved he became not only a good friend, but also my favourite drinking partner. We'd often end up going out Friday night and then turn up for our Saturday shift shattered after having an hour's sleep and nursing the worst kind of hangover. But it would be all right because Saturday was when we were allocated 'Lost and Stolen', which usually meant that the people ringing up were more hung over then we were. People who had lost their wallets, purses, clutchbags and tights the previous night would ring up moodily hung over, but still as stupid as ever.

'Can you remember when you last used your card?'

'No.'

'Can you remember what city you were in?'

'No.'

'Can you remember your own name …?'

'Lost and Stolen' was great because the boot was on the other foot. We could take revenge on all those customers who had been rude and stupid over the previous week. We would talk quite stuffily and ensure that our voices were tinged with the right amount of condescension as they sheepishly revealed their drunken antics. Tutting and rolling our eyes as we took the moral high ground, little did they know I was dashing to the toilet every ten minutes myself to throw up.

But even going to the toilet was becoming a cause of concern for the eagle-eyed, penny-pinching Barclaycard bosses. They introduced a time-saving initiative where you had to put down how long you were in the toilet and write down what you did in there, ironically, in a log book. We were told it was three minutes for a wee and five minutes for the other. They were right to scrutinise our toilet breaks because after a couple of horrible ranting customers, sometimes you did need to just get off the phones, and the toilet was the only place, sadly, to go for a breather.

To be fair, Barclaycard did give their workforce some rights to protect us from the often mentally ill customers. If two swearwords were said to you during the conversation, you had every right to hang up. Knowing this, I used to egg them on.

'Can you speak up, fatty?'

'Can't read your statement, twatface?'

'Tell me to F off … please!'

We came drastically close to getting a huge compensation payout when there were stories in the press that wearing a headset for eight hours a day could cause cancer, but thankfully, after a scientific investigation, this proved to be unfounded. However, it didn't stop the office hypochondriac, Paul, from accusing Barclaycard of giving him a brain tumour. Obviously, this was a serious matter that affected us all, or it would have been, if it hadn't come from a complete fruitloop such as Paul. He'd already had a fortnight off for an ingrown toenail, when he would hobble into the call centre on crotches grudgingly, only to discard them at 5 p.m. and mince unaided down Canal Street for a night of dancing. The illnesses continued. Then he started having weeks off for his deceased grandparents, other people's grandparents, my grandparents, the supervisor's grandparents who hadn't even died yet. This went on until Paul's work effort had been reduced to making cameo appearances in the morning before contracting TB or a tapeworm during his lunch break and disappearing for the afternoon.

Hypochondria, ironically, is an illness, and Paul had it badly. Guess whom he latched on to? Yes, me. Every phone call would begin with a groan, or an 'Ooooh!', and for the next year I was burdened with all his illnesses. Before long, I wasn't a friend, but a human landfill site for his miseries and woes, as a result ruining a wonderful friendship. We all have friends like that, dung beetles. Creatures that make it their jobs to wade through shit. I, of course, will be there for anyone if they're depressed or ill, but some people really exploit this kindness. I find it all a bit wearing myself. Look, look at me suffering, I've got it so bad, oh will I ever make it to the dawn? I hope not.

I confronted him once about this, and he replied sharply, 'Friends are there for the good times and the bad times.'

'Paul,' I said, 'there haven't been any good times.'

Don't you think I'm lonely? Don't you think I'm unhappy? Don't you think I'm making the best of a bad situation? I don't go around knocking on people's doors going, 'Boo hoo, I'm single, I'm ugly, I hate myself.' No, I do a tour and charge people to hear me moan.

The last time I heard from Paul was when he phoned me to tell me that he'd just walked in and found his flatmate dead. Charming. This news put me right off my meal-for-one. Why would you ring anyone up out of the blue and tell them that? This was all too much, and I changed my number.

My situation probably would have been a bit more bearable if I hadn't been struck down by psoriasis. The ongoing brawl that I'd had with my body had entered the next round, it seemed. Funny, isn't it? How people's bodies cope differently when they're run down. Mine has always excelled itself with its perverse logic. You can't get a decent job, you can't get a man, you live in a dump, so what does my body say? You know what, Alan? I'll give you skin like flaky pastry – my treat. If you ever needed proof that your skin gives out telltale signs of how you're feeling inside, then look no further than me in that call centre, a scabby battery hen. I suffered with plaque psoriasis, a skin condition that covers you in scaly red blobs, which on my flabby body looked like I'd been self-harming with a bingo dobber.

Plaque psoriasis rarely attacks the person's face – guess where I got mine? Yes, on my face, and on my body, on my legs, on my arms, believe me, everywhere. It was awful. I stopped going out at night drinking, which as you can probably tell was my one way of letting off steam from such a drab job. I would go out, positive that everyone was retching at my skin. I'm sure they weren't, but my self-consciousness overpowered me, and I just stayed at home and watched telly.

As with all my humour, the negative experiences of my life after some contemplation and positive retrospection are absorbed into my act and (hopefully) become a funny routine. Identity fraud, rat infestations, being mugged, all real events that have started out as very grim scenarios, but have ultimately saved me from inflicting huge psychological damage on myself as a good punchline. That is definitely true of my times with psoriasis; it eventually became a stalwart of my act, always getting a big laugh and sometimes a round of applause. It made me feel like at least I was coping with it, if not getting my revenge on this horrible, disfiguring skin disorder.

That's why I found it particularly depressing receiving countless venomous and vile letters from psoriasis sufferers after I joked about it on the Royal Variety Performance. Apparently, I shouldn't joke about it, it's a serious condition. I know, twats, I have it! I've performed my stand-up shows in front of hundreds of people, covered head to toe in scabs; I can't think of anything more empowering to a psoriasis sufferer, can you? Maybe I should just do what they do and lock myself away in a darkened room with a vat of calamine lotion and become a human scratchcard. For God's sake, psoriasis sufferers, chill out – stop being so flaky. Yes, I know what I said.

* * *

I'd spent a whole year with Cherry and Sarah at that terraced house in Rusholme Place and our lease had come to the end. We all decided that it was time to move on. Sarah and Cherry wanted to start a family and settle down as a couple. Also, we were being terrorised by slugs. I don't know what attracted them, but slugs were everywhere. You'd open the cutlery drawer and see a slug trail snaking its way across the knives and forks. Some would actually go slithering up the wall. They would be on the bed, they would go in our shoes, and the little buggers were quick – at mealtimes you would have to keep taking a second glance at your food to check that one wasn't doing the backstroke across your chilli con carne.

Another factor for leaving my first Manc home was the amount of rat shit we found behind the chest of drawers when we moved it. It seems it's not just millions of hungry humans that flock to the Curry Mile every year. Evidently, the overflowing bins and curry scraps that littered the cobbled streets around our house were like an 'All You Can Eat' buffet to a self-respecting rat, and judging by the droppings, they'd come back for seconds.

Look who it is!

Looking for a house is for me one of the most exasperating ways you can possibly spend a day: the travelling around, the disappointment, and – most exasperating of all – the lies! It doesn't take you too long to decipher what the descriptions actually mean and that 'up and coming' means 'dump', 'intimate' means 'tiny' and 'Chorlton Borders' means 'Moss Side'. If you ever see an intimate, up-and-coming, bedsit in Chorlton Borders, do yourself a favour and cross it off the list. After several infuriating bus trips, and countless disappointments, I went to visit a place, a beautiful road off Chorlton Green, and for once it actually matched the description. A grand Victorian house with wonderfully big airy rooms, all high ceilings and large windows and with what I thought was the best feature of all, an eccentric landlady, Ruth.

We instantly clicked. She had been a glamour model in the Seventies and had won numerous awards, including 'Penthouse Playmate of the Year' and 'Oldham Carnival Queen'. That accolade had been won at the age of 30. The age limit for the award was 21, and Oldham Council had found out her real age and demanded the crown back. It was just another fabulous anecdote in the world of Ruth. She was still an attractive woman, with her dark eyes, curvaceous figure and impressive *décolletage*, and it didn't take much imagination to see how stunning she must have been in the Seventies. I'm assuming it was the Seventies because her age and any reference to precise dates were either never mentioned or destroyed.

Ruth was a lady, and you never ask a lady her age. She was a camp icon in the making, and that was sealed the day I saw her stumble through the door after visiting the cash and carry, holding countless bags of bleach and toilet rolls and recollecting dreamily in the doorway, 'I remember when this would be caviar and champagne.'

I knew we were going to get on so well, and that is what we did. Most nights, you would find us with a bottle of wine, putting the world to rights. Sometimes we'd be joined by her friend Cynthia, an ex-bodybuilder in a mac with Mr Whippy hair. We would always get through a few bottles. The trouble is I would go to bed and Ruth would stay up. Still a bit merry on the old wine, she would start ordering things on QVC, and a few days later jewellery, lamps, shawls, facial saunas and gym equipment would all turn up. One day I remember signing for not one, but two massage chairs, which, along with the other stuff, went in the downstairs reception unpacked. It was a real Aladdin's cave in there, what with all the QVC purchases still in their boxes. It's what I imagined the upstairs at Argos would look like.

The house, like its owner, had an air of faded grandeur, and subsequently was always in the process of being 'done up'. The new housecat Mortimer didn't help. Ruth and I had rescued him from a cat shelter in Stockport. He was a lovely soppy thing, terrified of his own shadow, but would look up at you with such a dumb expression you couldn't help but fall for his charms. Why would anyone want to put him in a cat shelter? Because he shat and pissed everywhere, we soon found out. He was obviously urinating in the dining room because it reeked of ammonia, and you couldn't stay there for longer than a couple of minutes before the stench would start burning your vocal cords and making your eyes water.

He'd also done a couple of shits in my room. Obviously embarrassed, he'd tried to cover up his poo with my jumper. Any complaints to Ruth would be met by the usual 'Ah! He probably got disorientated,' and you would have to return to your room with a dustpan and brush and retch while you scooped it up and popped it in a carrier. It was impossible to be angry with him – he would stare up with his matted black and white face, eyes slightly crossed, and he was instantly forgiven. We strategically placed cat litter trays around the house to help him with his toilet training, and for a while it seemed to be working.

Ruth had found another tenant from a card in the local newsagent. Her name was Helen Highwater – something told me that that wasn't her real name. Helen was a hippy who played in a folk band and had turned her hand to interior decorating. I use the term 'turning her hand' because, looking at the wonkiness of the wallpaper and time she took to paste it up, you would think she'd only just started that morning.

As I worked on Saturdays, Wednesday was my day off from Barclaycard, and I would usually spend the day washing my clothes or lying on my bed reading. This much-needed 'me time' would often be interrupted by Helen's singing. Her voice was haunting, but not in a good way. The first time she 'sang', I started looking for Mortimer to see if he was in pain. Because she was wallpapering the hall, the higher she went up the stepladder, the closer the voice got. It seeped into my room like carbon monoxide from a dodgy boiler, and, ironically, she was a dodgy boiler.

* * *

Changing ends

Sarah and Cherry's decision to get themselves a new place and start a family prompted me to focus on my own life. Like the time I had worked as a degreaser on the outskirts of Northampton, something had come to shake me up and tell me to take control of my life. I was 24 and working in a call centre. Same old story – shit job, shit money blah blah blah. I was determined to make a break for it. Something really had to give. Surely one day I would be able to experience a job I enjoyed. One of the cruellest things about working in the call centre was the amount of time you had to think. Sometimes you could sit there for seven hours just thinking, re-evaluating all the life choices you'd made that had led you here to this one place in time. With customers reading out their Tesco Clubcard number instead of their actual credit card, it could seem a lot longer than seven hours.

What was I going to do? I can't actually pinpoint the time I chose to become a stand-up comedian. I sort of just fell into it, which is no help to anyone reading this for guidance on how to become a comedian. I think it was just a series of signs, of flashing green lights that frustratingly pointed to a career that after the nerves of the King's Head I'd vowed I'd never pursue. The germ of the idea had been floating around for years. I would always tell stories around the table to my friends, sometimes true, sometimes embellished, and that would always get them all laughing. Barclaycard customers would laugh at my voice and ask if it was a hoax. At first this was hurtful, but then it made me think, 'Why not use my voice for good instead of evil?' Then I would start to remember how well my routine at the King's Head had gone and what the gypsy fortune-teller had said. These instincts were all saying, 'Go on, do stand-up comedy. It makes sense.'

So I looked through the local listings magazine and found an 'Open Spot' night at the Briton's Protection. I rang them up, and they told me to come down on the Wednesday night. Although it was a week away, I instantly felt sick and couldn't eat for the whole day. I wanted to pull out on the day, but Sarah and Cherry said they'd accompany me and give me some moral support, so I went along regardless. I didn't have jokes as such back then. They were just stories about the call centre and my travels around Mexico and Thailand that had made people laugh around the dining table and that I hoped would have the same effect on the people in the room.

The Briton's Protection's Open Spot night was in a dingy room above the pub of the same name. I arrived all nervous, eyes bulging and green with nausea. I looked like ET, and I sat meekly at the back of the room after giving my name to the compere. I soon realised that none of the people in the audience was a member of the public, they were all Open Spots themselves. I foolishly thought that this would create an atmosphere of back-slapping, friendly camaraderie where anything goes.

I couldn't have been more wrong. As I finally made my way to the stage and sheepishly performed my routine, the other open spots just stared icily at me, cold as stone, unimpressed. I came off stage after what seemed like ages, dumbstruck, still no clearer about whether what I had said was funny or had even made sense. It had been a brutal introduction to the world of Open Spots. It was bitter, dog eat dog, a battle for survival, and unsurprisingly seven years on some of the people in that room are still jobbing Open Spots. How depressing is that?

My next one was at the Queen of Hearts pub in Fallow-field, the student heart of Manchester, and that gig couldn't have been more different. For a start, there were proper people who wanted to laugh rather than to sneer, and it was hosted by Toby Hadoke, a lovely man who was and is so supportive of comedy and, thankfully, of me. The gig was a success, and it filled me with enough confidence to carry on, to think that in fact I might have something here. If I'd had another gig like the one at the Briton's Protection, I would have given up. No, in fact, I would have topped myself.

I must have been buoyed up by that response, though, because I entered the *Citylife* Comedian of the Year Award. It was a brave move, as it was to be my third gig. *Citylife* was a magazine that annually held a competition to find the best new Manchester comedian. Even though the magazine was only available in the North West, its Comedian of the Year had a serious pedigree. Caroline Aherne, Jason Manford and Dave Spikey had all entered and subsequently won, while Johnny Vegas had entered and been beaten to second place by a young comedian called Peter Kay. To an up-and-coming comedian this award was important and in the North West hugely influential.

I performed my *Citylife* heat at the Buzz in Chorlton, which itself was a Manchester institution. Anyone who was anyone in comedy had appeared on that stage – Eddie Izzard, Lee Evans, Jack Dee, Steve Coogan, the list was endless. So the pressure of appearing on the very same stage as those greats was immense. I remember that night clearly. It was around the time that the petrol prices had gone through the roof. The lorry drivers had all created a blockade around the petrol pumps, and we couldn't get a taxi.

I arrived late, apologised to the compere, 'Agraman', the human anagram (don't ask), and sat down waiting to go onstage. The worry of finding a taxi had focused my nerves elsewhere, and I was relatively calm as I went on stage and did my routine. Well, you wouldn't believe the reaction. People were in hysterics, a woman at the front of the stage was rocking and crying with laughter. It was the same reaction I had had when I was performing at Middlesex University, but this time I was actually enjoying it, pausing for the laughter, soaking up the atmosphere, letting the timing do its thing.

I won the round. Not only that, but Agraman decided to book me for the plethora of gigs that he had in the North West. I've still got those diaries, and it makes me smile to see '£15, Preston' or '£10, Bury Arts Centre'. With the train fares, these gigs meant that I was out of pocket before I'd even left the house, but I was just proud to be getting money for something that I enjoyed for the first time in my life. Agraman was instrumental in getting my career up and running. Without his faith in me, I would never have improved as quickly as I did. In London, comedians have to wait up to a year to get an Open Spot, which must be terribly frustrating. To hone a comedy routine, you really need to take a run-up and have at least two or three consecutive nights to see an improvement.

Changing ends

I was lucky that Manchester was on the cusp of something big when I was there. There were no Printworks, Selfridges or Harvey Nicks yet – they would be coming in the following years – but brand-new shops, bars and restaurants were popping up all over town. Along with them were brand new comedy clubs including the Comedy Store, which were crying out for new talent to fill their comedy nights. For the first time, I felt like I was part of something new and exciting. A few years back it had been cool to say you were a DJ; now you were cool if you were a comedian. I'd never made a right decision before. I was well pleased.

The final of the *Citylife* competition for the best new Mancunian stand-up comedian came round more quickly than I would have liked. I was so nervous, as you can imagine, the butterflies in my stomach had wings the size of a pterodactyl. To prolong the agony, the final was being held at the brand new Comedy Store on Deangate Locks in Manchester. This was too much. At Barclaycard, all day my heart wasn't in it, the customers just seemed more irritating than usual, and my concentration level was wedged at zero. The competition hung like a fog at the forefront of my mind.

I turned up at the Comedy Store for a soundcheck and walked onto the stage. It was so daunting, it was brand new, and unlike the one in London it was set out like an amphitheatre. At least with this Comedy Store I didn't have the added pressure of a star-studded heritage to make me shake even more. I tried to relax and for the 5,000th time I went through my routine. It only had to be seven to eight minutes long, so I picked my best seven minutes and started mouthing the jokes up and down the corridor, gesticulating and pulling faces in all the right places. I could hear the audience coming in, finding their seats. One by one, like lambs to the slaughter, we went on stage. Finally, it was my turn.

Terrified, I went on stage, and the first few minutes were great. They were laughing, and I felt for once that I might actually have a chance of winning it. I completed all my jokes and embellished stories of working in the call centre and then … I forgot, I totally forgot what came next. I froze, I went dry, as we stand-ups call it. Of course, now when I 'go dry' I step over to my table, have a few sips of water and rethink, and the audience just thinks I'm thirsty. But then when I hadn't even done more than ten gigs, I panicked, my head cleared and my lips dried up. I couldn't remember any of my jokes, I couldn't even remember a why did the chicken cross the road joke. Even my dad's jokes which would inevitably involve two nuns in a bath remained elusive. It was awful. I mumbled something and then had to leave the stage.

What a disaster! Justin Moorhouse quite rightfully won that night. I was distraught. Damn my bloody nerves, my body yet again sticking its oar in when I least wanted it to. It took me a while to get over it, but it did me the world of good. It was a sign that Rome wasn't built in a day and that there was still a long way to go for me as a comedian.

I am often asked what my parents said when I told them that I wanted to be a stand-up comedian, and the truth is I never told them. If I'd told them, they would only have just rolled their eyes and muttered, 'What's he up to now?' Don't get me wrong, they were wonderfully supportive of me. It's just

I was always the kid who ran through the door, fired up by my imagination – 'Mum, I want to be a detective!' 'Dad, I want to be an archaeologist!' I would watch one documentary and that would be it. It would have a direct effect on me, and I would channel all my energy into getting into that profession, writing letters, asking for information packs. It must have been wearing for my parents. If I had told them, 'I'm going to be a stand-up,' they would have politely said 'Yes, Alan' and added it to the ever-growing mental list of 'Alan's potential jobs', filed behind store detective for good measure.

Anyway, the *Citylife* final had been so dispiriting for me that I didn't even class myself as funny, let alone as a stand-up comedian. Nevertheless, I persevered, and in the ensuing months I raised my game. I had to, call centres couldn't be my *raison d'être*. In fact I was living a double life. I would finish my shift at Barclaycard and then run to Piccadilly train station and head off to some destination to do my thing. Sheffield, Burnley, Bury, Preston, New Mills, Buxton, you name it, I've graced the stage for a tenner. If I was lucky, I could get a lift back with another act and would not have to wait on my own at a train station till the early hours.

I find it a bit naive of people when they come up to me today and say, 'Don't ever forget, we made you.' I don't actually remember seeing them standing with me at Sheffield station in the rain at quarter past midnight waiting for the train, or sitting with me on the National Express coach to London because I couldn't afford the train. Believe me, on those rainy bus journeys home to Manchester, clutching a fiver in my hand, I paid my dues. It's like Linford Christie training for years for the Olympics and just as he crosses the winning line a spectator joins him and shouts, 'We did it!' I really am flattered that people think I make success look easy, but it really wasn't.

Travelling to gigs in a car full of comedians sounds like it should be hours of fun, but that wasn't always the case. Sometimes I didn't know what was worse – getting the sleeper train that stopped at every little village or accepting a lift from the other comedians on the bill. The younger ones were great company, the brilliant Jason John Whitehead, Jim Jeffries, Steve Hughes. However, the older ones, already made bitter by years and years of comedy, would find it hard to suppress their resentment. You would always get the feeling they weren't 100 per cent behind you when you left the dressing room and went onto the stage. Sadly, that resentment would spill over into the car journey, especially if you had had a better gig than them. Sometimes you'd get the older ones who'd be going through a divorce and you would have to sit there listening to a sob story from Manchester to Carlisle and back again: 'Why would she leave me, Alan?' I don't know, Jeff, but we've just missed the turning for the A43. Flashbacks to my days as a driver's mate came back to haunt me, but at least I was getting paid to listen to that drivel.

* * *

My set was developing well. I had crept past the five-minute and ten-minute mark and nearly had fifteen minutes of comedy material. With the help of such comedy promoters as

Agraman, Silky, Toby Hadoke and Toby Foster, I was getting lots of practice. The Open Spot circuit, though, is depressing. Not only are you not getting paid, you often have to sit through a lot of rubbish, terminally unfunny people with hack jokes, stolen jokes or at worst hack, stolen jokes. Then again, some nights would sparkle with talent, and you would be on the same bill as people who are now formidable headliners or fronting their own TV shows. You have to remember that everyone has to start somewhere, and like every other job it's at the bottom.

One Open Spot night in London is particularly memorable, not because of the abundance of talent, but because a comic dressed as Hitler came on stage with a carrier bag, some crappy Nazi jokes, said that he had Princess Diana's head in a bag, and then jumped out of the window. Just another night on the Open Spot circuit. Sometimes it's the audience that's weird. I had a blow-up doll thrown on stage in Maidstone. I told my agent who said: 'Was it with a hen party?' Well, I don't think it came by itself.

Seeing how despondent I'd got over my Alzheimer's during the *Citylife* final, Sarah had – without my knowledge – entered me for the BBC Comedian of the Year. At first, I was put out by it. After the last experience I didn't want to do any more competitions, but then I talked myself around. Winning a stand-up competition is one way of leap-frogging over your fellow comedians and standing out from the crowd. It was the equivalent of being in a bus lane, whizzing down the inside, giving the V's to the lorry drivers stuck in the traffic jam. My stand-up was progressing nicely, the times when I was dying on my arse were gradually decreasing, and I was getting more and more confident. I could actually eat stuff now on the day of a gig. Plus, I'd got myself an agent.

I had been doing my usual twenty minutes back at the Buzz Comedy Club, probably for about a pound. Regrettably, I still wasn't earning enough to leave Barclaycard, but I was getting there. I'd finished onstage and went and sat down to watch the other comedians. I was approached by this tall, slim, attractive, blonde woman.

'Oh no!' I thought. 'My first groupie.'

As it happened, I couldn't have been more wrong. She was an agent.

'Hello, I'm Mary Richmond, and I'm interested in representing you.' I couldn't believe it. I tried to play it cool.

'Who else do you represent?'

'Johnny Vegas, among others.'

'*The* Johnny Vegas?'

'Yes!'

I was incredulous. I took her card and said nonchalantly, 'I'll think about it,' and then skipped all the way back to Ruth's.

Of course I accepted the offer of representation. Mary Richmond, I found out, ran Big Eye Management with her husband Steve Lock, who was just as lovely as her. Their office was in the Northern Quarter, and I would go there to write. The difference in getting comedy gigs yourself and having someone to do it for you is immense; it automatically gives you a more professional air. It means business, even if you are in an office above a kebab shop. They rang around all the clubs, bigged you up, raved about you, filled your diary, all for 10 per cent of your fee. It was money well spent, plus I got to support Johnny Vegas at the legendary/notorious (delete accordingly) Frog and Bucket Comedy Club.

Naively, I thought his ranting, drunk persona was a sophisticated character that he slipped into once he got on stage, but no, he really was pissed. He turned up with a pack of four Guinnesses in a Spar bag, and after he downed those he moved onto a bottle of red. Then he went on stage and ripped the roof off. I was in awe, at both his stage presence and his liver. It seems I still had a lot to learn.

As the drudgery of Barclaycard filled my days, comedy filled my nights, and before long I found myself in the semi-final of the BBC Comedian of the Year. It was being held in Nottingham at the Just the Tonic Comedy Club. Unlike the *Citylife* competition, the talent wasn't just Manchester-centric. I was up against the best new comedians in the country, and guess what? Yes, I was really nervous. I wasn't the only one. As always, the time just evaporated before our eyes and before we knew it we comedians could hear from behind the velvet curtain the audience taking their seats, and the first act was cued to go on.

Where you are placed in the running order can have a huge effect on how you are received by the audience. If you go on first, the audience may still be cold and you end up becoming a sacrificial lamb, an appetiser before the main course. I was seventh out of the eight, which meant that although the audience would be warmed up they might also be tired and all funnied out. Everyone had had a good one; the audience seemed nice and friendly. There was no reason why I should worry, but of course I did.

Then in what seemed like a flash it was my time to step out from behind the velvet curtain. Sometimes something happens that you can't explain. I was filled with a confidence that I'd never had before. I was enjoying telling my jokes, I was actually enjoying it. People were roaring, in fact one of the BBC judges fell off his seat with laughter, which I took to be a positive sign. I left the stage with a huge roar of applause. All I needed was for the eighth comedian to be a bit shit, and I was in the final for sure.

He was. Hooray!

The judges put me through to the BBC final, and I was ecstatic. One of my best mates, Karen Bayley, who was also in that semi-final, never fails to remind me that it would have been her in the final if I hadn't had such a good one. Competitions can be infuriating, as I'd learnt at the *Citylife* final. You can have complete stormers every night of the year, but in a competition it's all about how you perform on the night and whether the gods are smiling down. In Nottingham, they definitely were. To add to the excitement, the BBC Comedian of the Year final would be held up in Edinburgh during the famous festival. I'd never been to Edinburgh before and to think that I would be part of that prestigious festival, albeit in a little way, was mind-blowing and spurred me on in my quest to be a full-time professional comedian.

The problem was I couldn't get the time off Barclaycard. I could get the actual day off, but that meant coming back down to Manchester the day after. I didn't want to miss this

'DO YOU WANT TO SEE SOME PUPPIES?'

ME AND MINSTRAL ON THE NORTHERN LINE

ME AND SARAH ON CORONATION STREET

WITH CAROLYN IN KOH PHANGAN

ME, BAIT DIGGING

WITH CATHERINE IN SANTA MONICA

SEXY, YET PRACTICAL

'I'M TAKING OVER THE WORLD'

'OH, NEIL! JUST ASK ME OUT!!!'

UP ARTHUR'S SEAT, EDINBURGH

ME AND PETER KAY

2005

The Royal Variety Performance
Monday 21st November 2005
Wales Millennium Centre

In the presence of HM The Queen
HRH The Duke of Edinburgh

LIZ MEETING A QUEEN

| The Skating Willers |
| Il Divo |
| Alan Carr |
| Will Young |

A TYPICAL DAY DOWN THE HARLEY ARMS WITH LILY, PETE AND AMY

NOT CAMP AT ALL

'YO, BITCHES!'

HAVING A LORRA LORRA
LAUGHS WITH CILLA

THAT'S THE PRICE OF FOAM!

opportunity, so I handed my notice in without a second thought. I was going to quit the call centre the day before the final and become a stand-up comedian full time. This move, although bold, now seemed a bit foolish. I was still an Open Spot, and the most I was earning for a night of comedy was £20. I'd need to work a lot of nights to get near to my £13,000 a year salary. The relief was immense, though, and I felt strangely exhilarated by the fact that I was actually now freefalling through my life without a proper job. All I needed was a can of Tennent's Superstrength and I'd be like one of those people off *Jeremy Kyle*, and I loved it. What was I thinking?

I remember my last-ever phone call at Barclaycard. The matter wasn't even a Barclaycard matter. It was a haughty-sounding woman with a clipped voice and a personality disorder.

'I want to make a complaint. I've gone to use my Barclaycard in a shop, and the woman's just called me a c**t.'

Oh God. What fresh hell is this? I forget the ins and outs of the story, but the shop owner had called her the C-word, and to be honest, the more I heard this women's crazy witterings, the more I sided with the shopkeeper. Obviously, this wasn't a credit card problem, it was a problem between her and the shopkeeper, but she was adamant.

'I want to speak to your supervisor,' she barked.

'I'll just get her for you.'

It was one crazy person too much, and with a quick scan of the clock, I could see it was 4.30pm – home time, so I gently hung my headset up and tiptoed out through the revolving doors to freedom. In my more malicious moments I like to think that the woman is still there on hold, shouting abuse and waiting for my supervisor.

Chapter Nine

MATCH FIT

SEA SIDE TOWN

wish you were here ...

The next day I went up to Edinburgh on the train for the competition final. The BBC were paying for our expenses and giving us a room for a week in the centre of Edinburgh's New Town, and I'd packed for the whole week. I was definitely going to make the most of it.

It's sad really. Because I've been to Edinburgh so many times, I sort of take it for granted now, but when I first stepped off the train at Waverley Station it took my breath away. It was so dramatic, with the Castle high up on the hill, the dark grey cobbled roads snaking wildly around the city and the shadowy passageways and back streets that lead to yet more shadowy passageways and back streets and, if you're lucky, a cosy little public house. The drama and excitement that I felt inside seemed to be mirrored in my surroundings.

At the Festival it is so easy to immerse yourself in the world of comedy. With a pint in your hand, you could watch the best comedians in the world perform for your delectation. It was my first taste of this kind of lifestyle. I'd never gone to a stand-up comedy club in my life before. I wasn't really sure what to expect, but what I saw was a revelation. How had I missed it? The after-hours scene in Edinburgh was like a cabaret performance itself, late-night drinking in smoky rooms with burlesque being performed in the corner, world-famous comedians doing stand-up on a box in the back of a pub at half one in the morning. The night time for me is better than the daytime. I saw the sublime Daniel Kitson host 'Late N Live', a comedy night that starts at midnight and finishes at three (if you're lucky) in the morning. It is a bear pit, with the whole audience intoxicated and baying for the comedians' blood. But Daniel would effortlessly control the audience's heckles and deflect witty putdowns back at them with great aplomb. When you see someone like that at the top of their game, you realise how far you have to grow as a comedian yourself, with the very real chance that at the end, after all your growing, you still might not get to be that good.

The BBC final was being held at the Pleasance Dome, a huge building with – yes, that's right – a very large dome on the top. On seeing the cameras, the all-too-familiar butterflies were let loose in my stomach. Sometimes I think my body must have wondered what had hit it. In those days it was constantly on edge, and a solid poo was something to write home about. The wonderful comedian Ross Noble was hosting the final, and he was someone that we all wanted to impress, along with the judges of course.

Sarah and Cherry and Karen Bayley, the comedian, had come up to support me, which took the edge off some of my nerves at least; you can never underestimate the sight of a smattering of friendly faces in an audience. The final started and my body went into auto-pilot fear, worry, nerves, stress, but this time I was resilient. The humiliation of drying up at the *Citylife* final overrode my fears and I went on stage determined.

I had been watching through the gap in the curtain. I could only see three of the judges, Dr Graeme Garden, Ralf Little and Sean Lock, and they hadn't laughed hysterically at any of the acts so far so I knew there was no clear winner. I could also see that each of the acts had brought mates, and they were only laughing at their friends and remaining stony-faced for the others. Please, Cherry, Sarah, Karen, don't let me down – laugh! I stepped on stage and gave it my best shot.

As with all those early gigs, I can't remember much of what happened in those seven minutes. The blood seemed to be rushing around my head so fast, it had drowned out the audience. Whether they were clapping or booing, I will never know, but whatever they were doing it must have been positive because to my complete shock – I won.

Yes, I won, and the man who beat me in the *Citylife* final, Justin Moorhouse, came second. I was over the moon and so proud that I hadn't fluffed or cocked it up again. I ran straight to the phone and told Mum, who advised me cryptically, 'Don't do anything stupid now.'

If I thought the final was a blur, the party afterwards was even more of a blur. There was a bit of friction as I went into the party. The girl at the door refused to let me in to the party. 'I've just won the BBC New Comedian of the Year.'

'Anyone can say that.'

Which I totally understand, but when you're standing there holding a bright pink award with 'The BBC New Comedian of the Year' in your hand, the odds are considerably in your favour.

She grudgingly let me pass. Cow.

The party was great. I got VIP tickets which meant I could get free drinks in this special room only for VIPs. I walked in nervously and saw Trev and Simon from 'Swing Your Pants' fame at the bar, which left me in awe. I nervously sat down with Cherry, Sarah and Karen, drank the free drinks and tried not to do anything stupid. The rest of the week was such fun. I got to do interviews with different papers and magazines, people stopped to chat in the street and Nan rang to say that she'd seen my name on Teletext.

* * *

I was walking on air, and on the way back to Manchester on the train I couldn't quite believe what had happened to me. The excitement only began to fade once I'd stepped out onto the Piccadilly Station platform – I didn't have a job. I'd sacked off Barclaycard in a fit of pique and now I couldn't pay my rent. However, rent was the last thing on my mind when I returned home and opened the door to my bedroom.

I found my possessions covered in a layer of dust and debris littering the floor and a massive gaping hole in the side of the wall. I could see the garden from my bed. Ruth had been 'doing up' the house again, it seemed, while I had been away, and rather than give the wall a fresh lick of paint she had chosen to use a demolition ball. Yes, the room was quite dark, and the skylight that was in the roof only let in limited light. Ruth in her wisdom had decided to put another window in, without telling me, while I was in Edinburgh. She said it was meant to be a surprise, and she was right – it was a big surprise. The hole was lower than expected, so once the window was put in the neighbours around the back would be able to see not my face but my body from the waist down, which is probably the part of your body that you would want covering up, especially when there are people sunbathing and children playing in the gardens below.

We'd also got some new flatmates, Eva and Pauline, which didn't help in any way to rebalance the madness. They were both German. They did not know each other, but had both responded to Ruth's advert separately and liked the house. You couldn't have had two more different flatmates. Pauline was a stick-thin, pink-haired punk with piercings, and Eva was this curvaceous nymphomaniac who worked at Little Chef. Eva was lovely but had a voracious sexual appetite, and when not bringing blokes home with her from the Little Chef would scour the lonely hearts for more single men. I lost track of the amount of times I came down for breakfast to find some shifty-looking Little Chef customer muttering under his breath 'only popped in for an all day breakfast.' I don't know if Ruth believed that the string of gentleman callers that turned up at the house every week, or the ones that rang the landline, were her 'friends' or 'work colleagues', but she certainly didn't let on. There were a few times when she came close.

Ruth had come into the kitchen one morning and said to the man sitting with Eva in the kitchen eating breakfast, 'Hello, what is it that you do?'

'I paint.'

'What do you paint?'

'Women. Naked women.'

Ruth managed to muster an 'Oh'.

'I usually have them just wearing kitten heels or stilettos.'

The atmosphere was electric. Thank God Mortimer had started pissing next to the fridge or I wouldn't have known where to look.

* * *

Now I was 'Alan Carr, BBC New Comedian of the Year', I naively thought that things would change, but they didn't. I had one meeting with the BBC's Jon Plowman, the producer of some of my favourite comedies ever, such as *The Office*, *Absolutely Fabulous* and *The League of Gentlemen*. It was one of those meetings they give you, just to save face. You turn up and have a cup of tea. They do it to give you the impression that the wheels are turning, when in fact it's the scenery moving. To be fair to the BBC, what could they offer me? I'd just won a competition with seven minutes of comedy. No one gets their own show after just seven minutes, you don't even get that after seven years of comedy, (well, OK, I did with my *Ding Dong*, but let's not go into that right now) but I was new and I naively thought that *The Alan Carr Show* was just around the corner.

They were impressed with my stand-up, they loved the fact that I talked about call centres. It was 'now', it was very much in the general public's minds. I didn't dare tell them that it was my job, well, it had been ten days ago, but I let them talk, sipping my tea expecting every next sentence to start, 'We have a show for you primetime Saturday night ...'

It never came, but they loved my call centre material nevertheless. The news that call centres were relocating to India to save money, and British workers were losing their jobs, was all over the papers. I was talking about what it was like to work in those very call centres. It seems by complete accident I'd ridden the zeitgeist. For once in my life, I was this trendy comedian talking about the week's hot potatoes and the issues that counted. Can I have my primetime show now?

However, my comedy was appreciated elsewhere. Don Ward of the Comedy Store had spotted me playing in a half-empty room at the Frog and Bucket and had decided to give me my own Sunday show at the Manchester Comedy Store. Once a month I had carte blanche to hold a cabaret night. I was so excited, but as usual nervous. Sometimes being given carte blanche is worse than being told what to do. What or who would I have on the bill? Would we have a band, or a celebrity, and how much do you charge? When does the night start? I could see it was going to be a tough one. The Comedy Store helped out loads, what with the bookings and every-thing. I'd already come up with the name 'Alan Carr's Ice Cream Sunday', and the flyer was printed with me holding aloft a Mr Whippy ice cream, *à la* Statue of Liberty.

When it came to booking the acts, I knew I wanted a whole different selection. I didn't just want comedians, I wanted the whole gamut of performers that ply their trade upon the stage. I told them what I wanted, they rang around and if it was within the budget we would have them. The nights were definitely different. No one could say it was boring. We had headlining stand-ups, we had contortionists, jugglers, celebrities, lap dancers, rappers, it really was a smorgasbord of talent. Obviously, the level of quality would fluctuate wildly, but it would always be fun.

I had an amazing coup one night. We had booked Neil and Christine Hamilton for the 'Celebrity Interview' part of the show where I would pull out a leopard-skin sofa and chat to the celebrities for about twenty minutes. Now, as we all know, a Neil and Christine Hamilton interview is not really something that conjures up 'hottest ticket in town', but that Sunday morning splashed all across the *News of the World* was the luridly eyeball-popping story of an alleged sexual assault at a sex party by the Hamiltons, the very people who were on my show. Of course, it was all lies, but the salacious details of Christine sitting on the victim's face whilst Neil ejaculated over her breasts strangely seemed to attract my kind of audience and the Comedy Store that night was packed to the rafters with fans and, dare I say it, perverts.

Neil and Christine turned up (thank God) and seemed oddly unfazed by the flurry of media attention that surrounded them. Once on the sofa, they were really great sports. Every naughty question I asked them was taken in the right spirit, and every *double entendre* and insinuation was camped up to the max by both Neil and Christine. I know it was unfashionable to like them, but I liked them. They send themselves up relentlessly at every given opportunity, so much so that I think some people miss the point, as if the Hamiltons have a point, but you get what I mean. The night was a huge success, the audience loved it, and so did the Hamiltons to the extent that the night ended with Christine on stage holding a glass of Chardonnay while sitting on an escapologist sandwiched between two beds of nails. A truly wonderful evening was had by all.

The problem with having such an eclectic mix on stage is the fact that you are only as good as the acts you book, and for every Hamilton/escapologist/sex scandal night there would be a ropy one. Yes, I could come on stage and do my monologue at the top, do my topical jokes and spoofs, but when it came to the other acts it was out of my hands. One night which was a disaster was the one after the success of the Hamiltons. We'd had escapologists, ventriloquists, dancers and singers, so I needed something a bit different. Then it came to me: a clairvoyant! Now that's different and hasn't been done before. What a great idea! I got Heidi in the Comedy Store office to ring round, and before long we had found a comedy psychic. Wonderful!

Sunday came and the audience were buzzing, expecting another great night of entertainment. My psychic turned up in good time, which was a relief. He was unassuming but nervous – and quite rightfully so, as he'd never done clairvoyancy at a comedy club before. This was his first time, and after what I witnessed on that stage it would be his last.

All the other acts had gone down really well, everyone was all excited for the headliner, so I went on stage and introduced him. The crowd whooped and cheered, and I left him to do his thing. As usual when the headliner was on, I headed to the dressing room, packed up my stuff, signed the acts' contracts, folded up the costumes and basically pottered about till it was time to have a glass of wine.

'Heidi, have you turned the volume down on this telly?'

There was no laughter coming from the backstage television which shows what's happening on stage.

'No, I haven't touched it,' she said.

I pressed the volume button. It was up to the maximum.

'Shit.' I ran out the dressing room, up the stairs and pressed my ear to the stage door.

'Boo! Get off. Wanker!' It wasn't going well at all. I could see on the television and hear through the door that he was getting through to the other side, but the messages they were giving him weren't going down too well in the land of the living.

'Please, watch out for buses … You won't make it to your thirties … Your dad's with me and he's in a lot of pain' were just some of the gems he was telling the audience. I could see some people were walking out. One woman had shouted, 'You're sick,' before grabbing her handbag and storming off.

I came back on stage. I couldn't leave him out there to dry. You never know, with me out there on stage it might pacify the crowd and inject a bit of well-needed humour into the proceedings. I came on to a cheer and asked the audience to be patient and let the psychic carry on, and for a few minutes they calmed down.

He then wheeled out a white board and said, 'I can also analyse handwriting. Please, someone, anyone, write something on the board, and I will use my supernatural powers to analyse it.'

This young man came up to the stage, took the marker pen and wrote on the board, 'You're shit!'

Well, that did it! Half of the audience roared with laughter, the other half got up to leave. They'd had enough, and to be fair I don't blame them. I quickly said the psychic's name, declared the evening over and watched forlornly as the audience started to filter out, muttering. I don't blame the psychic – that's why I haven't put his name down here. I blame myself. Just because you are told that you can have a night where 'anything goes', it doesn't mean that you can have 'anything'. I misjudged the evening, and should have realised that punters who have paid their money and come deliberately to the Comedy Store for a laugh may not want to be told about their dead relatives and when they are going to die.

* * *

Although the Edinburgh Fringe Festival takes up all of August, if you want to take a show up to the Festival the decision to go must be made by February at the latest. You need to tell them the title of the show and a short synopsis of what it's about. This must be finalised in February, which is ridiculous because most of the comedians I know haven't even started writing their shows at that time, let alone know what the bloody thing is going to be about. What I always do is pick a title that is so oblique that it could encompass the meaning of life, the beginning of the universe and the essence of 'being'. Then whatever I write can fit nicely in between those brackets. One year I chose 'Me 'Ead's Spinnin'. But why was my head spinning? Hmm! Complex. No, actually, it just sounded quite funny, and I'd let the critics read into it what they wanted.

Although I never got paid for my 'Ice Cream Sundays', we never made a profit – don't laugh! What I'd been doing unintentionally was having to write new material each month to fill up the compere bits, so I was clearing a fresh twenty minutes every month. Now, faced with having to fill an hour at the Festival, this material was heaven-sent. I could cherry-pick the best bits of my monologues and add them to my routine and cunningly wind them into a story. All I needed was the story.

It wasn't long before my prayers were answered, and God moves in mysterious ways, he even rides on the number 43 bus up Oxford Road because that's when he answered them. A grubby teenage girl with scruffy hair and a donkey jacket got on the bus. She didn't sit down on the copious amount of empty seats that surrounded her on the bus, which I thought was strange, she just stood there distracted. When the bus stopped at a designated stop, she grabbed an old lady's handbag and ran for the door. The quick-thinking bus driver closed the door and it jammed on her neck.

'I've got Asthmaaaaaarrrrr! I've got Asthmaaaaaarr,' she croaked in her broad Manc accent. She managed to squeeze through the door with the handbag and ran off, while some passengers on the bus braver than me took chase. I did my bit and rang the police.

'An elderly lady has just had her handbag stolen off the bus outside the University on Oxford Road. The assailant is being chased by some of the passengers. She is a teenager …' I continued my description.

She told me to hold. I waited about thirty seconds.

'What's your name?' she asked. 'Can I have your mobile number? Where are you?'

'On the Curry Mile, outside the Sangam,' I replied.

'Wait a minute!' she said suspiciously. 'A moment ago you said you were at the University on Oxford Street.'

'I was. I'm still on the bus.' What the police officer had thought were gaps in my story were actually the bus stops I was passing through.

The whole robbery and chat to the police officer had not only jolted my sensibilities as a law-abiding citizen, it had jolted my imagination. As I have always done, I took inspiration from what on the surface was a pretty grim situation, neutralised it, and decorated it with comic touches and, *voilà*, a comedy routine for all the family to enjoy. I used most of what happened that day; fact is stranger than fiction, and it's also funnier.

Audiences have this amazing sixth sense where they can tell if a comedian is bullshitting them. They allow you to be a bit liberal with the truth, but if they get a whiff of an outright lie they can be horribly unforgiving. As soon as I got home I started writing the whole scenario down and using it as a basic framework and hooking certain jokes onto certain events. Obviously, I allowed myself a little artistic licence, and the conversation took on a more humorous tone.

'There's a woman who's been mugged. A girl grabbed her handbag, pushed her on the floor and ran off.'

'Do you want police, fire or ambulance?'

I was that close to being sarcastic, but I thought, 'No, there's a woman lying on the floor dying. The last thing she needs is a lifeboat turning up.'

A healthy dose of over-exaggeration can do wonders for even the most tired routines, and there is nothing more satisfying than watching it fit into place and seeing the beginnings of a new routine start emerging from the page before your very eyes. My home life was becoming a rich breeding ground for material. Pauline's pink hair and piercings, I'm afraid, were not figments of my imagination, but harsh realities. The mild, timid little doormouse that had walked through the door all those months ago had evolved into a feisty, confrontational tigress. If anyone did not do their washing up, they would wake up to find their dirty dishes outside their door with an abusive note in broken English pinned to their door.

One morning I came down the stairs to see Ruth and Eva shaking their heads on the porch. On closer inspection we found an A4 piece of paper with 'Which Son of Bitch steal my Shampoo? No Shampoo, no electricity!' We assumed she meant that she wouldn't be paying the electricity bill, rather than climbing up on the roof and cutting any cables. We were all horrified at this note. I don't know whether we were more shocked by the language or the fact that we would want to steal and use any shampoo that would leave our hair in as bad a condition as the straw crash helmet she called a 'do'.

As it happens, we were all innocent of such a heinous crime. The bottle of shampoo had fallen down behind the sink. I think it had thrown itself down there to avoid making contact with her hair, but that's another matter. The next morning there was another A4 piece of paper pinned to the front door with 'Sorry!' on it, but after that she kept a low profile, eating up in her room and laughing raucously to *You've Been Framed!* She used to love that programme; unlike the rest of the nation, she never used to be able to tell what was going to happen next. A man on a stepladder painting, next to a closed door, she would seriously be surprised when the door opens and he's knocked off the ladder and the tin of paint falls on his head. She would burst out laughing, completely shocked at the turn of events. I would love to say that her innocent childlike humour was magical, but I found her howls of laughter irritating. After you've seen three videos of a cat jumping up to flush a toilet, you get the gist. I would retire to my room indignant.

The preparations for my first-ever full Edinburgh show were proceeding nicely. 'Me 'Ead's Spinning' had been accepted by the board who run the Festival, and my time slot and venue had been confirmed – 9.30 to 10.30 p.m. at the Pleasance Upstairs just off the Pleasance Courtyard, the true hub of the Festival. Wandering around the cobbled square, you are likely to see famous comedians mingling with punters, promoters flyering frantically, and if you're really unlucky, hear people slagging off your show.

I got on the train at Piccadilly station in Manchester with my suitcase. I knew I'd be away for a month so I packed everything. Dreading what people would say, I packed lots of 'comfort' things – my Aretha Franklin albums, photos of my family and Rennies. I knew it was going to be tough, and I wanted these things around me.

The journey up to Scotland was all right. I had my Walkman and listened to that, not because I wanted to listen to the music, but to drown out the inane chatter of a student Drama group behind me, poisoning the atmosphere with their hoity-toity witterings. How quickly I had defected. A few years ago it would have me in a lime green leotard talking with affected camp about Stanislavski, and now I was tutting loudly and turning the volume up so high my ears bled.

There was so much to worry about. Would anyone turn up? If they did turn up, would they like it? What would the critics say? Where was I staying in Edinburgh? That last question was answered more quickly than the other ones, as I was taken straight there when the train pulled up at Waverley station. My agents Steve and Mary had done well, my accommodation was this beautiful apartment on the third floor of this old town house with huge windows that overlooked the Royal Mile at the front and the graveyard of Canongate Kirk at the rear.

I must admit I was a bit alarmed at the graveyard, but it hadn't been used for a while and a lot of the graves dated back to the 1700s, ancient enough not to arouse thoughts of your own mortality. It was well maintained and, strange as it sounds, I found the graveyard quite relaxing. I would often open the window and sit with a cup of tea and absorb the silence. The serenity was only disturbed a few times by goths having a fumble behind a gravestone, but more often than not it was just the chirping of the birds and my thoughts.

My bedroom at the front of the apartment was above the Royal Mile. At first, it was quite thrilling, living on the same road as the Palace of Holyroodhouse, the Queen's residence when she's ever in this neck of the woods. But the thrill lost its sparkle as I was awoken every morning by a double-decker tourist bus stopping outside my house. The top deck of the bus was parallel with my window, so every morning I would be woken up by the same piece of historical trivia.

'Robert Burns visited Canongate Church in 1780 to look for the grave of ...'

Every morning Robert Burns would haunt my morning dreams. It would be the first thing I'd hear as my head laid on the pillow. On the first morning I got out of bed to see who the fuck was shouting historical facts through my window, and I was greeted by a bevy of German tourists in cagoules staring through my window. I had a good mind to greet them every morning dressed as Robert Burns and tell them to 'Tak the high rood'.

In Edinburgh you have previews of your show for the first few days just so you can get your show in order, get used to the stage and iron out any creases that may still linger in your routine, but after that you're on your own. 'Me 'Ead's Spinning', I'm proud to say, was a success. It never won the Perrier, but then again that never appealed to me. It was a success on my own terms. I never cancelled a performance because no audience members had turned up, I never got an awful review, no one walked out of my show. All these fears that had clung to me on the train journey up to Scotland never materialised. I had survived intact and, as Edinburgh's standards go, that was enough to say your show had been a triumph.

To be honest after the first week I got bored and was starting to count the days to when I could return home. The Edinburgh Festival is too long, if you ask me, and halfway through the run the paradise turned into purgatory – a whole month trapped in a city full of Drama students and poets, unable to escape because you have to perform for one hour in the evening. I felt like a dog on one of those extendable leads. Even the endless socialising and drinking at all the after-hours bars can get monotonous, same old faces, same old hangovers. The exhilaration I had felt the previous year had been replaced by boredom, mainly due to the fact that I had stayed too long, and was beginning to see the sawdust beneath the sparkle.

I had stopped walking up the Royal Mile towards the Castle in fear of getting flyered to death. The turning point for me was when I had ventured up there, ironically to clear my head. Costumed performers just seemed to come out of the woodwork begging you to go to their shows. 'Five Stars, *Observer*', 'Unmissable, *The Times*' echoing from every corner of the old town. I politely declined and turned the corner only to get nearly knocked down by a tank being driven down the street with Drama students clinging to it singing 'Oh, What a Lovely War!' Sometimes it gets too much.

My friends came up at regular intervals, and they were a comfort. We would picnic up at Arthur's Seat or we would leave the city and visit some of the pretty towns and villages along the coast. We would do anything and everything, as long as it had nothing to do with the bloody Festival or stand-up comedy. Spending time with them proved to be a real tonic. They were the constant in my world, helping me deal with the loneliness and isolation of living alone above a graveyard or the frenetic, chaotic social whirl of the Pleasance Courtyard.

Chapter Ten

SLIDING
TACKLE

wish you were here ...

SEA SIDE TOWN

You would think that, being in a city gripped by an artistic frenzy for a whole month, I would have at least have got lucky at some point – but oh no, I couldn't even get a shag in a city full to the brim of Drama students, actors and theatre types. I had pulled one man but it hadn't lasted even to the morning. He was a Pole called Vladimir. I invited him back to my apartment, and over a cheeky glass of Merlot he asked me in broken Polish, 'What would you do for love?'

'I don't know,' I replied.

'Would you steal for love?'

'Yes, if I was really in love.'

'Would you give someone a thousand pounds for love?'

'Of course. Money means nothing when you're in love.'

Then something changed, and his eyes became all serious and steely. 'Would you kill someone for love?'

'I don't, er, really, er …'

'Forget it,' he said seriously and changed the subject. Was he expecting me to murder someone? Well, if he did, he can forget it, no chance – I had to think of my career. I've been talked into some things before, but never homicide. It was like something out of an Alfred Hitchcock movie. He sensed my discomfort and said, 'I will leave.'

To be honest, I was pleased and lied, 'Maybe we can meet again sometime.'

He turned and said, 'Yes,' with those piercing eyes. I closed the door behind him and without a second thought popped on the latch and turned the Chubb. Let the weirdo try and get through that lot.

Thankfully, it wasn't just psychopathic serial killers that visited my humble abode on the Royal Mile. I had comedy legends, too. A mutual friend was good friends with Peter Kay who'd heard about me from the Manchester comedy scene and wanted to meet me. I gave my friend the key to the flat and said I would meet him once my show was over. I was a bag of nervy excitement, and throughout my performance that night I couldn't take my mind off the fact that afterwards I would be meeting *the* Peter Kay. I walked up the stairs and opened the door, went in and instantly got tangled up in my wet washing that was hanging from the ceiling on a pulley-operated wooden clothes horse. I freed myself and in the process knocked a painting off the wall.

For some reason, I couldn't stop making a twat of myself. Peter probably thought that I was trying to get a part in *Phoenix Nights* or something. He was sitting on the settee quietly with his tour manager Gordon, and it was a real honour finally to meet him. Although I had never met him, I had felt his presence on the Manchester comedy scene for the past five years – whether it was Manc comics trying to do Peter Kay-style material or working with the cast of comedians from *Phoenix Nights*, like Toby Foster and Steve Edge, whom he had cherry-picked from the scene itself.

He sat there taking it all in, quietly listening to what I was saying, absorbing everything. I could see the cogs going and couldn't help thinking that he was taking notes on me, sculpting a character out of my mannerisms or storing up a saying or a comment to be used in a sketch. Peter Kay, as we all know, is the ultimate people-watcher. Well, if he could make any comedy out of the nervous mumbo-jumbo I was muttering, then he was welcome to it. Needless to say, meeting Peter was the highlight of my Festival.

The Festival rattled along nicely, and before long we had reached the end of August, and it was time to go home. It's surprising when you return home from living in this artistic bubble – living in fear of the reviews, praying you have an audience – that no one actually gives a shit. No, they don't. Up there, it was so ridiculously intense, you felt that you were the centre of the earth and that the whole world's eyes were pointing towards Edinburgh. I returned to Manchester with a loud 'I'm back!' – only to get a 'Where've you been?'

'Edinburgh!'

'On holiday?'

'No, the Festival!'

'Oh ...'

Lay people don't really care about the Fringe. They think that it's full of affected thespians, attention-grabbing comedians and tourists – and, come to think of it, they're probably right. As any performer who's been to Edinburgh will tell you, you come back totally drained, needing a serious detox, and just as you're finally getting your mind and body round to recovering, a big fat bill from the Fringe pops on your doormat. The bill amounts to what you owe the Festival after they've taken the money for ticket sales off the price of hiring the venue. Added to that is the cost of flyering, accommodation, the list truly is endless. If you're really lucky, you break even. If you don't, you could be left with a bill of up to £10,000. I was lucky, I just had to pay £3,000. I don't know why I used the word 'just', but hearing what some performers had to pay I felt incredibly lucky to get away with three grand.

* * *

My stand-up work carried on regardless. Although financially I was down, my confidence had improved from performing each and every night. But after saying nearly the same thing most nights for weeks, I was desperate to get writing and come up with some new jokes. My agent must have thought I was confident enough because he had put me forward for a corporate do for Abbey National Building Society on the outskirts of Birmingham. I saw how much they were going to pay me, and my heart skipped a beat. It was what I would earn at Barclaycard in a month. Of course, being the corporate whore that I am, I accepted.

I started thinking of what I would buy with my money. Some new shoes, perhaps, a holiday – my imagination went into overdrive. Not once did I wonder why they would pay such an obscene amount of money for what was basically performing twenty minutes of stand-up comedy. I'll tell you why, because they're soul destroying, self-esteem-crushing, degrading, vile experiences that in all my years have left me considering quitting stand-up comedy for good. Like Princess Lea chained to Jabba the Hut, you have to dance and perform every time they tug your chain, and, boy, do they tug it!

I was oblivious to this as I turned up at the conference centre and was taken to my dressing room. It was only once I'd stepped on stage that I realised I had signed a pact with the devil. But that was later.

The branch manager of Abbey National met me and took me to the large hall in the conference centre to do my sound check. 'We're looking for twenty minutes of clean stand-up. No swearing or sexual jokes. We don't like smut at the Abbey National. Our staff are here for a good time and are like one big happy family.' Sounded really nice people. This is going to be easy.

The time arrived for me to go on stage. The branch manager came on and introduced me.

'Our host for the evening used to work in a call centre, and now he's a comedian, so you could say he's gone from sit-down to stand-up!'

SILENCE. Which I'm not really surprised about really, but anyway.

'It's Alan Carr!'

The lighting change happened, but not as promised. I was plunged into darkness, and the spotlight lit up a man in a wheelchair at the edge of the dancefloor. Then we had to wait while they repositioned the spotlight on me. A few people started to talk – I was losing them before I had begun. Finally I started my routine, but by then everyone had started to chat, and I was facing a wall of sound. I couldn't hear myself speak, but I persevered nevertheless, hoping that someone, somewhere in the room might be enjoying my act.

I was halfway through, getting nowhere, when I felt something tap the front of my glasses, and then another tap. I looked down. It was a Cadbury's Mini Egg! They were throwing Cadbury's Mini Eggs at me! It was hard enough remembering my jokes without having to dodge the confectionary friendly fire that was staccato-ing off my spectacles.

They were animals. I could see the branch manager's horrified look on the top table. This one big happy family he'd described was now resembling the Mansons! Alcohol was turning people who I'm sure were decent human beings when sober into monsters. I'm not blaming them for drinking – if I worked for a bank, I would, too. These workers who probably rarely left the house were being plied with free drink, and they were making the most of it, which is fine. The unforgivable thing was leaving on the tables massive pots of M & Ms and Cadbury's Mini Eggs – a chocolate treat in the hands of a sober person, but a silver bullet in the hands of a premenstrual, paralytic bank clerk with a bubble perm.

I was sick of this unnecessary abuse, so I told them all to fuck off. I added that they were in my opinion 'a load of ungrateful wankers!' and left the stage to go to my dressing room. Karen, who lived down the road from the corporate in Sutton Coldfield, had come to give me some moral support, and together we just sat there shaking our heads. My brain was trying to compute what had just happened. I was downhearted, muttering to myself 'Wankers'. The branch manager came in to apologise for his staff's behaviour.

Sliding tackle

'I've never ever experienced such a bunch of rude wankers in my life,' I said, slipping on my coat. 'I'm off.'

'Where you going?' he asked.

'I'm off. I've never been so embarrassed.'

'But you've got to present the raffle.'

'What?'

He was right. I had only scanned the contract briefly. A raffle was part of the deal. The most embarrassing moment of my life was about to be surpassed ten minutes later by giving prizes to people I had just called 'a fucking bunch of wankers'. Hmm! Nice.

'This isn't going to be awkward at all, is it?' I thought. So I took off my coat and returned to the stage where they had positioned a tombola. My reintroduction – 'It's Alan Carr!' – didn't even get the half-hearted ripple of applause that my first introduction had received. Silence greeted my ears, but at least they weren't pebble-dashing me with M & Ms.

So for the next twenty minutes I read out the raffle numbers and had my picture taken with the 'wankers' smiling cheesily. As I handed over the DVD player with a bow wrapped around it, I was hoping in my heart that when the winner plugged it in it would short-circuit and electrocute him. They were probably the most forced photos you would ever see this side of David Gest and Liza Minnelli's wedding. Mercifully, the raffle didn't take too long, mainly due to the fact that neither of us wanted to speak to each other, so pleasantries were kept to a blessed minimum.

* * *

I got to see Peter Kay again, this time not in my sitting room, but in action at the Lowry in Salford. He very kindly invited me along. As it was sold out, he had got me a seat in the back of the auditorium, basically next to a St John's Ambulance man with a comb-over and a bag of Murray Mints. The show was highly entertaining from the moment he stepped on stage to the finale – a rendition of 'Danny Boy'. For 'Danny Boy', he got everyone standing up, waving their arms in the air. I was so far back, I didn't bother and continued to sit, until I heard, 'Alan Carr! Get your bloody hands in the air!'

I told you Peter was a people-watcher. Of course, I jumped up and joined in, surprisingly not embarrassed but dead chuffed that he had remembered my name.

Post-Edinburgh, my gigs were proving successful. Obviously, there were a few awful ones, although admittedly some weren't my fault. One time I was gigging in Manchester above a pub on a busy crossroads, and my hand-held microphone had started picking up the frequency of a local taxi-rank. It's hard enough dealing with a heckle from within the room, let alone 'Foxtrot Alpha Bravo, we need a pick-up outside Morrisons' stamping all over your punchlines.

Taxi-rank heckles aside, I was making progress, and my life in Chorlton was getting more settled, although my flatmates' lives were anything but. Pauline had been arrested for drug smuggling in Munich. Terrified, she'd phoned us from the airport, asking if we could all club together and stump up £1,000 for a bond to have her released. We were all skint in that house and, after a group chat in the sitting room, we soon realised we couldn't get our hands on that kind of cash. Plus, it became apparent that even if we did have the money, she'd been so sharp and aggressive with us over the previous months that we wouldn't give it to her anyway. Also, who chose Pauline to be a drugs mule anyway? She was hardly the most discreet mule in the world. With her pierced face, pink hair, big thick leather boots and a leather trench coat, she looked like she must have been off her face when she got dressed that morning. Sad to say, we never saw Pauline again.

A lot of the time, I would have the run of the house. Ruth had started donating her body to science to get money. She would go to Medival for weeks on end and have drugs tested on her for such ailments as Alzheimer's, Parkinson's and angina, and then come back and go on holiday, leaving me to look after the ever-expanding Mortimer, who was still frustratingly not litter-trained. Foolishly, I had assumed that going to the Edinburgh Festival would transform my career and that I would immediately be spotted by some television bigwig and get my own show. But obviously, it never materialised. Everyone else had the same idea. Worse still, people more talented than me had the same idea. Damn!

I don't know why I expected television to come knocking. I'm not one of those comedians who took up stand-up comedy solely to get on television. But I get so bored so easily that the thought of just travelling around the country doing my routine in different cities until I died made me feel depressed. Already, I wanted more stimulation.

Edinburgh had in fact the complete opposite effect on my career – my workload had actually gone down. So I found myself at home a lot of the time, and I shouldn't be left alone in the house with time to think because that's what I do: think and think and think. Questions seemed to come out of the ether and buzz about my head like a bluebottle. I started wondering whether I'd made the right decision leaving Barclaycard. Was I good enough as a stand-up? Was that the reason why I wasn't getting any work? Sitting at home most days, you do wonder why anyone would choose to be unemployed. And believe me, some people do choose. Being off work is so soul-destroying. Everyone else is at work, and what do you have for company? *Diagnosis Murder*? *Flog It*? *Cash in the Attic*? Christ. I'd rather go back to the factories, personally.

My financial position at the time meant that any work that did come in I grabbed with both hands. When I was asked to perform a New Year's Eve show at Just the Tonic in Nottingham for £300, I nearly balked. The money was amazing and for me the equivalent of a fortnight's stand-up gigs, plus it was New Year's Eve and everyone would be in high spirits … wouldn't they?

I arrived at Just the Tonic to find that the other comedians on the bill were Justin Moorhouse and the Voice of the Carphone Warehouse, Ed Byrne. This should be fun, I thought. For some reason, the men urinating in the queue outside and the women with the inflatable cocks chanting 'Show us your dick' didn't register as potential hazards and I walked through the door of the comedy club like a lamb to the slaughter.

'I've never done a New Year's Eve gig before.'

Ed Byrne and the promoter Darrel Martin smiled knowingly at me. I didn't take this as a sign either, and carried on going through my jokes in my notebook while the compere introduced Justin to the stage.

I got suspicious when Justin Moorhouse re-entered the dressing room, looking visible flustered.

'They're fucking animals. Just do ten minutes and get off!' he said to me.

In my arrogance I thought to myself, you can handle this, they're just excitable because it's New Years Eve, once I've got into my flow they'll love it. As it happens, the only way I could have controlled that crowd was if I'd mounted the stage on a police horse in full body armour and twatted the pissheads with a baton. They were indeed animals. Now in the early years I used to just go on stage and do my set and try not to get too wrapped up in what was going on externally, but when a woman runs on stage, getting her tits out mid-routine, you have to put the jokes aside and say something. I can't remember what I said, but whatever it was it didn't assuage the jeers. If anything they increased. My £300 fee was looking more and more like danger money.

Then I felt something hit me on the head and fall to the floor. Someone had wrapped a cork in tin foil and had thrown it at me. I was outraged! I was only trying to make them laugh.

'Throw it back,' one rough-looking Nottingham woman screamed. Without a second thought, I picked it up, aimed it and threw it at the gang of lads that the missile had come from. I threw the cork up underarm, it hit a lampshade and fell limply to the floor.

'YOU THROW LIKE A GIRL!' YOU THROW LIKE A GIRL!' the whole crowd chanted. For a split second I was transported back to Weston Favell Upper School's playing fields. I couldn't compete with this and left the stage to cheers, cheers that I was leaving presumably, rather than that they had enjoyed my anecdotal tales of life in a call centre.

After that response I decided to get pissed – hey, it was New Year's Eve. I got a bit too pissed, however, and the promoter Darrell had given me a bag of party poppers to distribute, which I did. However, he never specified when – I didn't realise he meant at midnight. I'm sorry to say that the moronic crowd starting popping them all through Ed Byrne's act. Poor Ed, they were hard enough to control as it was and I hadn't helped things.

Darrell snatched the bag out of my hand and shouted angrily, 'What are you doing?' and I started crying. I didn't really care, I was just, like the audience, very, very drunk. It was the perfect ending to a perfect night.

* * *

My agent was adamant that I should do the Edinburgh Festival again.

'It's the place where stars of the future are spotted,' Steve proclaimed. 'It keeps you in the forefront of people's minds.'

I wasn't convinced, but then again, what options did I have? No comedy promoters were knocking on my door, BBC Manchester definitely weren't, and my diary was giving me snow blindness with all its empty white pages. Could I be bothered? Staying up there again on my own, being at the mercy of critics and audiences, wasn't very tempting, especially with the real possibility of losing another three grand or more if this show was a turkey. But eventually I decided to go for it again and started writing a new show with a new title. My agent set those all-too familiar wheels in motion – venue, time, accommodation, blah, blah, blah.

And to be fair, it was blah, blah, blah a lot of the time. I arrived up there in the August of 2003. I was performing at the Cavern, right at the rear of the Pleasance Courtyard; it was a sombre venue that resembled a bunker. It was dark and damp and seemed to me no place to perform comedy. Like the previous year, I got good reviews, but unlike the previous year, I wasn't the new kid on the block any more. The BBC New Comedian of the Year Award had gone to the ventriloquist Nina Conti and her monkey. I didn't have that all-important hook to draw people in, and some nights it showed. Monday and Tuesday were particularly grim, sometimes as few as twelve, thirteen people would shuffle in to the 120-seater. That was depressing, to say the least, especially when you could see they'd only come in because it was warm.

It was a great show, so I was naturally disappointed about the audience figures. We tried everything, even a two for one. But then people would come with the free ticket and, because they hadn't invested anything in the show, they would sit there and open sweets loudly, slurp their cola, chat. Thank God the Cavern was so embedded in the ground they couldn't get a reception on their mobiles, or they'd have been ordering pizzas. I wouldn't have said I'd do Edinburgh again if I'd known I would feel this underwhelmed.

When I had first arrived, I had sneered over-confidently at Geoffrey from Rainbow's show across the Courtyard, which was based on his favourite anecdotes about Zippy and George. How shit did I feel? He was selling out every night. People wanted to see him over me, it was like Bungle was giving me the wanker sign – shocking. What could I do to get people through my damp, dank door?

Sometimes I tried unconventional methods, which I'm not proud of. I photocopied a headline from a review of Jimmy Carr's show – 'THIS CARR IS THE ROLLS ROYCE OF COMEDY' – and pasted it on my own poster. He was furious (quite understandably) and was seen in the Pleasance Courtyard yanking them off my posters in a rage. Sorry, Jimmy. I just thought family should stick together.

At the beginning of the week, I used to dread turning up at the venue and seeing how many punters were lining up to come and see me. It was affecting my confidence, especially when I popped to the toilet opposite the Cavern and saw a pile of my flyers in a urinal with someone pissing on my face. It really was the final insult.

It was a pretty grim time for me up there that summer of 2003. That same old feeling came to haunt me, that everyone else was having fun without me, that I'd been left off the all-important guest-list. Even my parents seemed to be enjoying more exciting evenings. My mother had told me that Dad had passed out at the local Chinese restaurant and had had a near-death experience. Initially, I was distraught, but when I learnt the facts, my sympathy started to evaporate.

Sliding tackle

Ever the prankster, Dad had taken his remote-control fart machine to the restaurant. Unbeknownst to his friend, my father had slipped the sensor into his friend's pockets, and as his friend had bent over to look at the all-you-can-eat buffet, Dad had pressed the button and a huge fart sounded out across the room – much to the disgust of their fellow diners, but to the huge amusement of my father. Dad couldn't stop laughing – so much so that he had a whitey and passed out. He slumped forward motionless at the table, and Mum, horrified, started screaming, 'Graham, Graham!'

Thankfully, it was only for about twenty seconds that Dad was heading towards a bright light. I know it sounds harsh, but a bit of me thinks that it served him right.

* * *

Dad's near-death experience raised my spirits a little, but it wasn't enough. Going back to my apartment that night, I rang my agent and said I needed a pick-me-up. He rang round and got me some extra-curricular gigs. If the punters weren't coming to me, I would go to the punters, and it proved to be just the tonic. Steve and Mary had put my name down for 'Late N Live', the dreaded bear-pit I had experienced the previous year. What was I thinking? Underneath all the nerves, I knew I needed this. I needed to prove to myself that I was funny, that my jokes were good enough for people to come to the Cavern and see the show.

I arrived at 'Late N Live' at around midnight. I was on at half twelve, and I could hear the roar of the drunken audience already baiting the acts beyond the dressing-room wall. Daniel Kitson was the compere, and I really wanted to do well in front of him. I'd been so impressed with him the year before and didn't want to look the second-rate chancer that I was back then. The night started. Daniel went on stage and instantly started getting heckles from the pissed-up crowd. I didn't really know how I would cope with a heckle. At my show in the Cavern, it was like pulling teeth getting a smile out of them, let alone – heaven forbid! – prompting any banter.

Finally it was my turn and, do you know what? I loved it. Yeah, they started shouting abuse, but although I didn't say anything witty or Wildean, I held my own. Looking back, I think I could only muster, 'Oh shut up or I'll fist you,' which, strangely enough, seemed to settle them down. I deliberately played it cool. Audiences can smell fear at a thousand yards. One sniff and I would be a goner, so I never let my guard down once. I strode nonchalantly about the stage, looking as if I didn't have a care in the world, working the audience, which numbered in the hundreds rather than the paltry twenty I'd had to endure most nights.

Why shouldn't I be up there performing? I had every right to. I persevered, shouting over the pessimistic voice whispering in my ear that I wasn't a proper comedian. I pumped out my best jokes like a well-oiled machine. I was nearly put off my stride when a rough woman to the left of the stage shrieked 'Faggot', but I ignored her and glided nicely to my final joke. I had reached the end of my set – alive – and got a huge cheer for my troubles. I'm ashamed to say that all the devil-may-care attitude I had tried to muster on the stage evaporated when I screamed out at the end, 'I've survived Late N Live!' and skipped off. How uncool is that?

My success at 'Late N Live' had whetted my appetite for more late night comedy. The wonderful thing about Edinburgh is that it is a melting pot, where comedians good and bad, famous or infamous get thrown together and are forced to rub shoulders under the grimmest conditions. I turned up all excited to one late night comedy in the bowels of the Pleasance Dome. I at first thought that I'd got the wrong night because I couldn't hear any laughter from the auditorium. Looking through the glass I could see that the audience were agitated and shouting at the tall skinny man with big hair on stage. I shuffled to the back of the auditorium and said to the organiser:

'Who is he?'

'Russell Brand,' he replied.

'Never heard of him.'

To be fair, Russell was at a bad place in his life that night as he will tell you himself. Back then he hadn't morphed into the hifaluting, huge-barnetted Victorian persona he is today. At the time you would probably call him 'late Georgian'.

Probably annoyed with the lack of audience interest, he announced:

'Do you want to see my cock?'

No one replied but he still got it out and waggled it at the audience. Sadly his penis fell on deaf ears, but who'd have thought that on that very night I would get to see such a celebrated willy? OK, I know I hadn't joined the most exclusive club in the world, but nevertheless it provided me with a bit of light relief and an Edinburgh anecdote. I can think of worse things to dine out on than Russell's willy.

Chapter Eleven

FIGHTING RELEGATION

wish you were here ...

SEA SIDE TOWN

I went back to Manchester knackered, swearing that I would never go up to Edinburgh again. That was it. Finished. Kaput. Over. On returning, my agents dropped a bombshell – they would be leaving Manchester to go to Ireland, but they would still like to represent me. They reassured me that everything would still be the same as it was, it's just they'd now be in Ireland.

OK, I thought, everything's done over the phone and Internet, you can be anywhere in the world these days, and anyway Dublin is a vibrant, funky city with its own comedy scene. So what was I worrying about? The problem was it wasn't Dublin they were moving to – it was Roonagh Quay in County Mayo, on the other side of Ireland.

I know, I hadn't heard of it either. Basically they had moved to the last house in Ireland before you get to America. The nearest shop was half an hour away and even that was a Londis.

When I finally visited them in this Roonagh Quay place they spoke of, it was so barren and rugged that, bathed in the late afternoon sun, it looked like the surface of Mars. It was a lovely house, with a beach at the end of the road and fields that seemed to roll on and on for eternity, but it was hardly the epicentre of the showbiz world. There weren't any power lunches happening in Roonagh Quay, let me tell you. But I was happy for them, and their son Cormac seemed excited by the surrounding fields and deserted beaches ripe for exploring.

I wasn't going to complain and spoil their move by moaning. Moving house is stressful enough, and besides, they had got me a job compering a nationwide tour. Although it would drag me all over Britain – not ideal, so close to Edinburgh – it was a godsend financially.

The tour was sponsored by Durex condoms. We wouldn't be performing in theatres and art centres; we would be performing in a giant big top, pitched in various towns across Britain with 'Durex' written in massive letters across the canvas. The tent was a dubious shape to say the least, not helped by the pelmet that at certain angles resembled a bell-end. Yes, it seemed that for the next few months I would be performing inside a giant inflatable phallus. God, I needed this, didn't I? To add insult to injury, the rain would penetrate the canvas and we would have to dodge the puddles to get on to the stage. If this was in fact a Durex condom, I would have been inseminated on the first night. Someone had obviously thought about the image Durex wanted to promote – willies. If only they'd thought about the marketing and locations as well. No one seemed to know that we even existed, and when you've got such great-quality acts as Daniel Kitson, Jo Caulfield, Milton Jones and Rob Newman on the bill and no one is turning up, it's a travesty.

The locations didn't help. I had naturally assumed that these big tops would be erected in the actual town centre to lure people at least out of curiosity, but no, our first date in Newcastle was in a car park outside Byker, the arsehole of Newcastle. Winter was drawing in, and before we went onstage we would be sitting huddled around a gas heater in this freezing tent, with the sound of boy racers circling the big top in their Vauxhall Gulfs. At least the fumes that seeped under the canvas were keeping us warm. Despite the cold, I did enjoy these gigs in a perverse way. I felt like I was in a circus. Once we'd performed and the audience had left, we would all pack everything up and head to the next city.

After two months away, I finally made it back home to Manchester, and nothing much had changed. A few of my flatmates had left and been replaced, sadly with even weirder ones. Eva had gone back to Germany and been replaced by Sue, an Irish woman in her forties studying Ancient Greek Language, one of those useless degrees that you can buy in the back of a Sunday magazine for five pounds a month. She had come to the house and starting kicking off. She said Mortimer had given her fleas, and not only that, they had bitten her on the nipples. Ruth had called her a 'liar'. Sue had then approached Ruth in the pantry, lifted up her tie-dyed T-shirt and asked, 'Would you like to see my nipples?' At which point, Ruth had called her a lesbian.

As a fitting footnote, whilst the drama was unfurling, Mortimer had gone upstairs and shat on Sue's pillow. I realised how much I'd missed being in that house, the drama, the weir-does and my lengthy chats with Ruth over a glass of wine.

The chaos and madness that encompassed my home life was now in stark contrast to the vacuum that was my love life.

To say I was unlucky in love would give the impression that I'd actually had some loving to be unlucky about. Of course, the usual drunken one-night stands had continued unabated. The Sunday bus ride home from some unfortunate-looking council estate was becoming a regular occurrence. However, one Saturday morning sticks in my mind. I was roughly shaken from my sleep and, naturally disgruntled, I looked up to see a traffic warden staring down at me. 'Oh no, Alan, you've slept rough!' I daren't look down, just in case I'd been clamped. Once I'd found my glasses I could see I hadn't slept rough, I was in a bedroom – thank God for small mercies. Apparently, I'd pulled a traffic warden and he was just starting his morning shift and wanted me off the premises. Once I'd focused on the traffic warden's face I decided to take my glasses off, not so I looked more attractive, but more because my myopia took the edge off his face. He was sweet enough and very kindly walked me to the train station, enthusiastically writing out tickets and plonking them on window screens as we went.

In fact these one-night stand shenanigans were taking their toll on my health – it was beginning to hurt when I urinated. I thought: 'Typical, I've spent the last month in a condom and now I get an STD. Great.' So sheepishly I arranged an appointment to visit a doctor at a clinic and deliberately chose an early morning appointment where I could slip in and out before too many people could see me.

I went in and saw the nurse, a lovely, plump woman who had such a big smily welcoming face that it came as a complete shock when she started quizzing me on my sexual habits. Well, some of the things she asked I'd never even heard of! I thought Nongonococcal Urethritis was a fishing village off the Canaries. She then told me to take off my pants and as I lay there quivering, she stuck the swab right up my urethra. My scream pierced the whole clinic – I swear it nearly cracked my glasses.

I had to wait a week for all the tests to come back. What would it be? Syphilis, chlamydia, gonorrhoea – the excitement was killing me. So the next week I turned up, only to be told that I didn't have anything. I was disease-free, clear, my penis was as clean as a whistle. Although I was relieved, this really pissed me off. I was still in pain. Why did it still hurt when I urinated? I confronted her: her tests must be wrong.

'Look, it really hurts, can you double-check? I'm concerned.'

'No, Mr Carr, I am happy with the results,' she insisted, quite smugly if you ask me.

'Well, can you explain why it still hurts when I wee?'

'There is only one thing that it can be.'

'What is it?' I demanded.

And then without looking up from her papers, she delivered her killer blow. 'Excessive masturbation.'

I got my coat and decided to take what little dignity I had left. I mean, who's going to hang around and question the point? I left with not only my victimised willy firmly between my legs, but my tail too.

As the year progressed my work diary sadly started to mirror my love life. Empty, minimal excitement with long journeys for little rewards, although at least I had never been heckled out of bed yet.

Scarily, I didn't have anything in for the month of December, and December in the comedy world offers rich pickings. The run-up to Christmas is full of tempting lucrative corporate dos, Christmas parties, extended comedy nights. They hang like shiny baubles from a Christmas tree – all you have to decide is how many you want to scoop up for yourself, and you're laughing all the way to the bank.

I asked my agent to get me some work. I mean, that is what I paid him for, and he said he would. A week later, I rang him again.

'Look, Steve, I'm skint. I've got my rent to pay. Have you got me any work?'

'Alan, have you tried temping?'

Did he just say what I thought he said? For a minute I thought he'd said, 'Have you tried temping?' He was serious, and it cut me to the quick. No way on earth was I going to go back there, to that gloomy grey place of clocking in and clocking out. My whole comedy act was about the dreary world of office politics and call centres. Oh what delicious irony; stand-up comedy had been my ticket out of that crappy existence, and now it was my ticket back. Great.

Steve could sense I wasn't happy. 'It's not permanent. Why don't you have a month off and a month on?'

What kind of comedian says, 'It's all right, I'll take December off and come back in January'? January is diabolical for work. Everyone's skint, and all the comedians worth their salt are staying at home counting all the money they'd made in December. Oh brilliant! I had an agent who thought my next career move should be envelope stuffing. It was hard to get angry with Steve and Mary because they are lovely people and they were there for me from the beginning. However, if they're honest, the move to the other side of Ireland had isolated them both from me and from the British comedy circuit. This was my career. How could they ring up promoters and say they had a hot new comedian called Alan Carr when you could distinctly hear the sound of a cow mooing in the background?

So I left. No way was I temping. My days of wearing a headset were officially over. I had to look for representation – and fast. During the Durex tour I had made friends with Matt who worked for the promoter, Karushi. I found Karushi's number in my phone and asked them if they would be interested in representing me. The lovely Lisa Thomas at Karushi said 'Yes', and my diary started filling up nicely. I was funny after all. Phew!

Now comedy is a cut-throat business. If anyone thinks comedy is a laughing matter, they're wrong. Behind the scenes, it's ruthless, vicious and every man for himself. Typically with me, nothing is simple. One day I had no agent, the next I've got three after me. But Lisa Thomas had saved my bacon. She was there when I needed a knight in shining armour, and I am a loyal chap through and through, and I will stand by my word. Well, that's what I thought anyway.

I had been doing some work for the comedy agency Off the Kerb. Judging by the amount of work I was getting off them, I must have been doing a good job. It was coming in thick and fast; in fact, they were giving me more work than Karushi. With Karushi, I was in the middle of doing a pilot for a new show on E4. It was called *The Gay Computer* –

wait, hear me out here. Yes, it did involve me being inside a cardboard box, painted metallic and making barbed comments at a celebrity through a slat in the side, but don't let that cloud your judgement. Yes, we put gay rights back twenty years, but it was absolutely hilarious. Because the celebrity couldn't see me and I was a computer I could say the most outrageous, near-the-knuckle things. It was a bit like what I do on *The Friday Night Project*, but in a cardboard box.

The pilot went really well. Once I'd come out of the box, I had a glass of wine with the controllers at E4 and talked about how promising it all looked. When I finally stepped outside into the street, I popped my phone on and found I had a message to phone Danny at Off the Kerb. Still a little tipsy from the wine, I called him.

'Alan,' he said, 'we've had someone pull out. Could you do the warm-up tonight for the Jonathan Ross chat show?'

Well, that sobered me up. 'Yeah, of course,' came out my mouth, whilst the voices in my head screamed, '*Jonathan Ross – AHHHHHHHHHHHH!*'

'We need you to be at the BBC Studios in Wood Lane for half six tonight. Is that all right?'

'*AAAAAAAAHHHHHHHHHHHHHHHHHHHHHHHHHHH-HHHHHHHHHHH!*' the voices in my head screamed. 'Fine,' came out my mouth. 'Thanks, Danny.' I closed my mobile.

It wasn't the actual warm-up that scared me, it was doing it for Jonathan Ross. He's a national treasure, he's television royalty, plus it's a cool show. I'd done warm-up before. I'd gone down the road to Granada in Manchester to entertain the audience for *Vernon Kay's Celebrities under Pressure*. How hard could it be? If these people had ventured out on a Monday night to watch Liberty X try to beat a family from York at a game of ping-pong, let's face it, their standards weren't particularly high in the first place.

As you'd expect, the night at Granada was pretty uneventful. The audience were those people who scour the Internet for free tickets to any show. I could tell they went to everything because when filming continued for longer than necessary, one woman who was dead behind the eyes shouted out, 'On *Stars in Your Eyes* you get biscuits!'

A few people grumbled and nodded. Although the audience were a bit tetchy, Vernon was absolutely lovely. He must have been standing in the wings listening to my material because in the commercial breaks he teased me by calling me 'Psoriasis Boy' – something I remind him of whenever our paths cross.

I made my way to BBC Centre for my stint warming up Jonathan Ross's chat show. I got there dead early as I wanted to make a good impression. I sat in my dressing room and waited. The dressing room was pretty bleak: a tatty old recliner chair, a wardrobe to hang your costumes up in and some torn flowery wallpaper that I swear was giving me hay fever just looking at it. Seriously, my heart would skip a beat if it had a window! As the weeks progressed, I realised that the dressing rooms were based on hierarchy and hierarchy alone. If there was an *EastEnders* actor on the show, I got the dressing room with a toilet – if it was a Hollywood A-lister, I gave up my dressing room for one of their entourage and was put in a dressing room without a toilet. If there was a proper diva like J-Lo or Puff Daddy with all their entourage and hangers-on, I was actually put in the toilet. There is nothing more humiliating then having your ear jammed up against the toilet wall, hearing bottles of Cristal being decorked from the other side. If the cistern wasn't in overdrive I could actually hear J-Lo talk. Oh yes, I knew my place, and sadly it was in a toilet.

'How do the stars put up with staying in these vile dressing rooms?' I muttered to myself. Of course, the stars never ventured into these dressing rooms. They have the posh ones further up the corridor. I got to experience these dressing rooms for myself when I filmed *Alan Carr's Celebrity Ding Dong*. A shower, two settees, rugs, complimentary champagne, bouquets on every table, three plasma screen televisions, even one in the toilet – a whole world away from the broom cupboard I had inhabited three doors down.

Finally, my time came, and I made my way to the studio, nervous but relieved to be out of that room. I went through the doors and saw the Four Poofs and their piano. They were really sweet and said nice things, which put my mind at rest. I just sat in the corner on a chair taking in the madness of it all. Four hours ago, I was a gay computer. Just as I was getting calm, Janet Jackson walked past with her four bodyguards, and my stomach knotted even tighter.

* * *

It's a really strange experience being a warm-up act. You seem to dwell in a no man's land. You're a part of the show, but you're not. You're integral to the show's atmosphere, but you don't get any credit. You are superfluous, but essential. Being on a well-established, popular show like Jonathan's is even stranger. I had to do my routine in front of that set that everyone knows and then introduce Jonathan Ross as if I'd known him all my life. 'Go mad, go crazy! It's the one and only Jonathan Ross!'

My warm-up went well, really well. The camera guys were laughing, the audience were laughing, the Four Poofs were laughing, but most importantly I could hear Jonathan Ross laughing. I did my thing and introduced Jonathan, who came over and shook my hand and said 'Bwilliant!' So for the remainder of the show I stood with my microphone at the edge of the studio floor, just in case there was an unexpected blip in filming or Jonathan needed a wee. I was on call all the time, just in case.

It was only when I got back to Manchester and checked my emails at the local Internet caff that I got a phone call from Danny at Off the Kerb again. 'You must have done well last night. Jonathan Ross wants you to warm up his shows every week.'

'Liar!' I remonstrated.

'No, it's true.'

And it was. Every Thursday I would drive down to London from Manchester, and I got to see in the flesh some of the most famous people in the world: Elton John, U2, Cameron Diaz, Jane Fonda, among others. They would all glide past me in the corridor, and I would be literally star-struck, just staring at them, not daring to say anything. After a few months this feeling began to subside as I realised that in fact these stars were disappointingly just like us. I had seen them in the make-up room foundationless, I'd seen them pissed in the Green Room, I'd seen them asking a runner, 'Where are the toilets?' I'd seen them desperately nervous, which in some ways was cute but disconcerting for the rest of us. Fear doesn't go away just because you're an A-lister. I should know.

Then you get the other side of the coin: the demands, the strops, the tantrums, which can really turn you off a celebrity, especially when they seem so nice on the telly. One star asked a bamboozled runner whether he could get him some coke. I usually take a Rapid Remedy to pep me up, but each to his own. Fans of the stars appearing on the show would usually pack the audience out, and this would often mean it would be a lively show. Weirdly, they would mirror the stars they had come to support. Marilyn Manson's would be all gothed out. Aerosmith's would be long-haired rockers, and with Janet Jackson, it would be a middle-aged woman with her tit hanging out.

Jonathan Ross would always close his show by telling the viewers who was coming on the show the following week. I would always wait with bated breath to hear the next batch of stars. When he said 'Paul Newman' one week, I nearly jumped for joy. I loved him. He was a proper, bona fide Hollywood star, and where else would you ever get the chance to be in the same room as Paul Newman? I couldn't wait.

Thursday came round, and I drove down in anticipation, as I did every week. But when they say 'Don't meet your idols', they're not joking. I knew something was wrong when they put the show forward a couple of hours so Paul could have an early night. The image of the chiselled, bronzed matinée idol I had in my head was shattered when this old man in carpet slippers, trackie bottoms and glasses on a chain shuffled in. Yes, I know he's old, but that doesn't mean you have to dress like an old person. Madonna's 50 and she still dresses like a twenty-something – a twenty-something streetwalker, but a twenty-something nevertheless. Maybe Paul didn't know what he was wearing, perhaps those beautiful blue eyes had become misted over with cataracts. Even when he got on the settee, his chat was a bit of a disappointment. He didn't want to talk about *Butch Cassidy and the Sundance Kid*, he just wanted to talk about his new flavour of mayonnaise. I could do that.

Over those months and eventually years of doing the warm-up, I started to dread seeing my idols because I didn't want the illusion to be spoilt. When the late great James Brown came onto the sofa, he started talking about his prostate problems. No one wants to hear that, do they? The man Carolyn and I had got on the good foot to at Carwash all those years ago was now sitting in front of me telling the world he had problems 'downstairs'. If the Godfather of Soul can't get it up, what hope is there for me?

* * *

I'd changed agents by this time. I'd left Karushi and joined Off the Kerb. It was horrible having to phone up Lisa and say that I was jumping ship, but in the end it had to be done. I felt awful because they had been there when I was at my lowest and had thrown me a lifeline. But that horrible feeling of betrayal eased when I got a round-robin email from Karushi saying that they were having to 'let go' two of their other acts. Everyone, it seems, is dispensable, even agents. Let's face it, we all have to be ruthless sometimes, and I bet they would have got rid of me if I wasn't funny. Anyway, I don't feel bad now because joining Off the Kerb was the best career move I'd ever made.

Meeting the team in the office was definitely an experience. It was like auditioning for *Oliver!* These cockney wide boys with their dropped aitches, Cockney rhyming slang and Blitz spirit nearly had me doing the Lambeth Walk over to the old Joanna and starting up a chorus of 'Knees Up, Mother Brown'. But for all their 'Gawd Blimey', East End swagger, they meant business. Sitting with them having a cup of tea in the back room, I was eyeing up all the tour posters and awards they'd won over the years for such people as Lee Evans, Jack Dee, Jo Brand and, of course, Jonathan Ross. There was no doubt that I was in very good company. Although I was born in Weymouth, Off the Kerb made me feel so welcome that I mistakenly thought I heard the sound of the Bow Bells tingling in my earholes as I left their office.

Moving to Off the Kerb was just the shot in the arm I needed; the live work flooded in and even, on the odd occasion, a bit of telly. Most of it was dire and not worthy of note and was banished to the cable channels that you find the other side of God TV on your Sky box. A lot of my first-ever television appearances were in those dreadful talking heads programmes where you have to sit there in front of a fish tank or lava lamp and wax lyrical about some subject or other.

They are awful shows but when you're starting out the money can be so tempting for what looks like very little work indeed. Five hundred pounds to talk about Duran Duran, count me in. It's money for old rope. The trouble is these shows never die, they are circulated forever and ever on the satellite channels, they have become the television equivalent of rats – you are never more than six channels away from a shitty talking heads programme. They don't go away – they're like Cher. The amount of times I have switched on at half past midnight only to see a younger, more enthusiastic version of myself slagging off Mick Hucknall, I've lost count.

The worst culprit was the *I Love …* series which in essence was a good idea, a nostalgic look back at trends and attitudes, but when they ring your agent up and ask you to do *I Love 1976* you do wonder who's running the show. When I told the researcher that I wasn't born then and that I was in fact a foetus, worryingly it didn't seem to phase her. 'You can still talk about space-hoppers though, can't you?'

A few of my first television appearances were all right, I suppose. *Flipside* is worth mentioning because it was the first time I worked with Justin Lee Collins. The show was a bit ropy, to be honest, three guests flicking through TV channels commenting on what they were watching. For legal reasons, we couldn't watch channels that showed sports, anything rude or any advertisements. Easy, you might say, but at midnight when the channels are filled with American football, porn and infomercials, it suddenly becomes harder than it looks.

For some reason, the show attracted the most unhinged viewers who would be invited to send us their comments through the website. The comments ranged from the weird to the downright offensive. One that sticks in my mind is 'I want to get a gun and shoot it up Alan Carr's anus' – I hadn't heard the like since Barclaycard. One poor female presenter was informed that they wanted to cut her breasts off. If the weirdo losers hated us so much, why did they bother watching the show then? At least I was getting paid to watch this shit.

A slightly better programme, but only just, was *FAQ U*, a show that yet again paired me up with Justin Lee Collins. This time, however, it wasn't on after the national anthem. It was on at ten o'clock on terrestrial television, on Channel 4 in fact. This was where new, up-and-coming stand-up comedians chewed the fat about various topics and news items. I had always liked Justin when he was on the telly, and I was pleased to see that he was full of enthusiastic, upbeat loveliness off camera, too. His wife was expecting at the time and I remember him talking all excitedly about becoming a dad, which to me is a bit surreal because those two strangers mentioned in a conversation then I now know personally as Karen and little Archie.

But it was on Channel 4's *Law of the Playground* that we actually became mates. I remember it clearly. We were in a school sports hall reminiscing about our schooldays with comedian Kerri Godliman and *Peep Show*'s David Mitchell. We were all in hysterics, enjoying each other's company, bonding over the fact that we were all horrifically bad at physical education. Had they, like me, been waiting all these years to get the humiliation off their chests?

I left that hall with a headache from laughing so much, little knowing that the exchanges between Justin and me had planted the seed in Channel 4's head for something bigger. My slight foray into late-night telly started to produce a fanbase, albeit a very meagre one, full of insomniacs and people who wanted to stick a gun up my arse. People in the audience for Jonathan Ross started knowing who I was and, sadly, knowing the punchlines to my jokes, which isn't so good. I even got some of the actual stars coming over to say lovely things.

Standing in the wings with my microphone as usual, I felt a tap on my shoulder. I turned around, and Robbie Williams was standing there saying, 'Hi, Alan. I was just wondering if you had a comedy DVD out in the shops?' At first I thought it was a wind-up, but it turned out to be a genuine request, proving that meeting the rich and famous can be an uplifting experience after all. The following week Charlotte Church came over and said, 'Hello, you're so funny!' which was really sweet and unexpected. Another complete surprise was when Nicole Kidman waved as she left and blew me a kiss, but looking back, she'd probably mistaken me for one of the Poofs.

Inevitably with praise comes criticism, and lo and behold nasty comments started appearing on the Internet, which I suppose is part of the remit of being a comedian. But still, considering that all I'm doing is trying to make people laugh, some of the comments seemed disproportionately harsh. I know my comedy is an acquired taste, but really – a *fatwa*!

Some of the criticism was more subtle and slipped below the radar. I turned up at one gig in Leicester to see on the poster under my name 'The New Ernie Wise'. I explained to the promoter that this was in fact an insult, and I wouldn't really want that on the poster. He apologised and popped some gaffer tape over the offending article.

'I got it off the Internet,' he explained – of course. It never fails to make me smile when the media says that the Great British Public are apathetic – believe me, stand-up comedians are living proof that they are not. Islamic fundamentalism, global warming, gun crime, not a flicker of passion or interest, but get on stage and tell jokes, you think you'd pushed a shit through their letterbox. For some obscure reason comedy seems to rub some people up the wrong way, which is silly really, because it's only words. The amount of times I've muttered under my breath, 'Calm down, dear, it's only a punchline.'

So despite the odd bit of vitriol, 2004 was proving to be a good year. Deciding not to go to Edinburgh had had a real calming effect on me. I could just enjoy myself and would not have to keep an eye on my finances. In fact, being free around the month of August meant I could go on my first holiday since I had arrived back from Bangkok. My friends were going to Mykonos, and I decided to tag along. It was wonderful, like an Alton Towers for gays. There was nothing to do there, the brochures told you that, but who would need distractions when you've got some of the most beautiful Europeans in skimpy swimwear as eye candy?

The place was a revelation to me. On the first day we headed to Superparadise, the gay nudist beach – don't worry, I had my windbreaker – and found ourselves a good spot, within whistling distance of a gin and tonic. It wasn't essentially a nudist beach; there were lots of people in their trunks bathing and swimming. It was just the odd few exhibitionists who took all their clothes off and, boy, did they make up for the rest of us! I wondered whether I should join them and eat my egg sandwiches al fresco, but I decided not to.

I love to read. Especially books with a historical twist – if there's a woman wearing a ruff on the front cover it's straight in my basket. One of my favourite times to catch up on all the books I've missed through the year is when I'm on a beach. There's nothing more relaxing than lying there covered in Piz Buin enjoying a good old yarn. But lying there with *Inside Stalin's Gulags* in my hand, it became infuriating because every time my eyes fell upon the opening line they were distracted by a beautiful, bronzed, naked man sauntering past. I must have read that opening sentence a million times: 'Seven million died in the "forgotten" holocaust …' I couldn't stop staring – it was getting embarrassing. At one point I was going to ask one of the sunkissed hunks if I could use his penis as a bookmark, but alas the opportunity never arose.

Mykonos is one of my favourite locations ever. We did have some fun on that holiday, a lot of naughty fun. In fact, I'd never got so much sex in my life. It was amazing. What I didn't realise then was that Mykonos would be the last time I would be able to be naughty on holiday and throw caution to the wind without the fear of a well-positioned camera phone or some loser selling their story. Anyway, the holiday was just what I needed, and every time I think of gulags it makes me horny.

* * *

Off the Kerb, in their wisdom, had decided to make me the resident compere at one of their regular comedy nights. Being a regular compere is a great way of getting to try out new material and create a bond between you and your loyal audience. They see you every month and look forward to you coming on stage and having a bit of good-hearted banter with them – well, that's if they don't hate you. My residency was at Cabot Hall at the foot of Canary Wharf. Cabot Hall was, and is, a vast hall, hollow and soulless. It actually reminds me of the hall in the scene from *The Poseidon Adventure* where they have to climb up the Christmas tree to escape the rising water.

What was more dispiriting than the Hall itself was the fact that it would be full of suits. I was dreading it, and I was right to dread it – they despised me. They would groan when I came on, and I would groan when I saw them all in their cheap Matalan suits. There was enough static in that room to power a tram. I swear to God, if wet-look gel was flammable we'd have had an inferno on our hands. The night would chug along, and I would start to think: why don't you fuck off to Spearmint Rhino, like you do every other night? And so the pantomime continued, with boring financial types scowling from their tables every month while I tried to find a joke that would incorporate the FTSE index. One night Reginald D. Hunter, a wonderfully supportive comedian who was headlining, said, 'Give it up for your compere, Alan Carr.' Instead of a cheer, all I got was one suit shouting out 'Faggot!' Charming.

It was then that I made up my mind that I was going to quit. So I left them to their tedious financial world, thanking God that at least I was fabulous.

Fighting relegation

Although working flat out, driving all over the country to perform comedy in obscure towns and villages, can be very draining, the cheques I received at the end of every month were proving very welcome indeed. For the first time in my life I was doing well, so much so that it was time to fly the nest in Chorlton and get my own house. Somewhere with no mad tenants, no shitting cats and no revealing windows – even though, despite the drama and tension, I would still miss Ruth and all her eccentricities. Admittedly, our relationship had got a bit strained of late. She'd started drinking a little bit too much. She'd broken her ankle falling down a grassy knoll on the way back from the pub and spent that summer flat on her back on the settee with a bottle of painkillers and a glass of Chardonnay. 'I know you shouldn't mix them, but it's the only thing that makes the pain go away.'

I remember her asking me to do a big shop for her as she couldn't leave the house. 'Of course, Ruth,' I said, taking the shopping list from her.

I read 'Two bottles of Sauvignon Blanc, two bottles of Merlot and two bottles of Rosé (any)'. Then she'd grudgingly written as a footnote: 'Loaf'.

I ended up moving in with a friend called Hayley, while I got myself together. She had bought a house in Stretford and had invited me to take the back room. I hate moving, it's such a drag. You never really realise what possessions you've got till you have to bubble-wrap them or roll them up in newspaper and put them in a box. Plus, it's such a waste of money. I hired the van and drove the couple of miles from Ruth's to Hayley's. Hayley's house was an old bargeman's cottage that was part of a pretty terrace on a narrow lane stretching from the road to the canal.

I thought that packing up the removal van would be the hardest part of the move, but I was wrong – it was manoeuvring the truck down the lane to the front door. I thought I was doing really well as the truck made its merry way up the lane, but then again I couldn't hear the sound of my new neighbours' canopies being ripped from their doors and crashing to the floor. They all came out to see what was going on. I got out, oblivious to the carnage I'd created, and said, 'Hello, I'm Alan, your new neighbour.' Unsurprisingly, they weren't impressed.

That wasn't the only time I made an impression. Word soon got round that the man with the squeaky voice who lived at number 22 danced at the other end of the ballroom, and it wasn't long before a few of the kids would shout out 'Bender' and 'Gay' whenever I walked back from the Arndale. However, when they saw me on the telly they would knock on the door and ask for my autograph. Homophobes can be so fickle, don't you think?

I soon settled in, although Hayley's obsession with cleaning took a while to get over. She wouldn't clean, as such, just douse the house in bleach so every room smelt like a public toilet. If you bent down too quickly after Hayley had done her cleaning, you would drift off onto a psychedelic rollercoaster that would put Woodstock to shame.

Although Stretford lacks the bohemian and cultured ambience of Chorlton, it's not without its charms. My new home overlooked the Trans-Pennine Way which, if you followed it, would lead you through luscious fields and rivers to the Pennines themselves, if you weren't killed first crossing the M60. I'd been spoilt living in Chorlton, what with the delicatessens and Italian food specialists on Beech Road; all Stretford had to offer was the Arndale. Many a time I would walk through the Arndale to get my weekly shop. It was a strange place, full of card shops, for some reason. The Arndale marketing team had clearly decided that in Stretford you can never send too many cards. I can't imagine what anyone would be celebrating in Stretford – it wasn't 'Congratulations! You've got a job!' Well, definitely not, judging by the number of waifs and strays inhabiting the coffee shops and Poundlands.

The Arndale or 'The Mall', as it's now known since it reinvented itself, always had a distinctive aroma. On the upper level there was a butcher's and the smell would drift down to the shoppers below. The aroma that would drift down wasn't the usual delicious smell of crisp bacon slowly being grilled or mouth-watering plump sausages ready to pop in your mouth, but the stench of burning animal flesh. You never forget your first whiff, it made you wonder what the butcher was doing up there – cremating livestock? This gag-inducing stench would descend from the heavens and cling to your clothes like an all-in-one body-stocking.

You could always tell the true Stretfordians because they would walk around oblivious to the pork smog that enveloped them. Years and years of pushing a trolley around the Arndale had rendered them strangely immune. I am glad to say I became one of those people because in fact that year I spent a hell of a lot of time in that Arndale, mainly shopping for bargains, but partly slyly looking for comedy material for my routine. I've always said Manchester is ripe for comedy. You can take a journey on a night bus through Whalley Range and have enough comedy gold for two Edinburgh shows – let alone one. So, yes, I would idly spend a good couple of hours wandering the aisles, oblivious to the fact that, two hundred and eleven miles away in London, cogs were turning and wheels were being set in motion, and soon I would be swapping the stench of animal carcass for the smell of sweet success.

Chapter Twelve

THE FINAL WHISTLE

wish you were here ...

SEA SIDE TOWN

ortunately, the opportunities to shop at the Arndale were few and far between because my workload was so immense. With stand-up comedy, the more gigs you do, the more confident you get, and with more confidence comes more material. I was starting to get a name for myself and, for once in my life, it was a good one. I was even venturing tentatively into radio. I was a regular guest on Michelle Mullane's late-night BBC radio show and on BBC6 Music. I even got invited onto *Woman's Hour* to talk about my comedy, which was an experience, to say the least. I was lucky because it was recorded at BBC Manchester on Oxford Road, so was only a short bus ride away. I turned up at the studio nice and early and sat in the Green Room waiting to go in. As you'd expect, I was sitting with a selection of women, and we all waited, listening to the show's introduction over the speakers.

'Coming up on *Woman's Hour*, we've got Deborah Harvey, a new up-and-coming singer-songwriter.' We all smiled at the girl with the guitar. 'Jane Brooks, the Mancunian author, will be discussing her new novel.' We all smiled at the bookish woman with the glasses. 'Plus, I'll be talking to a convicted rapist on why he's found God.'

They all looked at me, and I looked at them: 'That ... that's not me!' I spluttered to the women, before hearing, 'Plus, Manc funnyman Alan Carr will be popping in for a chat about having a sports-mad father.'

'That's me! Alan.' Instantly the atmosphere defrosted. As it happens, the convicted rapist had wisely decided to appear on *Woman's Hour* via the phone.

Even in the realm of stand-up, I was getting fans, people asking for me specifically to play their clubs, and a few odd autograph hunters waiting outside the club doors – sadly they were few and odd. I could often be found compering at the Glee comedy clubs, both in Birmingham and in Cardiff, and my walk-on music, unknown to me, would often be adapted by the manager to suit my persona, shall we say? I would make my entrance and then the music would start: 'Killer Queen' by Queen, 'She's a Lady' by Tom Jones or 'W.O.M.A.N.' by Peggy Lee. Every time something suitably camp would blast from the speakers just as I placed my foot upon the stage, I would give the sound booth an icy stare. Then I would begin my act, secretly thrilled to have my own music and flattered that they recognised, unlike some comedians, that I never took myself too seriously.

The spectre of the Edinburgh Fringe started to loom again. My year off from it had been wonderful. Mykonos had been a delight, and I had raked in the cash whilst everyone had been slaving away in Edinburgh. I had ventured up and visited Karen, who was doing her show up there that year. I took a perverse satisfaction in watching Karen and the other acts flyering madly, trying to lure punters in or, worse, sobbing in the Pleasance Courtyard after some critic had given them a one-star review. This year was their turn. Thankfully, I was immune from this madness and sauntered round the different venues enjoying rather than enduring the chaos for once, just me and my *schadenfreude*.

In my new-found confidence I had started talking about my relationship with Dad, and it had been going down well with the audience. It seemed to strike a chord with people. I would get people approaching me after gigs, saying, 'My dad was like that,' or 'I felt like you as a teenager.' I was onto something, and it wasn't just confined to sports-mad dads either, as I discovered. It was dads in the police force, the army, plumbing, the navy. This revelation made me see Dad in a new light. It wasn't just my dad, it was all dads. Well, anyway, this reaction set up a spark, and when Off the Kerb asked if I'd like to go to Edinburgh again I heard myself saying 'Yes'. Here we go again, I thought.

* * *

But before Edinburgh, more amazing opportunities arose, even some abroad. That summer of 2005 was just filled with wonderful experiences I will never forget. In some respects they paved the way to where I am now. I was invited to perform at the Montreal Showcase at the Comedy Store. The two stand-ups who got picked from the showcase would go and represent Britain at the world-famous Just for Laughs comedy festival in Montreal in Canada. To my complete surprise, I ended up being picked alongside Rhod Gilbert – a very funny man with some great one-liners.

Considering I was up against some of the best acts on the circuit, some of whom had been going a lot longer than my pathetic five years, I was overjoyed. Looking back, they must have hated me. Performing at the Just for Laughs Festival is career-defining stuff, and I found out they would pay my travel and for a hotel once I got there! Of course, I now know this is commonplace, but back then I was thrilled. I'd always had to pay to go abroad – well, apart from the time I collected those tokens in the *Sun* – but now someone wanted to pay for me to fly and stay in their city just so I can tell a few jokes? I couldn't believe it.

Montreal is a bit of a disappointment really. I had heard how wonderfully picturesque and mountainous Canada was, so to roll up in a place that had the look of Milton Keynes about it was anticlimactic to say the least. There was no discernible architectural style or any landmarks that were worth using up a pixel for. Karen (she was fast becoming my travelling partner) and I had our photo taken down by the harbour on the cobbles in front of an old Victorian tavern. We were later informed that it was built in 1982, so we had in fact been photographed in front of the Canadian equivalent of an Eighties' Wetherspoon's. In disgust, I immediately deleted the picture from my digital camera.

We had been told that Montreal was perfect for whale-watching, so we had to endure the embarrassment of asking at the tourist information booth where we could see some whales.

'Can you see any blue on here?' shouted the information officer menacingly, shaking a map of Montreal two inches away from my face. For all his rudeness we had to admit he was right – we were landlocked. I had assumed the harbour led to something like the sea, but I was wrong. But then, knowing Montreal, the harbour was probably built in 1987 and the 'sea' was a piece of tarpaulin painted blue to look like water. Was anything real in Canada?

As a comedian, you always wonder whether your jokes travel. Is my routine universal? Say they don't get me. These thoughts had been plaguing my mind for the entirety of the days leading up to my first gig in Montreal. I had done all I could do, taking out all the British household names and chat shows. I doubt if a Canadian would really appreciate the joys of 'Trisha'. I kept in all my father material – even people in Montreal must have pushy dads, surely.

Just for Laughs grips the whole city, just as the Edinburgh Festival does. It is everywhere, and the venues can range from huge theatres to a tiny room above a pub. My first gig of the Festival was in a trendy bar next door to a cinema. I was on the same bill as a couple of Americans, a couple of French people, a Canadian and Rhod Gilbert – at last, a friendly face from Britain, someone to worry with and share such a bizarre experience. Everyone was doing really well, the audience seemed to be really friendly. So I relaxed and with a large gulp of air strode confidently on stage.

Said my first joke. Nothing. Said my second. Nothing. I was dying on my arse. This hadn't happened since Cabot Hall. It was painful, and because I'm like an over-protective father with my jokes and treat them like my own children who can do no wrong, I blamed the audience. I shouted angrily,

'Thanks a bunch, Canada! I've come all the way from Manchester, and you can't be bothered to laugh!' and walked off stage, furious.

The atmosphere in the dressing-room was horrible. Everyone looked at me pitifully, all the international acts thinking, 'If this is the best that Britain can come up with ...' To make it worse, Rhod went on and stormed it. I was depressed. Don't tell me, I've got a whole week of tumbleweed ahead of me. It was only when I looked at the programme that it all became clear. The night had been a Christian fundraiser for a new church roof. I was livid, not with them, they can't help it, but with the organisers for putting a blatant homosexual onto the bill. They should have known it would go down like a bacon sandwich at a bar mitzvah, the miserable bastards. I hope the roof caves in on their miserable heads!

As it happens, I had nothing to worry about as the rest of the gigs at the Festival went really well. In fact, there was so little to do in Montreal, I started looking forward to them. My last gig there was a gay night of comedy, and it deserves a mention just because it was so crazy and kitsch. It was hosted by a drag queen dressed as Peggy Lee – not Peggy in her heyday, but Peggy in her 80s when she had the shakes and a drink problem. The stage was set up like her front room: a settee, a minibar, pictures on the walls. Peggy would be in this ridiculous Purdy-style bob, slurring her way through 'Fever' or 'Woman', and then a doorbell would ring. She would answer the door (after crashing into a bookcase), I would have to come on and do my fifteen minutes of stand-up in her lounge, and then she would stagger back and finish her song.

It was an absolute scream, and the perfect end to a week that, if I'm honest, hadn't started out as the best.

* * *

Once back in Great Britain, it was work as usual. I had to get my Edinburgh show ready, and it was looking quite good. As always, you go to these out-of-the-way places to try out the show, and I was turning up all over the country, the Aldeburgh Festival on the east coast, pubs on the outskirts of Manchester, art centres in Devon, anywhere I could run through the show without some snotty critic mauling it and ripping it to shreds. The constant driving and eating Ginsters pasties at service stations at two in the morning with a surly trucker is not only bad for your diet, but also dangerous. The number of times I've nearly fallen asleep on the way home – I have to put the blower on full force directed at my crotch just to keep my eyes open. It's a bit drastic, I know, but it can be quite erotic at the right temperature.

Ask any comedian and they will tell you that it's a lonely business. Travelling around by yourself in a car can be very isolating, and if you're feeling a bit down or low, being on the actual stage can be lonely, too – even if there are a hundred people watching. You can sometimes feel a fraud telling these jokes on stage and acting out all these comic scenarios when on the inside you're thinking, 'God, I wish I was on my holidays.' The audience can be bent double with laughter and I'm saying to myself, 'I must pick those trousers up from the dry cleaners.'

I remember sitting with my family in a Chinese restaurant in Northampton when a man came in and said, 'Table for one, please.'

Mum, being a mum, went, 'Ahh! What a shame!'

'Mum, that's me!' I said. 'That's me! Most weekends.'

I swear she nearly welled up. But it's true. It was me asking for 'a table for one, please', quickly followed by 'nowhere near the window'. It's especially bad, if you are doing a weekend in Bristol or Glasgow or Birmingham, and you've got nothing to do in the day and you have to kill twelve hours, but still at the end of it be sober enough to get on stage and perform.

I've been known to pop into the Jorvic Centre in York, Louis Tussaud's Waxworks in Blackpool or Stockport's Hat Museum, just to make the time pass that little bit more quickly. God knows what kind of loser I looked like, as I walked around on my own, reading the little information cards to myself, or idly thumbing through the oversized pencils in the gift shop. I must have got some pitying looks, I can tell you.

Various distractions came along whilst I was writing my show, but I was soldiering on with rewriting it, so I turned most of them down. One show I just had to do, though, was *The World Stands Up* – not for the programme, but for the chance to go to Melbourne where it was being filmed. I had spent so much time in Sydney, but weirdly had always missed out going to Melbourne, which is, in Australian terms, relatively close by. As at Just for Laughs, the best comedians from the UK were asked to do a routine and 'battle' against the stand-ups from the other countries.

The final whistle

If I were offered it now, I wouldn't take it, because it nearly killed me. Travelling to Melbourne on a twenty-four hour flight, only to turn round and come back again three days later once filming had finished, is devastating. But I was so desperate to go on what I thought was a free holiday that I foolishly stuck two fingers up to my body clock and went ahead with it. My body clock retaliated by making me fall asleep and also get impossibly drunk on the smallest amount of alcohol.

After filming had been completed, I was enjoying a little tipple with the comedian Lee Mack, who was also battling against the world for Britain. I seemed to be getting louder and more flamboyant. I like to think that I am like Dorothy Parker when I'm pissed, keeping my audience captive with my witty epigrams. But it's more like Danny La Rue on poppers – believe me, I've seen the photos.

Before long I was trolleyed, and Lee and I decided to call it a night, in separate rooms, I might add. An older guy joined us in the lift and, seeing us both swaying and giggling, said, 'You like parties?'

Well I never, it was Peter Fonda. Before we knew it, Lee and I were sitting around at Peter's feet in his suite, singing protest songs while he accompanied us on guitar. I would usually avoid this situation like the plague, but it was one of the Fondas, for God's sake. The only way I could trump this drunken anecdote would be if I did a cardiovascular workout paralytic with his sister Jane. Maybe you had to be there, but it was very funny, especially when Lee sat Peter down and said, 'I know you must get this all the time, what with *Easy Rider* and everything, but – what's your favourite pie?'

Peter stared at us over his guitar but we were in bits. Anyway, the party fizzled out, and we retired graciously, after Lee distracted Peter and I took all the drinks out of his mini-bar.

Obviously, as I was staying in Melbourne for just three days – with one and a half of them filming and rehearsing, and the other one and a half falling asleep in restaurants – I didn't get to see much of the place. But the bits I did see were charming, although no one told me about the wind from the Antarctic. The bright Melbourne sun would shine cheerfully through my hotel window, slyly luring me out of my room, only for me to step outside and get instant botox from the wind as it bit my face. I'd be glad to get back to Manchester where at least you knew what you were getting when you stepped outside your house – rain.

Back in England, all eyes were on Edinburgh. Everyone, including myself, was putting the final touches to their shows. After the miserable time I'd had last time in Edinburgh, I decided to throw myself into the whole Festival thing this time and share with another comedian – then at least I wouldn't get lonely and could feel more a part of it. My agent said, 'Why don't you share with another Off the Kerb act?'

I thought 'Why not?' The only other act who was looking for a flatmate was Brendon Burns. Now anyone who's seen Brendon will know that we are chalk and cheese. He is a loud, brash, bandana-wearing political firecracker, while I am – well, you know what I am. But even though the alarm bells were ringing so loud I thought I had tinnitus, I said 'Yes', thinking that macho bravado was all an act. It wasn't. Soon word got round that I was sharing with Brendon and overnight the nicknames 'Poofy' and 'Shouty' were born.

Brendon was great and considerate and always did his washing up, but his entourage was the problem. It would get bigger by the day, with more and more women joining the fold. During one riotous party, I came out of my bedroom in my dressing gown to tell them to turn it down, and I was instantly surrounded by scantily clad women – I must have looked like Hugh Hefner at the Playboy mansion.

Every morning I would be saying 'Hello' to another strange woman whilst eating my Coco Pops. One morning I was sitting opposite a woman who had given me a shit review two years ago. I gave her a sharp smile and took my bowl of chocolately goodness to my room. To be fair, that was just me being a party pooper – why shouldn't everyone go a bit crazy? It's a festival, for God's sake.

We were there for a month, and everyone was saying, 'Let your hair down!' But I just couldn't, and I never can – there always seems to be something to worry about. If I ever did trash a hotel room, I'd be throwing the television out the window with one hand and giving the sideboard the once over with a damp cloth with the other.

My show, simply called 'Alan Carr', was selling out every night and getting rave reviews. Typical, the only year I could not be arsed to come up with a title and I was getting some of the best reviews of my life. The *Scotsman* – five stars, *Independent* – five stars, *Three Weeks* – five stars. The good reviews kept coming into the press office, and they were put straight on my posters. This time I didn't have to steal them from Jimmy Carr. Because the show was doing so well, other comedians came to see it. I had some of Dad's footballing mates in the audience, including the manager Gordon Strachan. Unknown to me, Channel 4's head of entertainment, Andrew Newman, who would play such an integral part in my progression at Channel 4, also came to the show.

* * *

As the Fringe lurches towards its denouement, talk of Perrier rears its ugly head. Perrier, or whatever it's called nowadays, is an award a panel of judges give out every year to the comedian they think has the best show. In the Eighties they bestowed it on Steve Coogan, Lee Evans and Frank Skinner. Sadly in the Nineties it became the kiss of death, and whoever won it was never heard of again. As you can imagine, I didn't want anything to do with it and, besides, the two previous years I hadn't even got on the long list, let alone the shortlist. Why would they bother with me this year? However, my agent started getting himself in a tizz about this damn Perrier and, against my wishes, must have asked the main judge, Nica Burns, to come along and see the show.

I really wish he hadn't because, five minutes in, she'd fallen asleep in the front row. It was quite off-putting, I must say, to see that bulbous head resting on her chest with her legs wide open. At least with a heckle you can use a witty putdown, but to have this lethargic lump directly in my eyeline was proving a real distraction. Nevertheless, the rest of the audience had a great time, and I got a wonderful cheer at the end, which warmed my cockles but woke Nica from her slumbers, disorientated. I knew at that moment I had absolutely no chance of winning that Perrier. As it happens, the fact that Andrew Newman was in the audience proved more useful to my career than any award, and later that week he invited my agent and me to dinner in Leith.

'Have you heard of *The Friday Night Project*?' Andrew asked.

'No,' I replied. I stopped myself from saying, 'It's on a Friday night, isn't it?'

'Well, we at Channel 4 would like you to co-host the show with Justin Lee Collins.'

'But I hate that big hairy Bristolian!'

Obviously, I didn't say that – I love him. I dithered instead and said, 'Can I have a think about it?'

You've got to understand that I'd never seen the show. I knew the first series had been hosted by Jimmy Carr and Rob Rouse. But I'd been jet-setting all over the globe to Melbourne and Montreal, darling, so I'd never had the chance to see it and didn't have a clue what the show was about. It could have been a programme about celebrity badger baiting, for all I knew. I don't mind going on a satellite channel at one o'clock in the morning, but if I'm certain someone might actually be watching, then I don't want to be saddled with a turkey.

I said I'd think it over once I'd returned to Stretford. Ahh! Beautiful Stretford. I didn't think I'd miss it like I did. I only had to last a few more days and I would be leaving Edinburgh for home.

When the final day arrived, my heart sank. Brendon and I would have to clean the flat, as it had stated in the lease: 'Leave it as you find it.' Looking around, I hoped and prayed that we'd found it graffiti-ed, trashed, cigarette-burned and with a dislodged toilet seat, but it was a long shot. However, before I could slip on my Marigolds and drop to my knees, Brendon, in that wonderful rasping Australian voice of his, said, 'Leave it to us lot, mate. We made the mess, so we'll clean up the mess.'

I can't remember what I said next. All I remember is running out of the flat with my suitcase, slamming the door, shouting, 'Thanks, Brendon,' out of the sunroof, and putting my foot to the pedal.

The Friday Night Project played on my mind. What did Channel 4 want? Could I deliver what they wanted? Stand-up comedy is one thing, but reading from an autocue and interviewing someone famous and trying to look interested is another. And there's that thing in your ear where you can hear the director talking in the gallery. I wasn't sure I would cope with that interference, but little did I know I would be putting these skills to use sooner than I thought.

I was sitting at home in my flat when I got a phone call out of the blue.

'Do you live near the Trafford Centre?'

'Yes,' I replied.

It was the producer of *Richard and Judy* asking if I would like to do an outside broadcast at the Trafford Centre – 'Live!'

'When do you want me?'

'Five o'clock today.'

'What? Live? You must be joking!'

That was two hours away. I didn't even have time to feel sick at the thought.

I drove down to the Trafford Centre and found out what I had to do. I had to run up to shoppers, drag them back to a podium and in the studio. Trinny and Susannah would dish out fashion advice to them all – live.

I have never even seen the footage of that day because I dread to see how terrified I looked. Just before they counted me down I had this awful fear that Tourette's would take over my body and I'd just shout out 'Hello, motherfuckers' instead of 'Hello, Richard and Judy.'

It really was a baptism of fire – I had the director talking in my ear, I had Richard and Judy talking to me in the studio and I had to interact with the shoppers, and pretend to give a shit about their outfits. Listening to the cacophony of voices whizzing through my head was making me dizzy – I don't know how Derek Acorah does it.

But I survived, and when I was back at my flat having a very large glass of wine Richard Madeley rang up and left a message on my mobile.

'You did a really good job there, Alan,' he said, which was lovely of him. He didn't have to do that and it really meant a lot to me. It stayed in my voicemail for ages. Richard must have meant what he said because soon after I started getting offers of more work to do outside broadcasts for *Richard and Judy*, this time, thankfully, not live. They were fun to start off with but then they started getting more and more surreal. I don't know who was coming up with the ideas but I think they must have been on drugs.

I was asked to dress up as a potato for National Chip Week, and also to have dinner at a man's house who made meals out of roadkill. Seriously. Mercifully I couldn't find a window in my busy schedule, so I missed out on those delights, but some I did do were delivering a giant birthday card to Buckingham Palace for Prince Harry and finding someone with a third nipple in Liverpool City Centre. That was fun to begin with but there's only so many times you can be told to 'Fuck off!' and put on a brave face. When I told them that it was for *Richard and Judy* some scouse wit would end up shouting out, 'Nick us a bottle of wine, Richard!' which wasn't just tedious but totally untopical and we'd have to stop filming and try and find another three-nippled scouse shopper to interrogate.

* * *

It seems that it wasn't just Channel 4 aficionados and Gordon Strachan in the audience at Edinburgh. I had received an invitation to perform at the Royal Variety Performance. It had come through the post, but I couldn't believe it. How had Liz found out where I lived? I rang up my agent, and apparently it was true. Well I never! I double-checked the invite to see that it was in fact Her Majesty Elizabeth II attending and not someone shit like Princess Michael of Kent or that bloody Edward. If I'm performing, I want the real deal, I want A-list royalty, I want ermine, I want crown, I want orbs. I mean,

Dame Shirley Bassey was headlining – Liz had a lot to live up to when it came to making an entrance.

The venue wasn't the Palladium, which was probably the only disappointment, but it was at Cardiff's Millennium Centre. I would be performing alongside Sir Cliff Richard, Dame Shirley Bassey, Charlotte Church and Will Young, so not camp at all then really … The only way it could have been gayer would have been if Dale Winton, Lulu and Christopher Biggins joined the Village People for YMCA as the finale. Thinking about it, wasn't that the year before?

By that time, I was still warming up the Jonathan Ross chat show and had mentioned – well, came screaming into the Green Room waving my invitation in the air – that I would be performing at the Royal Variety Performance. Everyone was so pleased for me, and Jonathan said I could have one of his suits to perform in. I graciously accepted, and the wardrobe mistress took them up for me. It was a very generous offer, but looking at the footage you can see my stubby frame inside a suit for a lanky six foot two person and it looks very unforgiving. The jacket hung down so low I nearly tripped myself up by putting my foot in one of the pockets, but it was a lovely gesture and I am forever thankful.

When the day came, understandably I was nervous. Rubbing shoulders with all these legends at sound check, I realised I was almost the only one who hadn't had extensive reconstructive plastic surgery. I was 28, and I looked the oldest there. Also the Royal Variety Performance is renowned for having a tough crowd. Hen parties, stag dos, yes, I can deal with them; but the prospect of a whole room of snooty

Welsh people and the reigning monarch slow-hand-clapping terrified me. At least if Sir Cliff Richard dies on his arse, he can wheel out 'Devil Woman'.

As it happened, I was sharing a dressing-room with McFly. They are lovely boys, but in their skinny-fit jeans and spiky hair they made me feel very old. My hair was beginning to recede around that time in November 2005 – I noticed it in the reflection of Sir Cliff's veneers. It had started slipping back down my head like a rug on a highly polished floor, but thankfully with a bit of hair wax I could still fool people into thinking I had a fringe. Just as I was feeling really old, watching McFly coolly strum their guitars without a care, their manager came in and told the boys off for eating too many jellybeans.

'If you have too many E numbers, you'll be bouncing off the walls.'

Who says rock 'n' roll is dead?

There wasn't much camaraderie that night. All the big stars stayed in their rooms. Charlotte Church was lovely to me, as she always is. I passed Cliff on the stairs and said, 'Good luck!'

He replied sharply, 'I've already been on,' which was a bit embarrassing, but to be fair, I'd had the runs and had locked myself in a toilet. I can't be everywhere.

There were rumours Dame Shirley had demanded more sequins for her dress, so they had sent it back to India to have more sewn on and it was in the process of being flown back first class to Heathrow just in time for the show. Oh the drama! Can you imagine getting them to fly a dress from another continent just for you?

I wouldn't mind, but they looked pissed off when I asked them to get me a cheese baguette and can of Tango, and that was only downstairs.

Before long, it was show time, and it was a huge success. All my worries were for nothing, I never fluffed my lines, I never fell off the stage. More importantly, I never mentioned Diana. I'd had the worst anxiety dream where I'd ended my set that night with the words, 'You've been lovely, I've been Diana the Princess of Wales.'

The Royal Variety crowd are notoriously difficult, and looking out at the OAP crowd with their furs and opera glasses, I couldn't really see what we'd have in common. I had deliberately picked my most universal material and hoped they would get it, and thankfully they did. Not only that, but on the televised programme there is footage of Her Majesty laughing at my Tesco Clubcard joke. How does she know about Tesco Clubcard points? I don't care; I'm just glad she laughed in the right places.

The night was a triumph, and little did I know that it would open so many doors for me. My performance wasn't finished there, however. I had to return with the rest of the performers who had graced the stage that night to wave arms aloft as Shirley Bassey brought the show to a fitting climax. In rehearsals, the plan was that Dame Shirley would emerge from below the stage via a trapdoor. It had gone smoothly in rehearsal, but standing there on the night waving, Catherine Tate and I noticed that the trapdoor had jammed. We could clearly see Dame Shirley shouting to the stage hand, 'Get this fuc—'

'Music is my first love,' she bellowed, as the trapdoor propelled her up mid-rant. Of course, Dame Shirley was amazing and sang beautifully, and by the end she had the whole of the Cardiff audience on their feet. Tearfully, she cried, 'It's great to be home,' before striding off stage to get in a private jet to take her to Monte Carlo.

The only person who could possibly upstage the Dame was the Queen, and I finally met her at the end for the curtain call. Although I'm not the biggest royalist, there is something about her. I bowed when she shook my hand and said, 'Hello Ma'am.' That's what Will Young had done, and he's posh, so I followed suit.

Then she said, 'You were very entertaining!'

Oh my God, can I have that on my posters for my next tour? By Royal Approval, I am entertaining. Somebody pinch me.

Then, I heard her say it to Il Divo, then to McFly, then to Charlotte Church, then to Ozzy Osbourne, then to these two acrobatic dwarves from Croatia whose act was to spin half-naked on what looked like a silver wheelie bin. Christ, if she thinks they're entertaining, she needs her head testing. When she started saying it to the woman who sold the ice creams, I realised I'd been duped. She says it to everyone; it's a line she dishes out to every Tom, Dick and Harry. Damn it!

Anyway, for that tiny moment I felt very special indeed. I felt proud and warm inside, and I wasn't going to let Her Majesty's cheeky white lies spoil one of the highlights of 2005. I received a lovely photo of when I met the Queen. The only problem is that one of the members of Il Divo, who was standing next to me, had such an orange face that your eyes are drawn away from me and onto him. His tangerine-hued face looked like a sun setting behind my head, and it totally upstaged my first encounter with our sovereign.

Like everyone in Britain, I had grown up with the Royal Variety Performance and to be on it was a dream come true. But it was also a personal highlight because it was the first piece of comedy that my parents had seen me do. I'd always kept my comedy world secret from them because I didn't want them to be disappointed or not to get the jokes. Plus, half the stuff was about them anyway, and I didn't want to be sued or get my head kicked in. The night it was on the telly, I was working (of course), doing stand-up in Liverpool. I came off stage and saw I had missed a call from my parents. I hesitantly phoned home. Mum picked up.

'So, what do you think?' I said, trying my best to sound confident.

'We loved it.'

'Really? What about Dad?'

'Oh, he thought you were funny. Really funny.'

'What about that bit where he calls me a poof?'

'Oh, he couldn't stop laughing. It was really good. We don't know how you do it. So brave.'

She'd liked it and, more importantly, Dad had liked it. The more I thought about it, the more I realised that of course he would like it. Why wouldn't he like it? What was there not to like? Screw the FA Cup, you try and entertain that lot on the other side of that curtain. Tonight the Millennium Centre had been my Wembley and the audience had been the away fans.

Yes, I'd had nerves, I needed to be brave, I had to be match-fit, I had to perform. So what if I was stepping out onto a stage rather than a pitch, feeling the polished floor under my feet and not turf under my studs? What's the difference?

But then I think that Dad always knew there was no difference and that it was me who didn't get it. For once in my life, I'd missed the joke – and I was supposed to be the comedian. At last I understood he'd always been proud of me. He didn't give two hoots about my sexuality, or the fact that I was shit at sport – no, he just didn't want me to be a loser.

Heading home that night, I was on top of the world. Well, it couldn't get better than that, could it? I thought I'd reached the pinnacle of my comedy career. Where would I go from here? It was only when I got back up to Manchester that I received DVDs of all the *Friday Night Projects*, but to be honest I couldn't be bothered to watch them. My agent rang and said, 'What about this *Friday Night Project* show? Do you fancy it?'

'Oh, go on then,' I said. 'What's the worst that can happen?'

Thank-yous

Mum
Dad
Gary
Nanny Carter
Sarah Atkinson
Cherry Boarer
Justin Lee Collins (you are the wind beneath my wings)
Steve Lock
Mary Richmond
Catherine Labram
Carolyn Currie
Melissa Davitt
Michelle Foreman
Karen Bayley
David Raikes
Danny Julian
Addison Cresswell
Channel 4
Manchester
Natalie Jerome (happy now?) and everyone at HarperCollins

Own Alan's hilarious new DVD!

Released Mon 20th Oct 2008